Centennial History
of the
National Society of the
Sons of the
American Revolution

1889 - 1989

Turner Publishing Company
Publishers of America's History
P.O. Box 3101
Paducah, Kentucky 42002-3101

Book Staff :
Robert A. Lentz, Executive Director
    National Society of the Sons of the
    American Revolution
Winston C. Williams, Editor
    THE SAR MAGAZINE

Book Coordinator: Mark A. Thompson,
    Independent Publishing Consultant
    for Turner Publishing Company

Book Outlay: Elizabeth Dennis

Library of Congress Catalog
Card No.: 90-72152
ISBN: 1-56311-028-8

Printed in the United States of America

Limited Edition of 1000 copies.

CONTENTS

FOREWORD

The decade of the 1980s. What an historic time to be Editor of The SAR MAGAZINE! It was during this period that the National Society, State Societies and Chapters celebrated our Centennial through programs that culminated on April 30, 1989 - exactly 100 years after the SAR was founded.

We also commemorated the Bicentennial of those numerous events that began at the end of the American Revolution and concluded with the proposal by Congress of the Bill of Rights for consideration by the several States. Encompassed here were the defeat of the British at Yorktown in 1781 by General George Washington; signing of the Treaty of Paris, which officially concluded the War in 1783; Washington's resignation as Commander-in-Chief and his eventual election as the nation's first President; development of the United States Constitution and its ratification; and formation of the three branches of government as specified in the Constitution. How the SAR recognized some of these is included in the pages that follow.

Preparations for making the SAR Centennial began several years before the actual date. A special Committee was appointed to plan a multi-faceted program - which ranged from articles in THE SAR MAGAZINE, as reprinted in this volume, to suggested activities to be carried out by State Societies. Throughout most of this phase, Compatriot William C. Gist, D.M.D., a prominent member of the Kentucky Society, served as Committee Chairman. He and the Editor worked closely together.

As you read the "SAR Centennial History" which appeared in four consecutive issues published during 1989-1990, you will note the distinctive full-page and smaller editorial spaces devoted to information about the State Societies. These were actually sponsored and prepared by the Societies themselves as a means of supporting the celebration effort.

We hope that you enjoy reading about how our Society has sought to preserve and further what the Founding Fathers and Patriots of the American Revolution gave us - The greatest nation in the world today!

Winston C. Williams
Editor, THE SAR MAGAZINE

ACKNOWLEDGEMENTS

When the plan was first devised in the mid-1980s to publish a refreshingly new history of the Sons of the American Revolution leading up to our Centennial date, the obvious choice for an author to prepare this momentous work was Maryland Society Compatriot Carl F. Bessent, who served as President General during 1984-1985. Without a doubt, his knowledge about our organization far exceeds that of anyone else. We congratulate him for a job well done on the Centennial Heritage Facts stories and the four-part Centennial History that follow. Meriting thanks for their contributions of painstakingly researched writings are Former Presidents General Howard L. Hamilton and Benjamin H. Morris - as are Compatriots Allen R. Yale and Duane L.C.M. Galles. And finally, we want to recognize all of those State Societies that supplied information about their own history and purchased space in THE SAR MAGAZINE in order to share it with all members; their support of the Centennial program is sincerely appreciated.

Col. James R. Calhoun
President General

DEDICATION

These pages are dedicated to the **"Real Sons"** of the American Revolution in whose character lives the stillness of a man called Washington. He was the spiritual leader of this nation after his death in 1799. He was its inspiration throughout the celebration of the Centennial in 1876 and he is the Cincinnatus of this Society today. He stands not only as a monument to a strong and rugged past, but he is a legend in a democracy that we Americans treasure greater than life itself. It is therefore fitting that we lay down the history of the **"Real Sons"** in the spirit of a man who made this nation possible.

"Real Sons" were the sons of those men who rendered active service in the cause of American Independence. Many of these sons were instrumental in founding our Society.

James A. Williams
Historian General

PERSPECTIVE

The search, preparation and writing of the history of the Sons of the American Revolution have given me extreme gratification and satisfaction.

It is particularly fitting that SAR members look at the history of the Society at this time, one hundred years following its organization. This Society may be defined as a group of men distinguished by mutual interest, companionship and dedication to love of country. The SAR through the years has refrained from boasting of its many accomplishments, and others have at times claimed them.

SAR members are proud of their ancestry, not because of an hereditary aristocracy, but because they descend from the people who were willing to suffer and die to insure that freedom would be enjoyed in this country. The roll of members whose ancestors achieved the Independence of the thirteen colonies is thoroughly democratic in its make-up. The most eminent -- as well as the least prominent -- Americans of patriotic descent are members. Members make no special claim to patriotism, but believe they carry a responsibility of preserving the Republic undiminished as our forefathers established it.

It was the organization where veterans of the Blue and the Grey, antagonists in the great terrible struggle between the states, came together in 1889 for the first time for the improvement of this wonderful nation.

We are justly proud of our achievements. It is an extensive account of dedicated service. The SAR rescued from oblivion the names and records of the men and women who took part in the Revolutionary War. It marked the forgotten graves and erected monuments to commemorate the people and events of the War for Independence. It has preserved historic sites. It established "Flag Day" and initiated the commemoration of the United States Constitution. The SAR prompted passage of laws forbidding the desecration of the American Flag. It encourages interest in American history by promoting contests on patriotic subjects for students. The SAR conducts special programs to observe the patriotic anniversaries. Today its role of service continues.

The chapter on the history of the first one hundred years of our noble Society is completed. SAR members eagerly look forward to the challenges of the 21st Century.

It was an Honor to have written the Centennial History.

Carl F. Bessent
Former President General

6

CENTENNIAL HERITAGE FACTS

CENTENNIAL HERITAGE FACTS

The SAR and "The American's Creed"

By Former President General Carl F. Bessent

There is a close relationship between "The American's Creed" and the National Society of the Sons of the American Revolution.

A group of literary scholars joined together after the Declaration of War between the United States and Germany in 1917 to centralize American thought into a patriotic slogan. This proposed creed was to embrace all the traditions and aspirations of every American. The group included such literary giants as Booth Tarkington and Irvin S. Cobb.

The group selected a special contest committee with Matthew Page Andrews, author from Baltimore, as Chairman. Andrews was a member of the SAR (#29850) and a descendant of Colonel Richard Kidder Meade, an Aide-De-Camp to General George Washington.

Dr. P.P. Claxton, United States Commissioner of Education, served as the Advisor to this special contest committee.

The City of Baltimore, through Mayor James H. Preston, offered a prize of $1,000 for the best submitted creed of American Citizenship. Mayor Preston was a member of the SAR (#18512) and served as the President General of the National Society in 1920. He was a descendant of Captain Jacob Bond of the Maryland Militia.

Over 2,000 creeds were submitted; creed #384 was adjudged the winner. It was the entry of William Tyler Page, Clerk for the United States House of Representatives. Page was a member of the SAR (#32401) and a descendant of Carter Braxton, Signer of the Declaration of Independence.

The contest committee presented the winning creed to the Honorable Champ Clark, Speaker of the House of Representatives, before an assembly of members of the United States Congress. "The American's Creed" was accepted on behalf of the nation and first printed in THE CONGRESSIONAL RECORD, #102, April 13, 1918 with the following explanation of the doctrinal origin of the Creed:

"The United States of America" — Preamble to the Constitution of the United States.

"A government of the people, by the people, for the people" — Preamble to the Constitution of the United States; Daniel Webster's speech in the Senate, January 26, 1830; President Abraham Lincoln's Gettysburg speech.

"Whose just powers are derived from the consent of the governed" — Thomas Jefferson in the Declaration of Independence.

"A democracy in a republic" — James Madison in THE FEDERALIST, #10; Article X of the Amendments to the Constitution.

"A sovereign nation of many sovereign States" — E pluribus unum, Great Seal of the United States; Article IV of the Constitution.

"A perfect Union" — Preamble to the Constitution.

"One and inseparable" — Daniel Webster's speech in the Senate, January 26, 1830.

"Established upon those principles of freedom, equality, justice and humanity, for which American patriots sacrificed their lives and fortunes" — Dec-

claration of Independence.

"I therefore believe it is my duty to my country to love it" — In substance from Edward Everett Hale's "The Man without a Country."

"To support its Constitution" — Oath of Allegiance, Section 1757, Revised Statues of the United States.

"To obey its laws" — General Washington's Farewell Address; Article VI, Constitution of the United States.

"To respect its flag" — National Anthem, *The Star-Spangled Banner*; Army-Navy Regulations; War Department circular on Flag Etiquette, April 14, 1917.

"And to defend it against all enemies" — Oath of Allegiance, Section 1757, Revised Statues of the United States.

The 29th SAR Annual Congress meeting in Rochester, New York, on May 20, 1918 approved and endorsed "The American's Creed." The Secretary General was instructed to send a copy of the Creed to each State Society with instructions to read same at the general meetings of the respective State Societies.

Subsequently, many State Societies included the recitation of "The American's Creed" as part of all opening ceremonies of meetings.

Many State Societies furnished framed copies of the Creed to the schools in their respective states.

The National Society published and distributed many thousands of copies of a pocket size volume "The American's Creed and Its Meaning," printed by Doubleday, Page and Company, for educational purposes.

CENTENNIAL HERITAGE FACTS

The SAR and Constitution Day

By Former President General Carl F. Bessent

As heirs of a unique legacy, the Sons of the American Revolution have the responsibility to translate the people and events of the Revolutionary War era into present day action and project the achievements into the future. The United States Constitution spreads its beneficial protection over all citizens of this great country. One of the outstanding achievements of the SAR was establishing formal recognition of Constitution Day and its observance.

It began when President Elmer M. Wentworth of the Iowa Society SAR (SAR President General 1916-1918) prevailed upon the Iowa State Legislature to provide for the observance of Constitution Day in the state in 1911. In that year this effort resulted in appropriate exercises being held in every school in Iowa.

In 1915 the SAR printed its pamphlet, "No. 3, The Constitution of the United States." There was a heavy demand for copies. Thousands of copies were sent to the fifteen hundred naturalization judges for distribution at swearing-in ceremonies. In Philadelphia on May 10, 1915 copies were given to the 4,000 new naturalized citizens who were addressed by President Woodrow Wilson.

At the 1917 SAR Annual Congress in Nashville, Compatriot David L. Pierson of the New Jersey Society proposed a resolution that every Constitution Day be celebrated with ceremonies throughout the country. The resolution passed, and Constitution Day became a patriotic day, firmly observed annually by patriotic, fraternal and service groups.

David Pierson served as Chairman of the SAR Constitution Day Committee. Many prominent SAR members actively served on his committee, including Calvin Coolidge, Charles G. Dawes, William Howard Taft, Charles Evans Hughes, John D. Rockefeller, Henry Cabot Lodge and General John J. Pershing. On June 2, 1937 Governor Harold Hoffman of New Jersey signed Joint Assembly and Senate Resolution Eleven which recognized and credited David L. Pierson of East Orange, NJ, as the originator of the nationwide observance of September 17 as Constitution Day.

In 1917 the Kentucky Society celebrated Constitution Day by holding a patriotic pageant at Cherokee Park in Louisville with over 65,000 people attending. The *Louisville Courier Journal* devoted an entire section of the newspaper to the United States Constitution.

The nationwide pattern was well established by 1918. Most governors of states and mayors of cities issued Constitution Day proclamations. SAR committees contacted newspaper editors, radio stations, churches, and school systems urging support. Many churches held Constitution Sunday. Over 200 school system superintendents had Constitution Day ceremonies in their schools. The SAR sent speakers to many of the schools.

In 1922 local SAR Chapters and State Societies reported over 60,000 Constitution Day celebrations held throughout the country.

The New York Chapter of the Empire State Society held a noon program on the steps of Federal Hall on Wall Street. Annually many thousands attended this ceremony to hear prominent speakers talk on the Constitution.

The Philadelphia-Continental Chapter of the Pennsylvania Society has continually held Constitution Day programs with hundreds attending. A wreath was usually placed at Independence Hall. For many years there was a large parade.

There was a constant SAR effort to have definite instructions on the Constitution in the public schools. By 1929 the legislatures of 38 states had passed bills requiring such courses.

In 1949 all governors issued Constitution Day Proclamations and all Superintendents of Education were requested to allot time for observances.

Through the years ceremonies were held at many graves of Signers of the Constitution. Some of the graves had been in oblivion for many years. For example, Georgia Signer Colonel William Few had moved to New York, where he served in the New York Assembly and as an alderman in New York City. The Georgia Society desired to mark Colonel Few's grave but its location was unknown. After considerable searching, his tomb was finally located at Fishkill-on-the-Hudson. On October 5, 1939 a Georgia granite tablet was unveiled by SAR President General Kimball with members of the Georgia Society and the Empire State Society present.

Prior to television, radio was an excellent medium for Constitution Day programs. Compatriot George A. Bunting, founder of the Noxell Corporation, was an ardent supporter of SAR programs. Through his efforts in 1944-1945-1946 the SAR planned a Constitution Day theme for the popular program, "The Mayor of the Town," featuring Lionel Barrymore.

In 1938 the San Diego Chapter suggested "National Citizenship Day" as part of Constitution Day for all newly naturalized citizens in the foregoing year to be recognized into American citizenship. Oddly, Constitution Day was eliminated for national observance by resolution of the United States Congress and approved by the President on February 29, 1952; and September 17 was designated as Citizenship Day.

In 1955 the Daughters of the American Revolution promoted the concept of devoting the entire week to include both Constitution Day and Citizenship Day. The United States Congress and Compatriot President Eisenhower approved the resolution for Constitution Week to begin on September 17 of each year. It continues as the national governmental policy today.

Compatriot Bessent has done extensive research over the past few years concerning the establishment of formal recognition of Constitution Day. He clearly documents that the Iowa SAR provided for the observance of Constitution Day in the state in 1911, the first public recognition. *State Societies and Chapters are encouraged to use this series of Centennial stories in promoting the SAR. These articles will appear through the Centennial in 1989.*

CENTENNIAL HERITAGE FACTS

The SAR and the National Archives

By Former President General Carl F. Bessent

For the first 120 years of the United States the valuable records of the nation were stored in various government buildings in the attics, basements, sub-cellars, and in rented warehouses. The lack of concern resulted in many being lost. There was no organization to the records, and they could not be consulted.

In 1881 although the United States Senate passed a bill providing for a National Archives, it did not become law.

The National Society of the Sons of the American Revolution was organized in 1889. The SAR's interest in gathering and publishing the records of the Revolutionary War began with the first SAR Annual Congress in Louisville in 1890. A resolution was approved recommending that the Revolutionary War records in boxes and barrels in various rooms in the State Department be removed and placed in a fire-proof storage area with proper indexing and public accessibility.

This SAR resolution resulted in the United States Congress passing a law on July 27, 1892 directing the War Department to collect the Revolutionary War records. Compatriot Senator Redfield Proctor, who had been the Secretary of War, influenced passage of this legislation.

In 1903 Congress authorized purchase of land for a National Archives building. Later the acquired land was used for the Department of Interior Building. Except for the patriotic societies, there was no great impelling public sentiment demanding an appropriation for a National Archives.

In 1907 the SAR Annual Congress passed a resolution that Revolutionary War Naval records be collected by the Navy Department. This resulted in the United States Congress passing legislation that such records be collected by the Navy Department.

At every SAR Annual Congress from 1890 to 1912 a Revolutionary War Records Committee was appointed.

Senate Bill 271 enacted on March 2, 1913 authorized the storage and compilation of Revolutionary War records by the Department of Interior.

In 1913 the United States Congress directed the Secretary of the Treasury to prepare designs and estimates for a National Archives building with a capacity of 8,000,000 cubic feet. The cost of the structure was limited to $1,500,000 but the funds were not appropriated. However, $5,000 was appropriated to prepare the design and specifications.

Public Law #402 passed on March 2, 1913 authorizing the collection of the military and naval records of the Revolutionary War by the Secretaries of the Navy and of War.

The appointment of a Special National Archives Committee by the SAR in 1914 was an expression of the interest by the Society to secure the erection of the archives building.

The District of Columbia Society SAR took the lead in the promotion of the National Archives. Compatriots who were active in attending the many Congressional hearings on the matter were: Admiral George Baird, Admiral T. F. Jewell, Commander John H. Moore and General Walter Howe.

The first World War curtailed the efforts for a National Archives. However, the SAR continued to promote the project by appointing the Special National Archives Committee.

Following the war the Special Committee was active in lobbying the United States Congress during the 1920s. Finally in 1926, $2,000,000 was authorized for a National Archives Building on the Mall Triangle. The depression years curtailed the construction.

Ultimately on June 19, 1934 the United States Congress created the National Archives to preserve all the archives and records belonging to the United States. The specially designed National Archives building was completed in 1937.

1984 was the 50th Anniversary of the National Archives. Robert M. Warner, at that time Archivist of the United States, wrote to President General Carl F. Bessent acknowledging the vital support of the SAR in establishing the National Archives.

Societies and Chapters are encouraged to acquaint the communities they serve with the long and distinguished history of the SAR and our objectives. This can be accomplished through appropriate and timely programs of action. The Centennial Observances Committee will be offering suggested programs in the future.

CENTENNIAL HERITAGE FACTS

The SAR and the Origins of Flag Day

By Compatriot Allen R. Yale, Connecticut Society

Jonathan Flynt Morris, in 1861, when he first proposed the celebration of "Flag Day," was a banker in Hartford, Connecticut. He was one of the founders of the Republican Party in Connecticut, active in historical and genealogical matters, a founder of the CTSSAR, (State #5; Nat. #392), its first Registrar and a member of the Board of Managers until his death in 1899.

"At its annual meeting, May 11, 1891 the Connecticut Society of the Sons of the American Revolution voted that a celebration should be held at Lebanon, to commemorate the completion of repairs and restoration of the War Office, and to rededicate the building to public uses. The anniversary of the adoption of our National Flag was selected for this purpose, with a view to establish an observance of the day, for which the society has adopted the title of **Flag Day**."[1]

At this celebration, one of the speakers was Jonathan F. Morris, whom the President, Jonathan Trumbull, introduced as the "originator of the movement providing for the observance of the anniversary of the adoption of our National Flag, and whose untiring interests in the matter and whose earnest efforts in promoting the movement fit him perculiarly to speak on the subject."

Compatriot Morris proceeded to give a history of "Flag Day," which he had proposed 30 years before, in 1861, when, after the secession of some of the States, the firing on Fort Sumter and the call to arms by President Lincoln, there was a "rising of the people; the rallying of the troops; the spontaneous and universal raising of flags. Never before in its history had it been so displayed!"

He recalled that in early June 1861, in the office of the *Hartford Evening Press,* he was talking to the Editor, Charles Dudley Warner, and suggested the propriety of celebrating the approaching birthday anniversary of the Flag. He said the Flag and the Constitution were both on trial.

Mr. Warner agreed and wrote an editorial in the *Press,* which was published on June 10th. He advocated the establishment of the 14th of June and the 17th of September as national holidays, the one to be known as Flag Day and the other as Constitution Day. "Mr. Warner's suggestion for the observance of the day was well taken by the citizens of Hartford. There was a very general display of flags and decorations — the 'red, white and blue' was displayed everywhere. Other towns and cities celebrated too."

A year later, in early June 1862, Mr. Morris wrote to Connecticut Congressman Dwight Loomis, "asking him to introduce in Congress, a resolution for the observance of **Flag Day** as a national holiday, to embrace **Constitution Day** also." The Hon. Loomis readily complied with this request and introduced a resolution on June 12th, which was taken up on the 13th, but laid on the table.[2] The vote to table in the House of Representatives was by a heavy majority as the feeling at that time was there were too many holidays.

He further recalled that in connection with the celebration of the centennial of the flag in 1877, that "a distinguished editor in the Southwest, the Hon. Henry Watterson of Louisville, Kentucky, had on Memorial Day, that year, paid a beautiful tribute to the "starry flag of the Republic." Morris wrote

thanking him for the spirit of the address and suggested the observance of Flag Day that year, and the making of the day a national holiday. Mr. Watterson wrote back that he thought the suggestion an admirable one.

The obituary of J. F. Morris says, among other things, he "took a lively interest in the establishment of 'Flag Day' as a legal holiday and had gathered a greater amount of facts about the stars and stripes than any other man in the country."[3] In his position on the Board of Managers of the CTSSAR until his death, he had a great deal to say on Board actions as regards the fostering of "Flag Day."

Rightfully, unless earlier evidence is uncovered, Compatriot Jonathan Flynt Morris of the Connecticut Society must be considered the originator of "Flag Day." Others copied his promotion of the patriotic holiday. Nevertheless, he is the "Father of Flag Day."

FOOTNOTES

1. *The Lebanon War Office,* The History of the Building and report of the Celebration at Lebanon, Conn. Flag Day, June 15, 1891. Pub. by the Connecticut Society of Sons of the American Revolution. Edited by Jonathan Trumbull. 1891.

2. The National Holiday resolution was reported on p. 2671 of *The Congressional Globe,* containing the debates and proceedings of the second session of the Thirty-seventh Congress. 1862. (Material supplied by Former President General Bessent.)

3. *Hartford Courant,* January 31, 1899.

CENTENNIAL HERITAGE FACTS

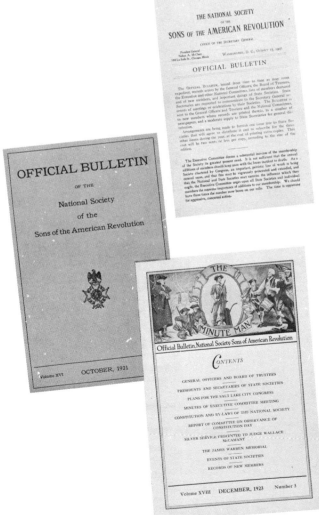

History of THE SAR MAGAZINE

By Former President General Carl F. Bessent

From the beginning of its organization, the National Society of the Sons of the American Revolution has depended on the printed word to disseminate information on activities and accomplishments.

At the outset THE SPIRIT OF '76 Magazine was the unofficial organ until 1906. This magazine contained general information on the SAR and other patriotic societies. Each issue contained sketched illustrations. Compatriot Louis H. Cornish, Secretary of the Empire State Society, was the Editor and Publisher.

In addition, during the early years many State Societies printed Year Books with the registry of its members.

The 1906 SAR Annual Congress authorized the publishing of THE OFFICIAL BULLETIN. The first issue was distributed to all members on October 15, 1906 and was published four times a year. Beginning in May, 1908 the volumes and issues of the BULLETIN were numbered. The BULLETIN issues were 5 inches by 7½ inches and contained an average of 46 pages, giving the President General's Message, National Society and State Society activities, and a listing of new and deceased members. Compatriot Howard Clark, Secretary General, served as Editor until his death in 1918.

Compatriot Philip F. Larner became Editor in 1918 and served until 1921.

From 1894 until 1921 the National Society published a National Society Year Book reviewing the proceedings of the SAR Annual Congress and the activities of the State Societies. It was a hardback book until 1916 when costs dictated a change to paperback; 1,000 copies were printed every year.

In 1921 the SAR Annual Congress eliminated the Annual Year Book and acted to enlarge the size of the BULLETIN. A 6-inch by 9-inch booklet was published in March, June, October and December with an average of 90 pages. A cover, giving a suitable appearance, was provided for the first time.

In December, 1923 the cover design was changed and the magazine became THE MINUTE MAN, OFFICIAL BULLETIN, NATIONAL SOCIETY, SONS OF THE AMERICAN REVOLUTION.

In 1931 the magazine title was changed and copyrighted to THE SONS OF THE AMERICAN REVOLUTION MAGAZINE. In July 1931 the size was increased to 7 inches by 10 inches and featured 150 pages including advertisements. The cover was yellow and white in color, and for the next 18 years averaged between 50 and 150 pages per issue.

Secretary General and Editor Steele became ill in 1949. Compatriot Gardner Osborn, Secretary of the Empire State Society, was named Editor by the Executive Committee. The magazine size was changed to 8 inches by 11 inches and averaged 60 pages per issue.

Compatriot Harold L. Putnam became Executive Secretary and Editor in 1950. The only change to

the magazine was in its cover. The yellow was replaced by a buff color. The Editor wrote a column to present his views on public issues. In the Spring of 1957 Robert S. W. Walker was appointed Editor.

The magazine cover format changed again in January, 1965. The magazine features were listed in bold print with light blue and white colors.

The magazine staff was augmented with the addition of George S. Carll as Assistant Editor.

Compatriot Harold Putnam retired as Executive Secretary and Editor in October 1966 and Compatriot Warren S. Woodward of the Empire State Society was employed as Executive Secretary and Editor. The most drastic change was again in the cover. It carried colorful illustrations of patriotic shrines and subjects, with the Annual Congress issue having a collage of Congress pictures.

After eleven years of service, Compatriot Woodward resigned in the summer of 1977. Lieutenant General Herman Nickerson was appointed Executive Secretary and Editor. There were no basic changes in the magazine.

Following the publication of six issues of the magazine and the relocation of SAR National Headquarters to Louisville, Kentucky in late 1978, Compatriot Ralph Godell of the Kansas Society was appointed Executive Secretary, and Compatriot Winston C. Williams of the Wisconsin Society was engaged as Editor of THE SAR MAGAZINE. Compatriot Williams is the current Editor.

CENTENNIAL HERITAGE FACTS

NSSAR Headquarters

By Former President General

Carl F. Bessent

Prior to 1927 the business of the National Society was conducted by each elected officer from his business office or his home. In reality the National Headquarters was the President General's home.

On May 18, 1925 at the 37th SAR Annual Congress in Swampscott, Massachusetts, a Resolution was passed that a National Headquarters be established in Washington, DC. In President General Harvey Foote's words: "We must establish a National Headquarters in Washington in our own building."

On June 6, 1926 in Philadelphia, Pennsylvania, the Board of National Trustees passed a Resolution that a committee be appointed to raise $250,000 to provide a suitable National Headquarters in Washington. Compatriot Henry F. Baker, a future President General, was appointed Campaign Chairman. He stated the dignity and prestige of the Society demands that there be established in Washington a Headquarters suitable to our needs.

The SAR Annual Congress meeting in Richmond, Virginia, in May 1927 authorized the purchase of the Norman Williams Mansion and its valuable furnishings, located at 1227 Sixteenth Street, Northwest, Washington, DC for $145,000. Compatriot Baker had raised $25,000 for the initial down payment.

On August 26, 1927 President General Ernest Rogers, Compatriot Baker, and Secretary General Frank B. Steels met in Washington to complete the purchase of the property. Due to certain legal restrictions in the SAR Constitution at the time, the three Compatriots individually signed a note for $120,000 and took the property. After the restrictions were cleared, the property was transferred to the National Society. The $120,000 was mortgaged with the American Security and Trust Company with a yearly interest of $6,600.

The National Society began operations at the Sixteenth Street Headquarters on October 1, 1927.

An unusual fact is that the first gift to the Headquarters Fund Campaign was $200 given by Mrs. John Miller Horton of Buffalo, New York. She was the Regent of the Buffalo Chapter, Daughters of the American Revolution. The gift was in honor of her father, Compatriot Pascal Paoli Pratt.

The 40th SAR Annual Congress was held in Washington, DC in 1928. Only $51,000 had been pledged to the mortgage. Former President General Louis Ames addressed the Congress on why the National Headquarters was important in the nation's Capitol and presented a new Headquarters Fund Plan.

By May 10, 1929 $110,000 had been pledged by Compatriots.

On November 1, 1929 President-Elect Herbert Hoover visited the Sixteenth Street SAR National Headquarters to be inducted into membership as a Life Member of the Pennsylvania Society.

The financial condition of the country after 1929 made the raising of large amounts of money extremely difficult, but determined Compatriots resolved to clear the Headquarters indebtedness.

In 1932, the Bicentennial of George Washington's Birth, after five years of Headquarters ownership, all but $40,000 of the mortgage had been paid. The mortgage was finally liquidated on August 26, 1935 by issuing Certificates of Indebtedness to SAR members, and these were paid off by 1955.

On May 20, 1940 a 47-inch by 34-inch bronze memorial tablet was unveiled at the Headquarters. It listed the names of Compatriots, State Societies and Chapters who carried the financial burden and generously donated to acquire the Headquarters. This tablet is at the entrance of the present Headquarters.

In 1956 the National Education Association desired the Sixteenth Street Headquarters property and offered a price of $250,000. A committee was appointed to explore the possibilities of the offer.

In 1957 at the 67th Annual Congress in Salt Lake City, Utah, Philadelphia tendered a very attractive offer for the National Headquarters to relocate there. President General Eugene Carver stated: "Our National Headquarters belongs in Washington as long as Washington is our nation's Capitol."

Admiral William Furlong was appointed Chairman of the National Headquarters Committee. He visited and inspected over 30 properties seeking a site in Washington.

On February 8, 1958 President General George Tarbox convened a Special SAR Congress in Washington, DC, with 88 delegates present. The Congress finally resolved to purchase the General Patrick Hurley home of 8,000 square feet located at 2412 Massachusetts Avenue, Northwest, Washington, DC, for $165,000. A Congressional Bill was approved by the 85th United States Congress to give the proper zoning for the SAR to purchase and occupy the property.

The new Headquarters was opened for business on September 1, 1958 enabling the staff to function with a greater degree of efficiency. The new building gave an improved office arrangement and offered better working conditions.

The transaction, the sale of the Sixteenth Street property for $294,000, the purchase of the Massachusetts Avenue property for $165,000 with alterations and improvements of $52,475, allowed $76,000 to be added to the Permanent Fund.

A Memorial Library and Auditorium to the Massachusetts Avenue Headquarters was proposed in 1963 for an estimated cost of $500,000. President General Charles Anderson appointed a special committee to develop plans and raise the necessary funds. At the 1964 SAR Annual Congress, Special Committee Chairman Herschel Murphy, a Former President General, reported the proposed structure would cost $1,500,000. A fund campaign was initiated with limited results.

The possibility of losing the District of Columbia real estate tax exemption and the increasing cost of operating the National Headquarters in Washington raised the question of establishing the Headquarters elsewhere. There were continual offers made to purchase the valuable Massachusetts Avenue property.

The National Trustees meeting in Washington, DC, on Febrary 12, 1977 authorized the sale of the National Headquarters property. On March 17, 1977 the SAR National

Headquarters on 2412 Massachusetts Avenue was sold to the Ivory Coast Government for use as their embassy for the price of $800,000.

Temporary SAR Headquarters were located at 2560 Huntington Avenue in Alexandria, Virginia, just off the Capitol Beltway. Over 4,700 square feet of office space was rented from June 1977 until January 1979.

On May 30, 1978 the 88th Annual Congress meeting in Louisville, Kentucky, approved a National Headquarters Acquisition Commission with the authority to acquire a National Headquarters property. President General Calvin E. Chunn appointed Former President General Walter Martin as Chairman. One Compatriot from each of the 13 SAR Districts was appointed to serve on the Commission.

Four particular properties were visited and surveyed: the Alcoa Building in downtown Atlanta, Georgia; a mansion property at University Circle in the Western Reserve section of Cleveland, Ohio; the large Emory Estate in the outskirts of Cincinnati, Ohio; and, the Kentucky Grand Lodge of the Free and Accepted Masons in Louisville, Kentucky.

After a careful evaluation, the Commission decided to purchase the Grand Lodge structure located at 1000 South Fourth Street and Kentucky Avenue for $404,000. The actual purchase was made on December 12, 1978 and the SAR took possession on January 1, 1979.

There was a special dedication ceremony held at the National Trustees Meeting in Louisville on February 3, 1979 with President General Chunn presiding. Local dignitaries attending included Louisville Mayor William Stansbury, County Judge Mitch McConnell and United States Congressman Romano Mazzoli.

The two-story steel and concrete fireproof structure of 14,000 square feet was built in 1954. In 1984 a 1,400 square foot extension was constructed on the southwest corner of the building to give an improved office arrangement and to provide space for automation equipment. Former President General and Mrs. Arthur M. King gifted the funds for the project. The $176,000 addition was dedicated at the 95th SAR Annual Congress on June 1, 1985.

There are continual improvements and enhancements to the SAR National Headquarters and it should satisfy all staff and Society requirements of the National Society for a long period into the future.

CENTENNIAL HERITAGE FACTS

The SAR Tricolors

By Former President General Carl F. Bessent

The original colors adopted by the National Society of the Sons of the American Revolution were blue and white. The Colors of the Society of the Cincinnati were also blue and white — although the SAR blue was a deeper color than the blue used by the Society of the Cincinnati. There was a general feeling by many that the SAR Colors infringed on the Colors of the Society of the Cincinnati.

A resolution was offered by Compatriot Archie Lee Talbot of the Maine Society SAR (SAR # 6411) at the 7th Annual SAR Congress in Richmond, Virginia, in 1896, calling for a tricolor combination as the SAR Colors.

The proposal suggested using the complete colors of the Revolutionary Army — blue, buff and white. General George Washington's uniform was a blue coat with a buff facing, white waistcoat and breeches. There was a desire to have SAR Society Colors distinctive and different from the colors of other societies. However, there was strong opposition to any change from the original SAR colors.

President General Horace Porter ruled the color resolution was out of order. It required an amendment to the Bylaws.

Compatriot Talbot conducted persuasive presentations in the next two years. He properly presented a Bylaw Amendment at the 9th Annual Congress, in Morristown, New Jersey, in 1898. The Congress approved changing the Colors to the present tricolors — blue, buff and white.

The shade of the SAR blue has varied through the years. In 1984, at the request of President General Carl F. Bessent, a color check was made against the blue of General George Washington's uniform in the Smithsonian Institute in Washington, DC. The blue uniform color is Pantone 282C on the Pantone Color Chart. This blue is to be used as the SAR standard.

Compatriot Archie Lee Talbot was born on September 14, 1846 in Phillips, Maine. He graduated from Maine Wesleyan Seminary at Kent's Hill, Maine, in 1867. He then took up the study of law. In 1877 he was appointed Deputy Collector of Internal Revenue under President Grant. Later he established a successful insurance agency in Lewiston, Maine. Talbot joined the SAR on February 11, 1893 and served as President of the Maine society. He passed away in Lewiston on December 29, 1932, at the age of 86.

FOR PUBLICIZING OUR 100 YEARS — The National Centennial Observances Committee, headed by William C. Gist of the Kentucky Society, has released for sale this bumper sticker to help spread the word that SAR will complete a century of service in 1989. Measuring 11½ inches long by 3 inches deep, it is printed in red and blue ink on a white background. It has a pressure-sensitive backing. The cost for one is $1.25; ten are $11. Orders should be sent to the Merchandise Department at Headquarters in Louisville; the item is identified as Catalog No. 0860.

THE COVER PHOTOGRAPH, taken in the President General's office at National Headquarters, shows these Compatriots examining the valued Charter: (seated) PG Nolan W. Carson; (standing, left) Historian General James R. Westlake; and Former PG Carl F. Bessent, the author of this article.

CENTENNIAL HERITAGE FACTS

The National Society Charter

By Former President General Carl F. Bessent

A charter is a written instrument executed in proper form by a sovereign power creating and defining a franchise with granted rights to a corporation or organization. It is essentially a contract between a governmental body and a corporation.

The Sons of the American Revolution Charter is a document issued by the United States Congress creating the National Society, defining its purposes, functions and organization. The Charter has an interesting history.

On January 17, 1890 the National Society was incorporated in the State of Connecticut through the efforts of the first President General, Judge Lucius P. Deming. The Society became truly national in character in its first years as it grew and prospered.

The General Board of Managers meeting at the Bellevue-Stratford Hotel in Philadelphia on December 4, 1904 questioned whether the Society was properly and legally constituted and incorporated. Thus, a special committee was appointed to investigate the issue fully and present recommendations to the next Annual Congress. Committee members were Judge Morris B. Beardsley of the Connecticut Society and John P. Earnest of the District of Columbia Society.

The special committee reported to the 16th Annual Congress, which convened on the second floor of Independence Hall in Philadelphia, May 1, 2 and 3, 1905. The report stated that the procedures incorporating the National Society under the laws of the State of Connecticut were not legally followed, resulting in the Society being primarily a voluntary association.

The Congress voted that another special committee be appointed to incorporate the National Society under the laws of the District of Columbia and to initiate efforts to secure a special national charter from the United States Congress. President General James Hancock appointed the following Compatriots to the committee: Judge Morris B. Beardsley, Connecticut Society, Chairman; Nelson A. McClary, Illinois Society; John Paul Earnest, District of Columbia Society; and Judge Henry Stockbridge, Maryland Society.

The committee reported to the General Board of Managers at the Waldorf-Astoria Hotel, New York City, on Saturday, November 26, 1905. Judge Beardsley reported it was "inexpedient" to incorporate under the laws of the District of Columbia because of local requirements and recommended that incorporation be secured by action of the United States Congress. The report was accepted and the special committee was directed to proceed.

During the first session of the 59th United States Congress on January 26, 1906, Compatriot Congressman Ebenezer J. Hill of Connecticut introduced House of Representatives bill #15332 incorporating the National Society of the Sons of the American Revolution. The bill was referred to the House Committee on the District of Columbia which gave approval. The bill passed the House of Representatives unanimously on February 26, 1906.

The bill was transmitted to the Senate and passed on May 23, 1906 with a minor amendment. The passage in the Senate was promoted by Compatriots Senators Brandegec, Bulkeley, Depew, Dillingham and Frye.

The bill was returned to the House of Representatives and passed as amended on June 5, 1906.

Finally Public Act Number 214 was approved and signed on June 9, 1906 by Compatriot President Theodore Roosevelt.

The first meeting of the Corporation under the new Charter, the National Society of the Sons of the American Revolution, was called pursuant to Section 5 of the Charter, to be held at the New Willard Hotel in Washington, D.C. on November 17, 1906. The new Charter was formally accepted and this action was communicated with a certificate of acceptance to the Secretary of State.

The Charter granted by the Congress of the United States made it necessary to revise the SAR Constitution and Bylaws. The original Constitution was not radically changed, only in wording to conform to the new Charter.

The main business of the 18th Annual Congress held in Denver, Colorado, on June 3 and 4, 1907 was revision of the Constitution. Much time was spent in deciding the number of Congress delegates, the timing of Annual Congresses and national dues. The problems at that time were similar to ones faced today. There was a move to increase the national dues from 25 to 50 cents. A new SAR Constitution and Bylaws consistent with the new Charter was approved, and the new Society incorporated by the United States Congress came into existence.

As an organization chartered by the United States Congress, the SAR is required to furnish an annual report to the Congress.

An impressive document preserved by the National Society is the Act of Incorporation passed by the 59th Congress of the United States. It bears the signatures of Theodore Roosevelt, President of the United States and a Compatriot; Charles Warren Fairbanks, Vice President of the United States and President of the United

States Senate; and Honorable Joseph Cannon, Speaker of the House of Representatives.

The beautiful engrossed copy of the Charter was received from the Department of State with a certificate signed by Compatriot Secretary of State, the Honorable Elihú Root. It is an outstanding example of the penman's art.

Section 2 of the Charter spells out the purposes and objects of the National Society.

This is the first of six pages that make up the Charter. The list of names beginning at the bottom were those of the National Officers, living Former Presidents General, the Board of Management and the Presidents of the State Societies in 1906.

President Theodore Roosevelt, an SAR, signed the last page of the Charter.

This document accompanied the copy of the Charter that was given to the National Society. Signed by Compatriot J. Elihu Root, Secretary of State, it attested to the fact that the copy was a true one. His seal is at the left.

CENTENNIAL HERITAGE FACTS

PIERCE'S REGISTER — A Valuable SAR Asset

By Former President General Carl F. Bessent

One of the most valuable assets of the Sons of the American Revolution is its 1786 copy of PIERCE'S REGISTER. It is rare in that there are only three such copies in existence.

PIERCE'S REGISTER is the final settlement account between the United States Government and the officers and soldiers of the Revolutionary War Continental Army. The Continental Congress on July 4, 1783 authorized the Paymaster General to settle all accounts with the Continental Army officers and soldiers by issuing certificates of indebtedness.

In accordance with this resolution, Paymaster General John Pierce prepared and issued certificates as final payment to the members of the Continental Army. The accounting did not include the offi-

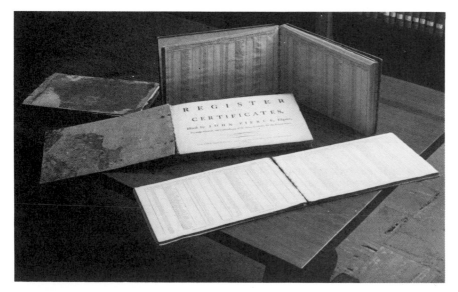

Former President General Carl F. Bessent, the author of this article, is shown viewing one of the four volumes making up the PIERCE'S REGISTER collection maintained in the Library at National Headquarters. The complete set is at the left. The books were obtained in 1912 for only $200.

cers and soldiers of the individual States' Militia Armies. Also, it did not provide for the officers and soldiers of South Carolina, due to a special fiduciary relationship between the Continental Congress and the State of South Carolina.

Arranged chronologically by the date of issue, 93,843 certificates were given out between July 11, 1783 and September 15, 1785. The certificates totaled $10,791,815.78. The register gives only the name of the officer or soldier to whom the certificate was issued and gives no reference to rank, military unit and organization, or state.

In 1786 a limited number of copies of PIERCE'S REGISTER for official use were printed by Francis Child at the New Printing Office, opposite the Coffee-House Bridge in New York City.

The original six volume PIERCE'S REGISTER under the title of *REGISTER OF THE CERTIFICATE, ISSUED BY JOHN PIERCE, PAYMASTER GENERAL, AND COMMISSIONER OF THE ARMY ACCOUNTS, FOR THE UNITED STATES* is preserved by the Manuscript Division of the Library of Congress.

The copies of the 1786 printing are in a four-volume set, each 8 inches by 13 inches with a total of 930 pages. There are only three complete sets of the 1786 copy of PIERCE'S REGISTER. One is in the Library of Congress, one is in the National Archives and the third set is owned by the SAR.

The SAR copy of the register was purchased in 1912 for $200 on instructions from President General Rogers C. B. Thurston.

In 1915 the Seventeenth Annual Report of the Daughters of the American Revolution included an alphabetically arranged content of PIERCE'S REGISTER. This arrangement was due to the effort of a special DAR Committee chaired by Mrs. Amos G. Draper. A reprint of this DAR report was published as Senate Document #988 of the 3d Session of the 63d United States Congress. Later it was printed by the Genealogical Publishing Company of Baltimore in 1973 and reprinted in 1976.

Acknowledgment: The author benefited in this presentation from the knowledgeable assistance of Dr. Marilyn K. Parr, Reference Specialist, Library of Congress.

CENTENNIAL HERITAGE FACTS

A Tribute to Patriot von Steuben

By Former President General Carl F. Bessent

During the past 100 years, the Sons of the American Revolution have honored Revolutionary War Patriots in many different ways. Probably the most unusual ceremony was held in connection with the 41st SAR Annual Congress.

Congress Headquarters was the Hotel Berkeley-Carteret, Asbury Park, New Jersey, June 1-4, 1930. The business sessions were held in the new Convention Hall on the beach near the hotel. The SAR was the first organization to use the Convention Hall.

The Airship Graf Zeppelin had just completed a record trip from Seville, Spain to South America and was now berthed at the Lakehurst Naval Air Station, New Jersey. The giant dirigible was scheduled to leave Lakehurst on Monday evening, June 2, to make the return trip back to Europe.

Contact was made with Commander Hugo Eckener who was eager to assist in honoring Baron Von Steuben by dropping a wreath over the Berkeley-Carteret Hotel.

The Congress delegates and their ladies were attending the Congress reception on Monday evening. Just at dusk they were notified that the dirigible was nearing Asbury Park. The assemblage left the Ball Room and went to the lawn and watched as the majestic airship, 800 feet long and 100 feet in diameter, came gracefully into view. It glided slowly, only several hundred feet above the hotel.

The bridge cabin trap-door opened and a wreath floated down to earth on a small parachute. It landed on a nearby solarium. The wreath carried SAR Colors and included an engraved card:

"In commemoration and honor of Baron Von Steuben who aided America's Cause in the

Participating in the wreath laying ceremony at the von Steuben statue were (from left): Baron Puttitz, Color Bearer A. A. Hoffman, Acting Secretary of War Davidson, President General Van Orsdel, Secretary General Frank B. Steele and Color Bearers John T. Finley and J. C. McGrew.

Revolutionary War, Dr. Hugo Eckener, Commander of the Graf Zeppelin presents compliments to the Sons of the American Revolution."

A special ceremony was held at the statue of Baron Von Steuben in Lafayette Park, Washington, on Monday, June 16. Honorable Josiah A. Van Orsdel, President General SAR, presided at the formalities. Baron Wolfgang Puttitz represented the German Government and presented the Graf Zeppelin Wreath to the Secretary of War, Honorable F. Trubee Davidson, who placed it at the base of the statue. There were many spectators at this event.

CENTENNIAL HERITAGE FACTS

SAR — Outstanding Quality for a Century

By Former President General Benjamin H. Morris

From the date of its founding on April 30, 1889 SAR has attracted leaders in government, business, the professions and the military. Our beliefs in patriotism, history and education have provided a common basis for participation by the men who have led this country for almost a century.

The organizational meeting at Fraunces Tavern in New York City was composed of outstanding men from all parts of the country. Among the officers elected were five Vice Presidents who were Governors of states: Buckner of Kentucky, Dillingham of Vermont, Francis of Missouri, Green of New Jersey and Hampton of South Carolina. Also present were an assortment of generals, admirals, senators and other governmental and business leaders. France, our valiant friend in the Revolution, was represented by M. Edmond de Lafayette of Paris.

As the SAR grew, men of outstanding ability, leaders in all fields, joined its ranks. Former foes in the Civil War were reunited in patriotism in the Sons of the American Revolution. Union Admiral David D. Porter and General Horace Porter (later President General) and Confederate Generals Joseph E. Johnston and Joseph Wheeler are a few of the many military leaders of that bitter conflict who became compatriots.

12 Served As U.S. President

Topping SAR's star-studded roster are twelve men who have served as President of the United States. Chief Executives whom we proudly call Compatriot are Rutherford B. Hayes, Benjamin Harrison, William McKinley, William Howard Taft, Theodore Roosevelt, Warren G. Harding, Calvin Coolidge, Herbert Hoover, Harry S. Truman, Dwight D. Eisenhower, Lyndon B. Johnson and Gerald R. Ford. Their pictures are on display in the Memorabilia Room at National Headquarters.

Although our Revolution was fought to gain freedom from Great Britain, one of Britain's most famous leaders, Prime Minister Sir Winston Churchill, was a member of SAR; his mother, Jennie Jerome, descended from an American Patriot, Lt. Reuben Murray, of the Albany County (NY) militia. In today's British government, the Lord Chancellor, Lord Hailsham, is an SAR.

Many Serve in Congress

In the Congress of the United States

Graduating third in the 1860 Class at the Military Academy in West Point, Horace Porter was President General of the SAR in 1892-96. He was on Grant's staff and attained the rank of Brigadier General. In addition to being President of the Pullman Company and a Director of Equitable Life, he was President of the Union League Club in Chicago. While Ambassador to France in 1897, he located the body of John Paul Jones and had it brought to the United States; it now is entombed at the Naval Academy in Annapolis.

SARs have played outstanding roles from 1889 to the present (space permits a listing of only a few of the senators and representatives who have worn the SAR rosette). The earlier days of our membership included Senators Chauncey Depew, Mark Hanna, Henry Cabot Lodge and John W. Daniels. Later came Senators Arthur Vandenberg, Robert A. Taft, Tom Connally, Homer Capehart, Leverett Saltonstall, Thruston Morton, Harry Byrd, Richard Russell and Harley Kilgore. Most recently we have had Barry Goldwater, Sam Ervin, Jr., Sam Nunn and Charles Mathias — while the durable J. Strom Thurmond still carries on.

In the House, "Mr. Sam", Speaker Sam Rayburn from Texas, was an SAR, as were two sons of President Franklin Roosevelt, Franklin Jr. and James. Hale Boggs of Louisiana was a former Majority Leader of the House. Today, Compatriot Jack Kemp

A 1915 graduate of the Military Academy at West Point, Dwight D. Eisenhower was our country's 34th President. He rose through Army ranks to become the Supreme Commander of the Allied Forces in Europe during World War II. He became Head of the Joint Chiefs of Staff in 1949-50 and Supreme Commander NATO 1951-52. The painting shown here was rendered in 1960 and donated to our Society by Laurens M. Hamilton, who then was Vice-President General for the South Atlantic District. Painted by Erik Haupt, a noted portraitist, it depicts Compatriot Eisenhower with an SAR rosette in his suit lapel. It is prominently displayed at National Headquarters.

is an announced candidate for the Republican nomination for President.

America's wars from the Civil War to Vietnam have given SAR some of its most famous members. From the Spanish-American War we claimed "The Hero of Manila", Admiral George Dewey. World War I's General of the Army, John J. Pershing, was SAR.

Winston Churchill took over the reins of the British government as Hitler marched on France during World War II. A world statesman of his time, he championed his ideals of freedom, democracy and justice.

From World War II, Generals Dwight D. Eisenhower, Douglas MacArthur, Jonathan M. Wainwright and Jacob L. Devers, and Admiral William F. ("Bull") Halsey were members — and from the cruel Vietnam conflict we list General William Westmoreland and Vice Admiral James Stockdale, a prisoner of North Vietnam for 7½ years.

Numerous Famed Jurists

To the United States Supreme Court SAR has furnished a number of distinguished jurists. Members have included Chief Justices Charles Evans Hughes and Fred M. Vinson, Justices David J. Brewer and Harold H. Burton.

SAR has also provided many leading jurists in the highest courts of our states. They include Walter B. Beale, former judge of the Washington Supreme Court; George H. Bradford, Justice of the Colorado Supreme Court; Edward S. Delaplaine, Chief Judge of the Maryland Court of Appeals; J. P. Dalton, former Chief Justice of the Missouri Supreme Court; Charles Loring, former Chief Justice of the Minnesota Supreme Court; Curtis G. Shake, former Judge of the Indiana Supreme Court; Harold J. Warner, former Chief Justice, Oregon Supreme Court; William M. Maltbie, former Chief Justice of the Connecticut Supreme Court and G. Mennen Williams, recently retired as Chief Justice of the Michigan Supreme Court (he also served as Governor). Currently serving as Chief Justice of the Nevada Supreme Court is Compatriot John C. Mowbray, former VPG and Chancellor General.

Other SAR leaders in government has been Frank B. Kellogg and Elihu Root, both of whom served as Secretary of State; Thomas E. Dewey, Governor of New York and twice candidate for President; Thomas Kean, Governor of New Jersey; Charles S. Robb, Governor of Virginia; Levi P. Morton, Vice President of the United States; Rogers C. B. Morton, Secretary of the Interior; Warren R. Austin, Ambassador to the United Nations and Secretary of State; Nelson Rockefeller, Governor of New York and Vice President of the United States; Paul Fannin, Senator from Arizona; Senator Mike Monroney, from Oklahoma; John S. Tower of Texas and the present Ambassador to France, Joseph M. Rodgers.

Professionals and Businessmen

In the professions and business the list of notable leaders from SAR is quite long. In education, religion, finance, journalism, law and medicine SAR members have been and are at the top. A few of the well-known leaders are:

EDUCATION: Daniel Cort Gilmer, President of Johns Hopkins University; Timothy Dwight, President, Yale University; Dr. Ernest M. Hopkins, President, Dartmouth College; Elvis J. Stahr, President of Indiana University; and Roscoe Pound, Dean of Harvard Law School.

PUBLISHING: William Randolph Hearst, Jr., Hearst Publications; Arthur Hays Sulzberger, New York Times; Frank Gannett, Gannett Newspapers.

BUSINESS AND FINANCE: George H. Swift, Jr., Chairman, Swift and Company; Count Rene de Chambrun, Chairman of Baccarat Company; Colonel Louis Annin Ames (PG 1918), President of Annin Flag Company, with whom we still do business; Bernard Baruch, Financier and Advisor of Presidents; Keith Funston, Chairman, New York Stock Exchange.

RELIGION: Rev. Norman Vincent Peale, Clergyman and Author; Ezra Taft Benson, President of the Church of Latter Day Saints (served under President Eisenhower as Secretary of Agriculture).

COMMUNICATIONS AND ENTERTAINMENT: Bing Crosby ("Der Bingle"), Singer and Movie Star, friend of Bob Hope, who received SAR's First "Distinguished Patriot Award" in 1986; Lowell Thomas, Commentator; Charles H. Goren, bridge expert.

Our last frontiers of air and space have found SARs leading in the mid-1900s as they did in the earlier years. Joe Foss was one of World War II's leading aces (he was later governor of South Dakota). The first American in space, Rear Admiral Alan B. Shepard, Jr., was SAR as was Air Force Colonel Charles M. Duke, Jr., Astronaut of the Apollo 16 Mission who walked on the moon.

Compatriot Alan B. Shepard became America's first man in space on May 5, 1961 when he reached an altitude of 115 miles while riding the Capsule *Freedom 7*. His 15-minute trip of 302 miles began at Cape Canaveral, Florida and ended with splashdown in the Atlantic Ocean. In 1971 he commanded the Apollo 14 flight to the moon and joined the ranks of moonwalkers. A 1944 graduate of the Naval Academy, he retired in 1974 as the first astronaut to become a rear admiral. This color photograph, which is now hanging at National Headquarters, is autographed by Compatriot Shepard.

To do its job effectively SAR needs men of varied interests and abilities. The great majority of our members do not achieve national prominence, yet they contribute the resourcefulness, the dedication and the elbow grease that keeps SAR growing and improving. What, then, is the importance to SAR of our more illustrious members? Many have worked hard for SAR. For example, Former President Hoover was a member of the Executive Committee in 1936. But, aside from that, an organization is judged by many by the achievements and standing of its members. Just as a nation needs heroes, an organization needs members whose careers have set examples of outstanding service and performance in their chosen fields.

CENTENNIAL HERITAGE FACTS

The SAR and DAR Working Together

By Former President General Carl F. Bessent

There has been a close and strong relationship between the Sons of the American Revolution and the Daughters of the American Revolution since their foundings. They are brother and sister organizations in every sense and have supported each other through the years.

The first SAR National Congress was held in Louisville, Kentucky, on May 30, 1890. At this Congress a new SAR Constitution was adopted and other major issues were decided. One of the decisions adopted was to have a military comradery fellowship type organization which ladies were not expected to join, and it was therefore "Sons" in the true gender sense. Up to this time much pressure had been exerted to include ladies in the new organization. Actually, ladies had been accepted into membership in some SAR State Societies.

Several ladies in Washington, D.C. were aroused by the action of the SAR Congress and made plans to form a ladies Revolutionary War patriotic society.

In the formation period of the "Daughters," Miss Mary Desha and Miss Eugenia Washington, two of the DAR founders, consulted with Dr. George Brown Goode, SAR Registrar General, and A. Howard Clark, SAR Secretary General. William O. McDowell, SAR #1, who had a lead role in organizing the SAR, gave continual advice.

At 2 pm on October 11, 1890, eighteen interested ladies met at the Stratford Arms in Washington to organize the DAR. A number of SAR members were present. Compatriot McDowell, who had presided at the organizing meeting of the SAR, was invited to preside, with Wilson L. Gill serving as the secretary for the meeting. The first DAR Advisory Board was composed of all SAR members: Dr. G. Brown Goode, Chairman; William C. Warlock.; William O. McDowell; Henry V. Boynton; General Marcus J. Wright; and Wilson L. Gill. At early DAR meetings, these advisors were asked to sit in an anteroom, offering their opinions when asked, but never participating in the meeting actions or knowing if the advice was being followed.

Compatriot Clark conceived the plan for having local level chapters with the National Headquarters in Washington. This scheme led to the rapid growth of the DAR.

MRS. RAYMOND FRANKLIN FLECK
PRESIDENT GENERAL
NATIONAL SOCIETY DAUGHTERS OF THE AMERICAN REVOLUTION

Our sincere and hearty congratulations to the National Society of the Sons of the the American Revolution on your Centennial. You are to be commended for your 100 years of service.

As we prepare for our own centennial, we are always reminded of the help given by the SAR when the Daughters of the American Revolution was being organized in 1890.

Thank you for your guidance in our early years. May both the SAR and the DAR continue to help each other as we begin our second century of service.

Ann D. Fleck

As pointed out in this story, Compatriot George Brown Goode designed the DAR Insignia. The symbolism is based on a spinning wheel that was owned by his mother. That artifact, now residing at DAR Headquarters in Washington, DC, is pictured here with DAR President General Ann D. Fleck.

The first membership application blanks were provided by the SAR. The Daughters scratched out "Sons" and substituted "Daughters." The Daughters used a copy of the SAR Constitution in drafting their own.

SAR member Dr. G. Brown Goode of the Smithsonian Institution designed the DAR Insignia, which is beautiful in its simplicity. He was granted Patent #401584 on September 22, 1891 for his design which he assigned to the DAR. His design was based on his mother's spinning wheel which he gifted to the DAR.

In the early period Mrs. Tulloch, the DAR Treasurer General, encountered problems with accounting procedures. Charles Waldo Haskins, Treasurer General of the SAR, reviewed and simplified the DAR accounting system.

In February, 1903 the SAR gave the Daughters a beautiful silk American Flag which was raised in the presence of the Delegates to the Thirteenth Continental Congress at the site of the proposed Memorial Continental Hall. SAR members Bernard R. Green, who had built the Library of Congress, and General M. Wilson served as advisors to the DAR Committee of Architecture in the planning and construction of the Memorial Continental Hall.

Many husband-wife teams took leading roles in the work of the two societies. A. Howard Clark was Secretary General of the SAR; his wife was a Vice President General and Registrar General of the DAR. Judge William Wirt Henry, grandson of Patrick Henry, was the first President of the Virginia Society SAR; his wife was the first Regent of the Virginia State Society DAR. Colonel Adolphus S. Hubbard was the first President of the California Society SAR; his wife was the first State Regent of the California State Society DAR.

In 1924 President General Louis Ames of the SAR worked with President General Mrs. Cook of the DAR and designed the DAR Banner.

Today the DAR is the strongest patriotic hereditary society in America. There have been more patriotic accomplishments by the DAR than would have been possible with a mixed patriotic society composed of men and women. Through the years the two societies with the same aims and purposes have walked hand in hand.

In the beginning the older brother took the little sister by the hand and helped her through the initial difficult days until she was able to walk alone. Through the past century the brother has loved his sister devotedly. Their mutual association has grown stronger with passage of time.

Together we share a love for our great country and knowledge that God is the foundation of the nation. Together, we pledge to pass our love for God and country to succeeding generations and hold steadfast to the faith of our forefathers.

CENTENNIAL HERITAGE FACTS

Society of the Sons of the Revolutionary Sires

By Former President General Carl F. Bessent

In marking the Centennial of our Society, it is appropriate to review how the Society of the Sons of the Revolutionary Sires started it all in San Francisco, the site of this year's Annual Congress.

The Fourth of July in San Francisco in 1875 featured a platoon of soldiers in Continental Army uniforms commanded by Captain F. C. M. Fenn, who subsequently became a member of the California Society of Revolutionary Sires. *The Daily Alta,* a San Francisco newspaper, on July 6th reported on the unit: "It was a marked feature of the procession. . . ."

Later a few descendants of Revolutionary War Patriots met on Friday evening, October 22, 1875 at the office of Dr. James L. Cogswell, 230 Kearny Street, San Francisco, and formed a temporary organization. Present at the meeting were: Dr. Cogswell, Major Edwin A. Sherman, Ira C. Root, Dr. P. W. Randle, Rush R. Randle, Joseph Weed and Dr. Emory L. Willard. Major Sherman suggested that a national society of Revolutionary descendants be organized. Dr. Randle was elected President of the organization; he was born at Sparta, Georgia, on November 9, 1806. His father was Josias Randle of the Maryland Line.

Thus initiated and nurtured by these men, the organization became known as the Society of the Sons of the Revolutionary Sires and was the seed which gave birth to the Sons of the American Revolution.

A letter from an unknown writer was published in *The Alta* on the 26th of June, 1876. It was suggested that in the coming Fourth of July parade of the Centennial Celebration of the Founding of the United States, "our grandparents of the Revolution should be represented by the grandchildren living in San Francisco."

During the Annual Congress this July in San Francisco, a contingent of SARs visited the site on Kearny Street where the Society of the Sons of the Revolutionary Sires was organized in 1875. A commemorative plaque, being pointed out by President General Charles F. Printz, was dedicated by Former President General Matthew B. Sellers on October 25, 1976. The original building was razed in the 1890s and replaced.

The next day, *The Alta* included a call for the descendants of Revolutionary Patriots to contact Dr. Cogswell at his office, 230 Kearny Street. The June 28th issue included an invitation for the descendants to meet on the evening of June 29 at the request of the parade Grand Marshall for the purpose of celebrating the Centennial Anniversary.

On that evening General Albert M. Winn was called to preside at the meeting, and Dr. Emory L. Willard was selected to serve as Secretary. The roll was taken and the group consented to meet again at the Palace Hotel on July 1, 1876 to make final plans for the Fourth of July Parade.

On July 1 the organization met at the hotel, with General Winn presiding. James P. Dameron was elected Treasurer and William Moses, Parade Marshall for the Society. It was resolved that signing the roll and paying the $1.00 initiation fee constituted membership. Also, a pledge of honor was taken that a "Signer" was a lineal descendant of an American Revolutionary Patriot.

The next meeting was held on the Fourth of July at the Palace Hotel. Eighty-eight men were present; eleven were REAL SONS (sons of Revolutionary Patriots). William Moses formed the group for the parade. Fifty of the group rode in carriages due to age. The other 38 marched carrying 13 shields of the original states. The men attracted the attention of everyone watching the parade. The descendants were enthusiastically received.

The REAL SONS were: John Paul Jones Davison, 87 years, son of George Davison, Connecticut; Samuel Graves, 82 years, soldier of War of 1812 and son of Russell Graves, New York; Captain J. S. Marston, 72 years, son of Samuel Marston, New Hampshire; Benjamin F. Penniman, 70 years, son of Amos Penniman, Massachusetts; Dr. P. W. Randle, 70 years, son of Josias S. Randle, Maryland; John M. Robinson, 62 years, son of Captain Noah Robinson, New Hampshire; Joseph Sumner, 71 years, son of William Sumner, Connecticut; Augustus C. Taylor, 67 years, son of Captain James Taylor, Vermont; General John Wilson, 87 years, son of William Wilson; Eben R. York, 57 years, son of William R. York, Massachusetts; John F. York, 50 years, son of William R. York, Massachusetts.

The Descendants returned to the Palace Hotel after the parade. James Dameron delivered a patriotic address. Prior to adjournment it was resolved to continue the association.

On July 11th a meeting of the Society was held at Dashaway Hall for the election of officers, with 50 men present. General Winn presided, addressed the assembly and was chosen President by acclamation. The officers were charged to prepare a Constitution and Bylaws.

On August 2nd the Society met again at the Palace Hotel and a proposed Constitution and Bylaws were presented. The formal organization, "Sons of Revolutionary Sires," was completed when the Constitution and Bylaws were approved. The Bylaws provided an Auxiliary Society of ladies and a Young Men's Auxiliary for men under 40 years of age.

On October 4th, a meeting was held at the Palace Hotel, with the President reporting a membership of 99.

The Society sponsored a public celebration for the Centennial of the Surrender of Yorktown at Union Hall, with 1,500 people attending including all the city's officials.

In the next few years with General Winn as President, the general interest of the Society declined. He continued as President until he moved to Sonoma, California in October, 1881.

At this time the Society received renewed energy through the interest of

Colonel Adolphus S. Hubbard, the Recording Secretary. Judge Caleb T. Fay was elected President in 1881. Captain Augustus C. Taylor, a REAL SON, served as President in 1882; Loring Pickering in 1884. Colonel Hubbard assumed the leadership in July, 1886 and held the position to February, 1892.

Meetings were held on a regular basis; bulletins were sent to the membership.

Upon the organization of the National Society of the Sons of the American Revolution, Colonel Hubbard guided the California Sons of Revolutionary Sires into the movement. Major George B. Halstead consented to represent the California Society at the organizational meeting of the National Society of the Sons of the American Revolution at Fraunces Tavern in New York City on April 30, 1889.

The office on Kearny Street boasts a painting of Washington by Rembrandt Peale.

After the organization of the Sons of the American Revolution, the California Society changed its name to "California Society of the Sons of the American Revolution" and immediately reorganized in compliance with the SAR Constitution and Bylaws.

SAR membership application forms were distributed to all members of the Sons of Revolutionary Sires. The total membership reduced from 175 to 75. Compatriot Hubbard continued as President. Compatriot Charles J. King was First Vice President and Colonel W. B. Eastin served as Secretary and Treasurer.

The National Society adopted at the First National Congress at Louisville, Kentucky, April 30, 1890 the following resolutions:

"Whereas, The Society of the Sons of the American Revolution was first organized in the State of California on the Fourth of July 1876; and,

Whereas, to Colonel A. S. Hubbard of the California Society, is due in a large degree, the credit of organizing that Society, and, in a still greater degree

the credit of maintaining that Society through trials which would have discouraged a less patriotic man; now, therefore,

Resolved, That in the publication of the names of the Presidents General of the National Society of the Sons of the American Revolution, the name of Colonel A. S. Hubbard be hereafter included."

At the Third National Congress, at New York City, April 30, 1892 it placed on record the following tribute to the memory of the late General Albert M. Winn:

"Resolved, that the name of A. M. Winn, first President of the California Society, shall hereafter appear in the roll of Past Presidents General of this Society."

At a special meeting of the Board of Managers of the California Society SAR held on Saturday, March 4th, 1893, Past President A. S. Hubbard presented the following Preamble and Resolution which was unanimously adopted:

Whereas, The initiatory and preliminary steps for the institution and organization of the California Society of the Sons of the American Revolution was taken Friday, October 22nd, 1875, which fact is established by sworn statements and documentary proof on file in the archives of the Society, therefore,

Resolved, That this Society claims October 22nd, 1875, as its natal day, and upon the papers hereafter issued by this Society shall in suitable form appear the following statement in substance:

Whereas, That a copy of this preamble and resolution be transmitted to the past and present officers of the National and State Societies of the Sons of the American Revolution; to all past and present officers of the National Society and Subordinate Chapters of the Daughters of the American Revolution; to the officers of the General and State Societies of the Sons of the Revolution; to the officers of the General and State Societies of the Daughters of the Revolution; to the Diplomatic Representatives of the United States residing in foreign countries; Order of the Cincinnati; to the American Historical Association and State Historical and Genealogical Societies; to the Commandery in Chief and State Commanderies of the Military Order of the Loyal Legion of the United States; to the U.S. Military and Naval Institutions; General Society of the War of 1812; the Aztec Society, and to such publications interested in the objects of our research and labors.

J. Estcourt Sawyer
Lieut. U.S.A.
President

Roscoe S. Gray
Secretary

CENTENNIAL HERITAGE FACTS

U.S. Presidents and the SAR

By Former President General Carl F. Bessent

George Washington is an important personage to the SAR, including the fact that our Society was organized on the 100th anniversary of his inauguration as President — April 30, 1889. (All paintings of Presidents copyrighted by the White House Historical Association; painting photographs by the National Geographic Society.)

A factor that has attracted men to the Sons of the American Revolution is that it is a Society thoroughly American, democratic, non-partisan and non-sectarian. The qualifications are good character and being a lineal descendant of a Patriot of the American Revolution.

The SAR membership roll of 133,000 Compatriots echoes the names of giants in all fields of endeavor, prominent men and inconspicuous men. Station in life is not a factor for SAR membership.

However, the SAR is justly proud of the Presidents of the United States who became members, because they have led our great nation to be a better America.

The importance of the Presidency of the United States has increased in the past 200 years from George Washington to George Bush. The President is one of the symbols of American Democracy. In the past 100 years since the organization of the Sons of the American Revolution, 13 men who have held this high office have become members.

RUTHERFORD BIRCHARD HAYES

Rutherford B. Hayes served for one term from 1877 to 1881 as the 19th President. He was born in Delaware, Ohio, on October 4, 1822 and graduated from Harvard Law School. At the outbreak of the Civil War he enlisted in the Union Army, was wounded five times and rose to the rank of Major General. Hayes served in the House of

Representatives and served as Governor of Ohio for three terms. The nation was still suffering from the pangs of the Civil War when he became President. One of his first actions was to withdraw Federal troops from the Southern States. Compatriot Hayes enjoyed being President but disliked politics and chose not to run for a second term. President Hayes died in Fremont, Ohio, on January 17, 1893.

President Hayes was very proud of his ancestry, especially his Revolution-

Rutherford B. Hayes

By Daniel Huntington

ary War ancestors. He became an early member of the SAR.

His great grandfather, Ezekiel Hayes was 52 years old and living in Bamford, Connecticut, when independence was declared. Ezekiel was appointed Collector of a special war tax passed by the Connecticut Legislature to conduct the war. He led a caravan of oxen teams carrying provisions to the colonial troops at the siege of Yorktown. He witnessed the surrender of Lord Cornwallis.

His grandfather, Rutherford Hayes, the First, was a blacksmith in Battleboro, Vermont, when commissioned at the age of 26 as an Ensign in the South Vermont Regiment of New York Troops. Later he received a grant of land in Chenago County, New York, for his service.

BENJAMIN HARRISON

Benjamin Harrison was the 23rd President, serving one term from 1889 to 1893. He was the grandson of William Henry Harrison, 9th President of the United States, and the great grandson of Benjamin Harrison, Signer of the Declaration of Independence. Harrison's term as President came between the two terms of Grover Cleveland.

Benjamin Harrison was born on August 20, 1833, at his grandfather's farm near North Bend, Ohio. He studied law, was admitted to the bar in 1853 and practiced law in Indianapolis, Indiana. With the outbreak of the war between the States Harrison was made Colonel of the 70th Indiana Regiment. Known as a fearless officer, he was promoted to

Brigadier General. He later served in the United States Senate.

In 1888 Benjamin Harrison was selected as the Republican candidate for President and defeated his Democratic opponent, Grover Cleveland.

The New Jersey Society SAR was organized on March 7, 1889 in Newark and many patriotic men answered the recruiting bugle. The first public activity of the new Society was on April 29, 1889 at Elizabeth, New Jersey, when President Harrison visited Elizabeth on his journey to New York City for the Centennial ceremonies of George Washington's Inauguration as the first President. At a reception by

Benjamin Harrison
By Eastman Johnson

New Jersey Governor Green at his home the individual members of the new Society were presented to the President. Later the Society members served as an Honor Escort for the President from the Governor's residence to the wharf where he boarded a barge for New York City.

Both President Benjamin Harrison and his only son, Russell Benjamin, became members of the SAR, by descent from the Signer Benjamin Harrison.

President Harrison's wife, Caroline Scott Harrison, was elected as the first President General of the Daughters of the American Revolution. Caroline Harrison and Rutherford B. Hayes's wife, Lucy Webb Hayes, were cousins.

WILLIAM McKINLEY

William McKinley, 25th President, serving from 1897 to 1901, was born in Niles, Ohio, on January 29, 1843. He attended Allegheny College in Pennsyl-

vania. He volunteered for the Union Army in the Civil War and distinguished himself in action, rising to the rank of Major.

McKinley served in the House of Representatives, later elected Gover-

William McKinley
By Harriet Murphy

nor of Ohio and became a national figure. In 1896 he was nominated at the Republican National Convention and elected President by a large plurality.

President McKinley was a man of great tact and personal charm with a marked religious attitude.

The outstanding event during his administration was the War with Spain.

President McKinley was reelected for a second term. On September 6, 1901 while welcoming citizens at the Pan-American Exposition in Buffalo, New York, he was shot by a fanatical anarchist who was later executed. McKinley died eight days later on September 14 saying, "It is God's Way. His will, not ours, be done." His death was mourned throughout the world.

McKinley joined the Ohio Society SAR on May 1, 1895 while serving as Governor. His Revolutionary War Patriot was David McKinley who served for two years as a soldier in the Pennsylvania Militia. In 1832 he received a pension for his service.

The California Society SAR held a reception for President McKinley on his visit to San Francisco in 1901 a few months before he was killed. The reception was held at the Palace Hotel on Friday, May 24, at 1:30 p.m. with many distinguished citizens of the city

attending. Compatriot William H. Jordan, President of the California Society, introduced the President to the assemblage.

The President spoke: *"Members of the Sons of the American Revolution, Daughters of the American Revolution, and my companions of the Loyal Legion: It gives me particular satisfaction and pleasure to be greeted here in this city of San Francisco by the members of the historic associations, and I salute with reverence and affection this Chapter which was the original and beginning of the memorable organizations known as the Sons of the American Revolution."* The President took the time to shake hands with everyone present.

THEODORE ROOSEVELT

Theodore Roosevelt, 26th President, served from 1901 to 1909, and was the youngest man to become President. He was 42 when he was elevated from Vice President to President when President McKinley was assassinated.

Theodore Roosevelt was born in New York City on October 27, 1858. He graduated from Harvard and attended law school. Young Roosevelt entered public service as Police Commissioner of New York City, Assistant Secretary of the Navy and Governor of New York. At the outbreak of the Spanish American War Roosevelt organized a volunteer cavalry unit known as the Rough Riders, and he became a popular American hero. He was selected as the Vice President candidate with William McKinley in 1900 and the ticket was elected.

As President, Roosevelt sponsored legislation conserving the nation's re-

Theodore Roosevelt
By John Singer Sargent

sources and created the United States Forest Service, promoted the construction of the Panama Canal, sent the "Great White Fleet" around the world on a goodwill mission. He was reelected to a second term.

Roosevelt continued active in politics after he completed his second term. He fought against America's isolation attitudes before World War I. He died on January 6, 1919 at his home on Oyster Bay, Long Island, New York.

Roosevelt was a profound writer, authoring over 40 books. He was a fifth cousin of a future president, Franklin D. Roosevelt, and an uncle of Franklin's wife, Eleanor Roosevelt.

Theodore Roosevelt joined the SAR on April 10, 1898 when he was Governor of New York. His National Number was SAR #12,000. He was a descendant of Jacobus Roosevelt who served as a Captain in the New York Militia and who died in 1777. Jacobus Roosevelt's son, Jacobus I. Roosevelt, served as a Commissary for the entire war.

Compatriot President Roosevelt visited New Orleans on October 26, 1905 and the city celebrated with a big parade. The officers of the Louisiana Society SAR rode in a carriage in a lead position in the parade. The SAR Colors were carried by an SAR Color Guard just preceding the President's carriage.

Compatriot John B. Richardson, President of the Louisiana Society, was wearing his SAR Insignia at the reception for President Roosevelt. In Colonel Richardson's words: *"The President noticed the SAR Badge and remarked with one hand on my shoulder while with the other he grasped my right hand, 'One of the Sons, I see.' I replied, 'Yes and you are one too.' With that manifested every mark of pleasure and appreciation and clasping my right hand in both of his, shook it most cordially. I can tell you it was one of the happiest moments of my life."*

Theodore Roosevelt's eldest son, Theodore Roosevelt, Junior, joined the SAR in 1919 while serving as a Lieutenant Colonel in the Army. The younger Roosevelt served as Governor of Puerto Rico and later as Governor General of the Philippines. In 1942 he reentered the Army as a General of Infantry. He died on the battlefield in France. He was awarded the Medal of Honor for gallantry. Two other sons, Kermit and Archibald Roosevelt, also joined the SAR in 1919.

WILLIAM HOWARD TAFT

William Howard Taft, 27th President, served from 1909 to 1913, never had any ambition to be President and never was totally happy in the posi-

William H. Taft

By Anders L. Zorn

tion. He was a reserved person and never captured the public with his personality.

William Taft was born on September 15, 1857 in Cincinnati, Ohio. He graduated from Yale, the University of Cincinnati Law School and was admitted to the bar in Ohio. He went into public service first as a state judge, then as Solicitor of the United States and next as a federal judge. He served as Governor of the Philippines and then as Secretary of War in President Theodore Roosevelt's cabinet. President Roosevelt decided not to be a candidate for reelection in 1908 and presented William Taft to be the man to succeed him. Taft was elected.

During the Taft Administration the Department of Labor was established, the direct election of senators was approved and the income tax was ratified.

There was a three-way race for the presidency in 1912. Taft and Roosevelt were defeated by Woodrow Wilson.

After leaving the White House, Taft became a law professor at Yale. In 1921 President Harding appointed Compatriot Taft Chief Justice of the Supreme Court serving until 1930. He died one month after his retirement on March 8. Taft was happy as Chief Justice. He is buried in Arlington National Cemetery.

William Taft joined the Connecticut Society SAR in March 1915 while teaching at Yale, as a descendant of Aaron Taft, who lived in Uxbridge, Massachusetts, and answered the alarm of April 14, 1775 by the Massachusetts Minutemen.

The Maryland Society celebrated George Washington's Birthday on Thursday evening, February 22, 1917 at the Hotel Belvedere in Baltimore. Former President Taft attended the af-

fair and was warmly received by the large audience of ladies and Compatriots. He was greeted with the audience standing and singing "America" when he entered the Ballroom; everyone was waving an American Flag. President Taft acknowledged the ovation and stated he was most honored to be with his fellow Compatriots on such an occasion as Washington's Birthday.

William Taft's son, Robert A. Taft, Junior, joined the SAR in 1943. He was known as "Mr. Republican" and was a close advisor to President Eisenhower.

WARREN G. HARDING

Warren Gamaliel Harding, 29th President, was the sixth President to die in office. President Harding was on a goodwill nationwide tour when he died suddenly in San Francisco on August 2, 1923.

Harding was born near Blooming Grave, Ohio, on November 2, 1865. He graduated from Ohio Central College

Warren G. Harding

By Hodgson Smart

and went into newspaper work. He purchased a small weekly newspaper in Marion, Ohio, which prospered. Harding was a tall handsome man with a pleasing personality.

Harding entered politics as a Republican and was elected Lieutenant Governor of Ohio in 1902. In 1914 he was elected to the United States Senate. In 1920 Harding was the Republican candidate for President and easily defeated the Democratic candidate on a promise to repeal the high income taxes. An oil reserve scandal embittered Harding in his second year in office.

Warren Harding joined the Ohio Society SAR on July 2, 1920. He was a descendant of Abraham McKinley, Junior, who resided in Walhill, Orange County, New York, at the outbreak of the Revolutionary War. Abraham Harding, Jr., served as a Lieutenant in the New York Militia.

President General Washington L. I. Adams invited President Harding to attend the 34th SAR National Congress to be held in Nashville, Tennessee on May 20-22, 1923. President Harding replied to the invitation:

"I have been particularly proud of my membership in this society, and of the fact that I am eligible to such membership. I look upon it as one of the worthy and uniformly well-directed engineries of patriotism that have sought to crystillize into national sentiments and public policies the best thought and purpose of the American Nation; therefore I have pleasure in wishing the success of the forthcoming Congress and the continuation of our Society's splendid service."

Most Sincerely yours,
Warren G. Harding

The White House, Washington,
D.C. February 1, 1923

(JOHN) CALVIN COOLIDGE

Calvin Coolidge was the 30th President and the sixth Vice President to become the Chief Executive on the death of a President when President Harding died in 1923.

Coolidge was a popular President, and the general public appreciated his shyness and referred to him as "Silent Cal."

Calvin Coolidge was born in Plymouth Notch, Vermont, on July 4, 1872. He was named John Calvin Coolidge but dropped the "John" as he preferred a single name.

Washington, DC was the setting for the 39th Annual Congress held in 1928. Attendees were the guests of President Calvin Coolidge at The White House.

Coolidge graduated with honors from Amherst College in 1895. In his senior year he wrote an essay on "The Principles Fought for in the American Revolution" and was awarded a Gold Medal by the National Society SAR.

Coolidge passed the Vermont bar and began the practice of law. He moved to Massachusetts in 1911 and was elected to the State Senate, as Lieutenant Governor in 1914, and Governor in 1918. Coolidge gained nationwide notoriety in suppressing the Boston Police strike. In 1920 the Republican Party selected Coolidge as the Vice President candidate on the Harding ticket which won the election.

During the Coolidge Administration the National debt was reduced substantially and involvement with the League of Nations was avoided. He did not seek reelection in 1928 and supported Herbert Hoover for President. Coolidge died of a heart attack on January 5, 1933.

Calvin Coolidge joined the SAR in 1921 while serving as Vice President. His Revolutionary ancestor was John Coolidge, who at the age of 19 answered the call in April 1775, joined the Massachusetts Militia as a private. He fought at the Battle of Bunker Hill and was discharged in 1778.

The 39th SAR Annual Congress was held in Washington, District of Columbia, on May 21-23, 1923. Many of the 280 delegates and 140 ladies marched from the Mayflower Hotel to the White House to be received by Compatriot President Coolidge on Monday at Noon. The President spoke briefly to the group and greeted many personally.

HERBERT CLARK HOOVER

Herbert Hoover, 31st President, came to public life by chance. He was a wealthy mining engineer when World War I began. He was appointed Chairman of the American Relief Commission, then Chairman of the Commission for Belgium Relief, then United States Food Administrator. He was recognized as a great humanitarian and an excellent administrator.

Hoover served in both President Harding's cabinet and President Coolidge's cabinet. When Coolidge chose not to run for reelection Herbert Hoover was elected President.

Herbert Clark Hoover was born in West Branch, Iowa, on August 10, 1874. He became an orphan at an early age and lived with an uncle in Oregon. In 1891 Hoover graduated from Stanford in engineering. He pursued mining engineering in many parts of the world — Australia, Africa, China. In China he directed food relief for victims of the Boxer Rebellion.

Herbert H. Hoover

By Elmer W. Greene

Hoover worked conscientiously at being a good President and is wrongly judged because of the Great Depression which occurred during his administration. In 1929 the stock market crashed and the economy collapsed. Many farmers lost their farms; workers lost their jobs. There was widespread unemployment. Hoover was defeated by Franklin D. Roosevelt.

At the conclusion of World War II President Truman appointed Hoover as Coordinator of the European Food Program. Later he was appointed

Calvin Coolidge

By Charles S. Hopkinson

During a ceremony in Washington, DC, President Herbert Hoover was inducted into membership. On hand were (from left): George Gosser, PASSAR; J. Howard Johnson, PASSAR; John L. Walker, PASSAR President; William Tyler Page, Clerk of the House of Representatives, DCSSAR; Mr. Hoover; A. W. Wall, PASSAR; Josiah A. Van Orsdel, SAR Director General; Mark F. Finley, DCSSAR Past President; and Frank B. Steele, Secretary General.

Chairman of the Commission to Reorganize the Executive Branch.

Herbert Hoover died on October 20, 1964.

Herbert Hoover's Revolutionary ancestor was Jacobus Wynne, a private in the First Regiment, Ulster County Militia, New York Troops. Another ancestor was Isaac Sherman, Lieutenant in the Second Regiment of the New York Line.

President Hoover accepted an invitation to join the Pennsylvania Society SAR and on November 1, 1928 visited the SAR National Headquarters on Sixteenth Street to be inducted into membership.

At this time Compatriot President Hoover said: *"This is a genuine compliment you pay me today. The Society of the Sons of the American Revolution, organized by those who originally fought for the establishment of this government, whose members throughout the one hundred and fifty years of our history have with uniform devotion sustained all its high principles and noble purposes, is one with which every American can be proud to be associated. I am glad to add my name side by side with that of my brother, Colonel Theodore Hoover, who for many years has enjoyed a similar distinction, and I appreciate your reminder of my ancestor who fought in the Revolutionary War."*

Many years after he left the White House, the Oregon Society spent much effort and resources to restore the boyhood home of Compatriot Hoover in Newberg, Oregon. Dr. Burt Brown Barker, President of the Oregon Society SAR, was a boyhood friend of the former President, and planned a program to have the former President speak at the dedication of the restored home on his 81st birthday, August 10, 1955. Many dignitaries attended the event.

FRANKLIN DELANO ROOSEVELT

Franklin D. Roosevelt, 32nd President, held the position of Chief Executive longer than any other President. He was elected for four terms.

Roosevelt was President during the country's worst depression and its greatest war. There is agreement that he was a dynamic leader. He generated both deep devotion and intense bitterness. He believed that government was the means to improve the betterment of its people. President Roosevelt pushed many revolutionary relief and reform legislative programs through a special session of Congress.

The United States assisted its allies in Europe after Germany and Italy waged war against them. The Japanese attack on Pearl Harbor led the country to enter the global conflict. The strain of leading our nation to victory in war led to the deterioration of President Roosevelt's health. One month prior to the surrender of Germany, the President died of cerebral hemorrhage at Warm Springs, Georgia, on April 12, 1945.

Franklin D. Roosevelt
By Frank O. Salisbury

Franklin D. Roosevelt's Revolutionary ancestor was Isaac Roosevelt who served as a private in the 6th Regiment, Dutchess County Militia, New York Troops.

On June 14, 1931 Franklin Roosevelt, then Governor of New York, attended the SAR Flag Day ceremonies and "Descendants Day" on the village green adjoining Saint Paul's Episcopal Church in the quaint village of Eastchester, Mount Vernon, New York. Many members along with the Color Guard of the New York Chapter of the Empire State Society attended. Theodore Roosevelt's and Franklin D. Roose-

velt's ancestor, Jacobus Roosevelt, was an original pewholder and vestryman of the church. The church's bell, prayer book, Bible and chalice had been secretly buried during the Revolutionary War. The bell hangs in the belfry today, and the books and chalice are displayed on special occasions.

On April 20, 1933 President General Frederick W. Millspaugh and General Fries called at the White House to inform the President that his SAR membership had been approved.

Two of President Roosevelt's sons joined the SAR: Colonel James Roosevelt and Congressman Franklin D. Roosevelt, Junior.

HARRY S. TRUMAN

Harry S. Truman became the 33rd President when Franklin D. Roosevelt died after only 83 days into his fourth term.

It was a critical time in American history. World War II was concluded with victory. The United Nations was organized. The country converted to a peacetime economy, and the armed forces were disbanded. Programs were initiated for economic and technical assistance to depressed countries. There was friction with the Soviet Union resulting in the Cold War. President Truman was reelected to a second term. When communist troops invaded South Korea, President Truman ordered American forces to assist the Republic of South Korea.

Harry Truman was born in Lamar, Missouri, on May 8, 1884. He was working on the family farm at the outbreak of World War I when his National Guard unit was called to active duty. He saw action in France and was discharged as a Captain. He entered business operating a clothing store in Kansas City which failed. Truman entered on a political career and was elected a

Harry S. Truman
By Martha Kempton

county judge. In 1934 he was United States Senator from Missouri. He was effective as a Senator, investigating fraud and waste in defense programs. He was selected as the Vice Presidential candidate for President Roosevelt's fourth term.

Upon completing a second term in office in 1953, President Truman returned to Independence, Missouri, and wrote his memoirs. Truman died in 1972.

Harry Truman's Revolutionary War ancestor was Lieutenant James Holmes of the 2nd Regiment of the Virginia Militia, who served from 1777 to 1781. The first SAR Membership Certificate signed by President General Len Young Smith was for former President Harry S. Truman. Truman's next door neighbor and longtime friend was Compatriot Rufus Burrus of the Missouri Society.

On March 7, 1968 President General Smith visited Independence, Missouri,

At his home in Independence, Missouri, President Harry S. Truman was presented his membership certificate by President General Len Young Smith (right) and Missouri Society Compatriot Donald C. Little, a close friend of Mr. Truman.

and presented Compatriot Truman with an SAR Membership Insignia Badge and the SAR Gold Good Citizenship Medal.

DWIGHT DAVID EISENHOWER

Dwight David Eisenhower, the 34th President, was born in Dennison, Texas, on October 14, 1890. Shortly after this time the family moved to Abilene, Kansas. He graduated from the United States Military Academy, West Point, in 1914.

Eisenhower commanded the troops that landed in North Africa in the early days of World War II. He became the Supreme Commander of all Allied Forces and led the Normandy invasion in 1944. He was President of Columbia University in 1948. He returned to active duty and served as Commander of NATO troops in 1950.

Eisenhower, the Republican candidate, was elected President in 1952, and

reelected in 1956. As President he eliminated wage and price controls, reduced taxes and initiated the Interstate Highway system. He negotiated a peace treaty ending the Korean War. When

Dwight D. Eisenhower

By J. Anthony Wills

his term of office was completed, he retired to his farm in Gettysburg, Pennsylvania. He died on March 28, 1969.

Eisenhower's ancestor was John Peter Eisenhower who furnished supplies to the Continental Army troops during the winter of 1777-78 at Valley Forge. Another ancestor was John Matter, a Pennyslvania Militia soldier who fought at the Battle of Long Island.

When accepted into SAR membership in 1945, General Eisenhower wrote to the President of the Empire State Society: *"I need scarcely say that I feel a great sense of distinction in the action of the Empire State Society of the Sons of the American Revolution in electing me as a member. Moreover, I am grateful for the trouble the Society has taken to look up and verify the genealogy. I hope you will express my sincere thanks to the members of your society and especially those individuals who have taken an active part in extending to me this valued invitation."*

President Eisenhower's son, John Doud Eisenhower, and his brother, Dr. Milton Stover Eisenhower, joined the SAR.

LYNDON BAINES JOHNSON

Lyndon Baines Johnson, 36th President, became Chief Executive upon the assassination of President John F. Kennedy.

Johnson was born in Stonewall, Texas, on August 27, 1908. He graduated from Southwest Texas State Teachers College in 1930. With the assistance of his wife, Ladybird Johnson,

he developed an extensive enterprise in farming and broadcasting. In 1937 Johnson entered politics and won a seat in the House of Representatives, returning to Congress for four terms. He was the first Congressman to enter active duty when the United States entered World War II. He was separated as a Lieutenant Commander after four years in the Navy.

Johnson was elected Senator in 1948 and reelected six years later. When the Democrats gained control of the Senate in 1955, he became the youngest Majority Leader in history. Kennedy asked Johnson to serve as his Vice President. In November 1963 Johnson inherited the Presidential position when Kennedy was shot.

President Johnson worked for welfare legislation, the establishment of Medicare and civil rights reforms. He was reelected for a second term in 1964. The war in Vietnam escalated; there was a turn down in the economy, there were anti-war demonstrations and race riots. The division in the country caused President Johnson not to run for another term of office. President Johnson retired to his ranch near Johnson City, Texas, to write his memoirs. He died on January 22, 1973.

Lyndon B. Johnson

By Elizabeth Shoumatoff

Compatriot Johnson's Revolutionary ancestor was John Johnson who served as a soldier in the Georgia State Militia.

With the promotion and support of SAR Legislators in the National Congress Compatriot President Johnson was able to have a law passed which outlawed the desecration of the United States Flag. He signed the bill (Public Law 90-381) which provided for severe penalties.

Senator Charles S. Robb, President Johnson's son-in-law, is an active member of the SAR.

GERALD RUDOLPH FORD

Gerald Ford, 38th President, is the only President and Vice President to serve in these offices without being elected in a national election. On October 12, 1973 he was nominated for Vice President by President Nixon when Vice President Agnew resigned. Gerald Ford became President when President Nixon resigned on August 9, 1974.

Gerald Ford was born in Omaha, Nebraska, on July 14, 1913. He was adopted by his stepfather and assumed his name. He was a football star at the University of Michigan where he received his Bachelor degree. He graduated from Yale Law School in 1938. He served as a Naval Officer for four years in World War II and was separated as a Lieutenant Commander.

Ford was elected to the House of Representatives in 1950 and served as a Congressman for 25 years. He was the leader of the House Republicans for eight years.

President Ford pardoned former President Nixon of any federal offenses he may have committed. The Ford Administration inherited double-digit inflation. Ford vetoed many bills to hold

Gerald R. Ford
By Everett Raymond Kinstler

#105,000, and an SAR Membership Insignia Badge. Also, President Ford was given a hand wrought porcelain, depicting the Declaration of Independence, as a gift from the National Society SAR.

In 1989, the SAR Centennial Year, former President Gerald Ford was presented the SAR Gold Good Citizenship Medal.

President Gerald R. Ford (left) was given his membership certificate and insignia in the Oval Office at The White House. Participating in the program were (from left): President General M. Graham Clark, Law Enforcement Committee Chairman Ordway P. Burden, Past Vice-President General Donald Baldwin, Compatriot Hugh G. Swofford and Former President General Marion H. Crawmer.

government costs in check. He survived two assassination attempts. In 1980 he lost a close election to the Democratic nominee, Jimmy Carter.

President Ford's Revolutionary War ancestor was Ezra Chase, who served as a Minuteman in the Massachusetts Militia.

In 1975 President General Graham Clark visited the Oval Office in the White House to present the President with his Membership Certificate, SAR

The Sons of the American Revolution is proud of its 13 members who have served in the high office of President of the United States of America. We honor these Compatriots who used their position as President to build a better America. Each remembered the founding of this great nation and the role of their Revolutionary War ancestor in making America the beacon of liberty and justice for all.

Kansans to Honor Dwight Eisenhower

The people of Kansas have launched a five-star tribute to their state's most famous native son, Dwight D. Eisenhower, also a prominent member of the SAR.

The Kansas Eisenhower Centennial officially began with Kansas Day festivities in January. It will continue through nearly ten months of celebrations and observances across the state before concluding on the 100th anniversary of the birth of the former President and General of the Army on October 14, 1990.

Though born in Texas, Eisenhower spent his entire childhood in Abilene, Kansas. Much of the attention will focus on that north central Kansas community.

Compatriot General Eisenhower is shown visiting with a soldier in Belgium during 1944.

The Eisenhower's simple white frame house on Fourth Street is one of five buildings that make up the Eisenhower Center. The complex also includes the Dwight D. Eisenhower Library, the Museum of the Presidential Library, a Visitors Center and "A Place of Meditation," the final resting place of Eisenhower.

A scholar portrayed Eisenhower in an address to a joint session of the state legislature in Topeka following the official centennial kickoff ceremony. The dramatic interpretation, titled "Eisenhower as Senior Statesman, " will be repeated several times at various locations across the state. A gala banquet; a reunion of members of the Supreme Headquarters, Allied Expeditionary Force; the first day issuance of an Eisenhower stamp; and a wreath laying ceremony at grave side are some of the major happenings planned for the October 13-14 grand finale.

In between, events will range from displays of vintage World War II military vehicles and aircraft to antique car and fashion shows to art displays (some featuring Eisenhower's own paintings) to a presidential library tour package in cooperation with the Harry S. Truman Library at Independence, Missouri. President Truman was also an SAR.

CENTENNIAL
HISTORY

COMPATRIOTS: LET OUR CENTENNIAL CELEBRATION BEGIN

The Sons of the American Revolution is celebrating its 100th birthday this year, 1989. There are few patriotic organizations in our country that have reached this age. To celebrate the beginning of the second century of the Sons of the American Revolution, THE SAR MAGAZINE is featuring this overview.

We SAR members have an obligation at this start of the second century of our noble Society to evaluate our historical development. It is the purpose of this presentation to review the conscientious and devoted service rendered to promote the aspirations of the Revolutionary War.

The history of the SAR is a narrative of love of country, fellowship among descendants of Revolutionary War Patriots, promotion of patriotic programs and the dissemination of patriotic and historical knowledge. In America today there is diminishing interest in the accomplishments of the people and events of the Revolutionary War. Therefore, it is more important than ever for the SAR to continue to carry out its founding purposes and objectives.

To justify itself, an organization should continually work for the purposes for which it was organized. The real test is what has it accomplished and what are its goals for the future.

The first American Revolutionary War hereditary society was the Society of the Cincinnati, founded on May 13, 1783 in Baron von Steuben's headquarters of the Catonment of the American Army on the Hudson River near Newburgh, New York, by officers of the Continental Army and Navy and a few French officers. A society was established in each of the 13 original states and in France.

Membership constituents were lineal or collateral descendants of commissioned officers of the Continental Army.

REASON FOR FLAG WAVING

The great American government underwent a critical test with the Civil War. Happily, in April 1865 the American states were reunited. In the early 1870s Americans were looking to the Centennial of the Declaration of Independence to further heal the tragedy of the Civil War, to wave the Flag, to celebrate the country.

Drastic economic, social and demographic changes were taking place, giving greater comfort to all. There was a general desire to celebrate the anniversaries of Lexington and Concord, Bunker Hill and other Revolutionary days together with the Centennial of the inauguration of George Washington as the first President of the United States. The public rejoicings of these anniversaries exerted a powerful influence on the public mind in every part of the country. They inspired a pride in Revolutionary ancestry and a new respect for the principles of America's government.

There was a high patriotic fever in California, particularly in San Francisco where a gala celebration was being planned for the Centennial of the founding of the country. This sentiment resulted in a meeting of descendants of Revolutionary soldiers, sailors and patriots held on Friday evening, October 22, 1875 at 230 Kearney Street in San Francisco. The resultant organization, known as the Society of the Sons of the Revolutionary Sires, was planned to be national in character and planted the germ which gave birth to the Sons of the American Revolution.

The organization was completed on July 4, 1876 when the Sons of the Revolutionary Sires participated in the gala parade. When the parade formed, 90 members of the Society were present; ten were REAL SONS — sons of Revolutionary War Patriots. Fifty members marched and 25 rode in carriages. They proudly passed through the streets and were greeted with enthusiastic loud cheers.

In the early 1870s efforts were made to induce the Society of the Cincinnati to change its policy so that membership could be extended to other Revolutionary War descendants. There was no change.

SONS OF THE REVOLUTION FORMED

On January 15, 1876 John A. Stevens of New York City held a meeting at the New York Historical Society to organize a new

This issue launches the commemoration of our Society's rich 100-year heritage. Highlights of the past will be related for an entire year by Former President General Carl F. Bessent — coupled with historical briefs sponsored by individual State Societies and Chapters.

society accepting Revolutionary War rank-and-file descendants. In 1883 an interested group of New York City men participated in the local celebration of the 100th anniversary of the evacuation of the city by the British. After the public exercise, the group organized as a permanent society under the title of "Sons of the Revolution." Societies of the "Sons of the Revolution" were organized in Pennsylvania, New Jersey, Massachusetts and other states.

Steps were taken for the institution of a national society to bind together the various new state societies. The "Sons of the Revolution" adopted a constitution providing that other state societies be auxiliary branches of the New York Society, thus creating a breach that finally resulted in the development of another organization.

The enterprising New Jersey Society of the "Sons of the Revolution" was a prime mover in organizing societies in the other states. On March 7, 1889 the New Jersey Society adopted a resolution to meet with the societies of other states to organize a national society. William O. McDowell of Trenton, Josiah C.

Pumpelly of Morristown and General William Strryker of Trenton were appointed to carry out the resolution.

Notices were printed in all the leading newspapers throughout the country. Letters were sent to the Governors of states. By the 30th of April 1889, 13 Revolutionary Societies were in existence.

MEETINGS AT FRAUNCES TAVERN

On April 10, 1889 a call was issued by the New Jersey committee inviting delegates to meet at Fraunces Tavern in New

FPG Bessent, shown here in the office he maintains in his Baltimore, Maryland home, possesses a great deal of knowledge about our Society's past. For this reason he was asked to prepare this refreshingly new history. Compatriots will recall that he also has produced a series of stories that began over two years ago aimed at detailing significant — and often little known — facts about our Society's heritage. Prior to being elected PG in 1984, his experience at the national level included being Secretary General, Treasurer General and as either Chairman or a member of a variety of committees. He is also a Past President of the Maryland Society and the John Eager Howard Chapter.

The National Society was formed in Fraunces Tavern in New York City. This photo of the historic structure appeared in a *Register* published in 1902 containing biographies of those who became members through December 31, 1901.

We the people, The Kentucky Society of the Sons of the American Revolution, proudly celebrate our Centennial year 1989;

We consecrate the Kentucky County, Virginia, part of the original 13 colonies, our ancestors and our Nation;

We commemorate those historic men who created our Commonwealth of Kentucky;

We salute the first member of our society, General Simon Bolivar Buckner, former Governor of Kentucky and honored Kentuckians who have been Presidents General of our National Society.

Major General Joseph Cabell Breckinridge 1900
Rogers Clark Ballard Thruston 1913
Marvin Harrison Lewis 1924
Walter Allerton Wentworth 1958
Col. Benjamin Hume Morris 1985

York City at 9 am on April 30, 1889 to discuss all aspects to organize a national society.

Twenty delegates representing 13 states, including the original California Society organized on October 22, 1875, were present in the famous "long room" on the second floor of the two-day national convention.

William O. McDowell of Newark, New Jersey, was called to chair the meeting and Lieutenant James C. Cresap, U.S.N., was elected secretary. A motion was presented to adopt the constitution of the New York Society of the Sons of the Revolution with other state societies being "auxiliary branches." Josiah Leach, the Pennsylvania delegate, stated the Pennsylvania Society refused to be an auxiliary branch of the New York Society. The assembly decided to organize a national society with each state society a member, equal and independent. The National Society of the Sons of the American Revolution was thus formed.

Only 11 of the 20 delegates at this convention became members of the Sons of the American Revolution: Major George B. Halstead represented California and later became a member of the New Jersey Society; William O. McDowell, New Jersey Society; Josiah C. Pumpelly, New Jersey Society; John J. Hubbell, New Jersey Society; Luther L. Tarbell, Massachusetts Society; Lt. James C. Cresap, U.S.N., Maryland Society; Hon. Gavius F. Paddock, Missouri Society; Hon. H. K. Slayton, New Hampshire Society; Frederick Leighton, New Hampshire Society; Hon. Andrew J. Woodman, Delaware Society; Dr. George B. Abbott, Illinois Society.

This session was adjourned to meet the next day after a committee was appointed to prepare a Constitution and Bylaws.

The second session of the convention was held on May 1, at 9:30 am at the Produce Exchange Building. The Constitution of the New Jersey Society was adopted as an interim constitution.

OFFICERS SELECTED

General officers for the new Society were elected: Honorable Lucius P. Deming, New Haven, Connecticut, President General; Lieutenant James C. Cresap, U.S.N., Maryland, Secretary General; James Otis, New York, Treasurer General; L. L. Tarbell, Massachusetts, Registrar General.

Vice-Presidents General were elected for 26 states and for a Society in France. However, only 18 of these elected Vice Presidents General became members of the Society: AR — Colonel S. W. Williams; CA — Colonel A. S. Hubbard; CT — Major J. C. Kinney; DE — A. J. Woodman; IL — Bishop C. E. Cheney; IN — Hon. William E. English; KY — Hon. S. B. Buckner; MD — Rev. J. G. Morris; MA — Hon. E. S. Barrett; MN — Hon. John B. Sanborn; MO — Hon. D. R. Francis; NH — Hon. H. K. Slayton; NJ — Hon. R. S. Green; NY — Hon. William H. Arnoux; VT — Hon. W. P. Dillingham; VA — Hon. Fitzhugh Lee; WV — Hon. J. J. Jacob; DC — Admiral D. D. Porter.

In the course of the winter and spring 15 new Societies were organized. On January 17, 1890 the National Society was incorporated in the State of Connecticut. The first social meeting of the SAR was held at Delmonico's Restaurant on March 1, 1890 at 7 pm, with 110 gentlemen present from all over the country.

There was a continual effort for union between the Society of the Sons of the Revolution and the Society of the Sons of the American Revolution. Meetings were held to accomplish a merger. There were difficulties; first, a name for the united society and second, admission requirements. All efforts for unification failed.

At the end of the first year the membership of the SAR was 2,500 in 28 Societies. The annual per capita dues were set at 25 cents.

INITIAL CONGRESS IN LOUISVILLE

The first SAR National Congress was held in Louisville, Kentucky, on May 30, 1890. A refined Constitution and other major issues were decided. Membership provoked a discussion on the admission of ladies. The New Hampshire, Ohio and Missouri Societies admitted ladies into full membership. It was brought out that membership in the State Societies of the Sons of the Revolution was restricted to men. In the interest of harmonizing differences and smoothing the pathway for union between the two national societies, it was decided the SAR would be an organization of "Sons" in the true gender sense. There was a compromise providing for the honorary registration of ladies of Revolutionary ancestry by State Societies.

Membership required lineal descent from a Revolutionary Patriot. A Resolution was approved recommending that the Revolutionary War records in boxes and barrels in the State Department be transferred to a fire-proofed storage area with proper indexing and public accessiblitiy. The SAR Resolution resulted in the United States Congress passing a law directing the War Department to collect and properly store the Revolutionary War records.

1889–1900: The Formative Decade

This was a decade of growth and prosperity. In the first years many distinguished Revolutionary names were represented by descendants enrolled in the SAR: 59 descendants of 25 Signers of the Declaration of Independence; 126 descendants of 49 General Officers; many members of the Washington Family. The great-grandson of Martha Washington, two great-grandsons of Marquis General de Lafayette and three great-grandsons of Benjamin Franklin became SAR members.

Many of national reputation were attracted to the Society: General Nelson A. Miles, Commander of the United States Army; Thomas F. Bayard, Ambassador to Great Britain; C. R. Breckinridge, Ambassador to Russia; William Strong, Justice of the Supreme Court; Daniel J. Brewer, Justice of the Supreme Court; Governor (later President) William McKinley of Ohio; Governor James P. Eagle of Arkansas; Governor Albert Morton of New York; Governor Baldwin Bigelow of Connecticut; Governor Morton G. Bulkley of

Connecticut; Governor Urban Woodbury of Vermont and Governor Hugh Thompson of South Carolina.

Men from the highest stations were elected President General: General Horace Porter, Ambassador to the Republic of France; Governor Franklin Murphy of the State of New Jersey.

Over 200 REAL SONS became enthusiastic members of the SAR. The Organizing President of the Minnesota Society was a REAL SON, Judge Albert Edgerton. The only officer who served as a General in both the Army of the United States and the Confederate States Army was Joseph Eggleston Johnston, a REAL SON. Chief Sophiel Selmore of the Passamaquod Indian Tribe was a REAL SON and a member of the Maine Society. His father, Chief Selmore Soctomah, served as a Captain in the marines and as an Indian scout in the Maine Militia.

A Chapter organized in Elizabethtown, New Jersey, on September 26, 1893 was the first local community Chapter formed in the SAR.

FLAG DAY OBSERVANCE LAUNCHED

The first SAR national program was the observance and general display of "The Stars and Stripes," the national ensign, on Flag

Massachusetts Society *of the* Sons *of the* American Revolution

Organized April 19, 1889   Faneuil Hall, Boston, Massachusetts

CELEBRATES CENTENNIAL OF NSSAR

OFFICERS: 1988-1989

President:
David Judson Gray
121 Medford Street
Arlington 02174

1st Vice President:
Duane T. Sargisson
311 Main Street
Worcester 01608

Secretary/Editor:
Cecil M. Daggett
P.O. Box 493
Northborough 01532

Treasurer:
Jerome L. Spurr
62 Fiske Road
Wellesley Hills, 02181

Registrar:
John T. Abbott, C.G.
118 Wilson Road
Bedford 01730

National Trustee:
Raymond F. Fleck
100 Cottage Street
Norwood 02062

*Pres. Generals
  from MASAR:*
Edward S. Barrett   1897
Francis N. Appleton   1905
Moses G. Parker   1911
Benjamin N. Johnson 1931
Eugene P. Carver, Jr. 1956

*Cont. Color Guard
  Appearances*

Bicentennial Events:
   Concord   1975
   Yorktown   1981
   Paris Treaty   1983
   Philadelphia   1987

Annual Congresses
USS CONSTITUTION
Bunker Hill Memorials
Grave Markings
*State and Town
  Historical events*

Nineteen of the thirty members of the MASAR Continental Color Guard participated in the parade and services in Paris, France in 1983 commemorating the 200th anniversary of the signing of the Treaty of Paris formally ending the Revolutionary War.

MASAR CREDO

The Massachusetts Society of the Sons of the American Revolution seeks to preserve the memory of the far-sighted, brave men and women who first left the oppressions of their homelands to establish their freedom in the colonies of a wild and undeveloped land.

We believe this preservation to be important to ourselves, our posterity, and to the principles of liberty and freedom which encouraged and sustained 92,562 of our grandfathers in Massachusetts to enlist in the cause. They served as crude soldiers and sailors, purveyors and merchants, financiers and statesmen, privateers and spies. Over 11,000 of their graves have been identified and marked.

We believe in making continuing commitment to the structure of government in which the people are the governors; and we believe in perpetuating those principles through the education of our own future generations, and by the education of others. We look to Massachusetts Society members at home, now residing in 20 other states and territories and 6 foreign countries to supply the resources of person, substance and energy to sustain those early dreams forever.

And, we are proud to continue to join with all brother Compatriots as members of this National Society of the Sons of the American Revolution.

MASAR welcomes Dual Memberships, and subscriptions to the Woodward Award winning MASAR BULLETIN. Contact the Secretary/Editor.

Day, June 14th of each year. The program and promotion was a result of a Connecticut Society Resolution in 1890. In 1891 throughout New England, New York City, Philadelphia, Baltimore, Chicago and Washington thousands of American Flags were flown on June 14th as a result of the SAR program. By 1895, with the cooperation of the Daughters of the American Revolution, the observance of Flag Day was national in scope, and the date was secure on the patriotic calendar.

An SAR Resolution in 1895 was adopted promoting the flying of the American Flag on all public buildings on every patriotic holiday. Shortly thereafter, the President of the United States ordered that the American Flag be flown continually from the White House. Previously it had been flown only on special occasions.

A National Society Flag Committee was appointed, chaired by Colonel Ralph Prime of Yonkers, New York, to secure legislation from both the National Congress and state legislatures to outlaw the descecration and improper use of the Flag of the United States.

BEGIN MARKING PATRIOT GRAVES

In the first year the Massachusetts Society initiated a program to suitably mark the graves of Revolutionary Patriots buried in the Old Bay State with an appropriate metal SAR marker. Many Massachusetts towns formally requested the Massachusetts Society to mark the Revolutionary graves in their cemeteries. Later, the grave marker was adopted as the official SAR grave marker. On October 19, 1894 Compatriot Nathan Appleton, an officer of the Massachuetts Society, placed the first grave marker, an SAR marker, on the grave of Marquis General de Lafayette in Picpus Cemetery, Paris, France.

On January 17, 1896, Benjamin Franklin's birthday observance, the Massachusetts Society placed an SAR grave marker on Franklin's grave in Christ Church Cemetery, Philadelphia.

CAPITOL CORNERSTONE COMMEMORATED

On September 18, 1893 the SAR had a prominent role in the centennial celebration of the laying of the cornerstone of the United States National Capitol when Judge William Wirt Henry, grandson of Patrick Henry and President of the Virginia Society, delivered the Speech of the Day.

In 1895 a Society was organized in Honolulu, Sandwich Islands (now Hawaii) with 17 members. The Society in France was organized on September 16, 1897 in Paris with General Horace Porter as President. He was the Ambassador from the United States.

General Horace Porter was President General for five consecutive terms beginning in 1892. A graduate of the United States Military Academy, he served with the Union Forces in the Civil War.

An early patriotic project of the SAR was presenting American Flags, portraits of George Washington and medals to schools and colleges throughout the country. In 1895 the Empire State Society placed 340 framed portraits of Gilbert Stuart's George Washington in high schools in New York City, Rochester and Buffalo.

In this decade the Washington State Society presented every high school in the state with a copy of Stuart's portrait of Washington together with a framed reproduction of the Declaration of Independence.

One of the first SAR programs was an essay contest, wherein medals were awarded for winning essays on "The Principles Fought for in the Revolutionary War." In May 1896 an SAR Medal was awarded to John Calvin Coolidge of Amherst. He later became the 30th President of the United States and a member of the SAR.

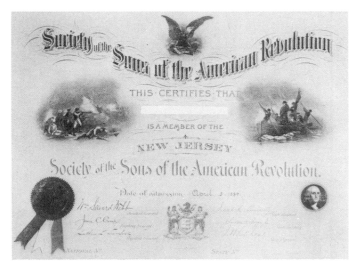

The original SAR Membership Certificate was a genuine work of art.

SAR COLORS ADOPTED

The colors of the Continental Army uniform — buff, blue and white — were adopted as the SAR Colors at the 7th SAR Annual Congress in Richmond, Virginia, in May 1896.

In 1896 the National Society appointed a special committee to secure appropriations by the United States Congress for the restoration of the frigate "Old Ironsides."

Compatriot John D. Rockefeller joined the Empire State Society in March 1896.

Senator Henry Cabot Lodge organized and was elected President of the Old Essex Chapter, Lynn, Massachusetts, in 1896.

Preserving historic sites, securing funds and erecting monuments to commemorate Patriots and events of the Revolutionary War was a prime interest of the SAR.

The Maine Society erected the first monument at Valley Forge, the famous winter quarters of General Washington's little army in 1777-1778.

The New Jersey Society placed a three-ton boulder with a plaque marking the location of a signal station on a hill ridge at Summit, near Springfield, New Jersey. An alarm cannon was placed on this station during the Revolutionary War to alert local Minutemen of impending British attacks. The cannon was popularly called "Old Sow." Also, the New Jersey Society placed a large granite monument with a commemorative tablet at the Presbyterian church graveyard near the Springfield Battlefield.

The Empire State Society erected an impressive monument at Dobbs Ferry on the lower Hudson River to commemorate the location where General Washington and Count Rochambeau planned the Yorktown campaign.

The New Hampshire Society erected a large statue of General John Stark in State House Park at Concord.

The Indiana Society promoted the erection of a bronze George Rogers Clark monument in Indianapolis.

The Connecticut Society secured title to a building known as the "War Office" in Lebanon, Connecticut, and restored it to original condition. The building had been used by the Connecticut Council

A National Society Congress was held in May, 1899 in Detroit.

of Safety during the Revolutionary War to plan their strategy against the British.

The Nathan Hale grammar school house in New London where the Patriot taught in 1774 and 1775 was purchased by the Connecticut Society. The Society relocated the structure to a prominent location in the town and restored it to good condition.

The Maryland Society erected a graceful 27-foot column surmounted by a ball in Prospect Park, Brooklyn, New York, to commemorate the gallant action of the "Maryland 400" at the Battle of Long Island.

The 19th Century closed with the Sons of the American Revolution composed of 39 different Societies and a membership of 9,671 Compatriots. Massachusetts had the largest Society with 1,400 members and the Empire State Society second with 1,205.

The opening decade of the 20th century was a boom period for America. The country was experiencing both social and economic changes. There were 76,000,000 people living in America in 1900. On December 17, 1903 the Wright brothers flew the first heavier-than-air flying machine. Assembly-line mass production by the Ford Motor Company made the automobile practical, and by 1910 there were 50,000 registered vehicles. The Great White Fleet sailed around the world in 1906 to demonstrate America's power.

Three Presidents of the United States served in this decade; all were members of the Sons of the American Revolution. Compatriot President William McKinley (SAR #2406) was assassinated on September 6, 1901 at the Pan-American Exposition in Buffalo, New York, by an anarchist. Compatriot Theodore Roosevelt (SAR #12000) became President. On March 4, 1909 Compatriot William Howard Taft became the 27th President.

President Roosevelt was highly visible on the SAR scene. The 13th SAR Annual Congress in 1902 was held in Washington and attended by many notable Compatriots: President Roosevelt, Assistant Secretary of State David Hill, Assistant Secretary of the Navy Truman Newberry, Senator Marcus Hanna of Ohio and Senator Henry Cabot Lodge of Massachusetts.

President Roosevelt attended the Vermont Society Annual meeting in Montpelier on August 30, 1902 accompanied by Compatriot Governor Wallace Stickney of the State of Vermont. The President attended the Empire State Society Annual Banquet in New York City on March 17, 1905.

President Roosevelt visited New Orleans on October 26, 1905. At the city's reception Louisiana Society President Colonel John Richardson was wearing his SAR Membership Badge on his left breast. The President saw the badge and took Colonel Richardson's right hand with both his hands and said, "A Son, I see. When I became a member I can tell you it was one of the happiest moments of my life."

CHARTER GRANTED BY U.S. CONGRESS

The original SAR Charter was not legally constituted under the laws of the State of Connecticut. A National Charter was secured from the United States Congress and signed by Compatriot President Theodore Roosevelt on June 9, 1906 constituting the National Society as a national body, defining its duties and powers. At the time there were only three national organizations chartered by Congress: The National Society of the Daughters of the American Revolution, the Society of the United States Daughters of 1812 and the American Red Cross.

The records of the Bureau of Census in Washington of the 1790 National Census, giving the names of 400,000 heads of families, were saved from proposed destruction through prompt action by the 13th SAR Annual Congress held in Washington.

The SAR promoted congressional action for the Pension Bureau to index the service and families of the 62,069 pensioners of the American Revolution. The index gave personal, historical and genealogical information. At the end of the decade only 15% of the cases had been catalogued.

Relations with our sister organization, the Daughters of the American Revolution, continued close. In February 1903 in the presence of the delegates to the 13th DAR Continental Congress, the SAR presented the Daughters a beautiful silk American Flag which was the first flag raised at the site of the proposed Memorial Continental Hall.

The SAR Flag Committee continued to promote legislation relative to preventing the desecration of the American Flag. The SAR was responsible for the organizing of 56 patriotic organizations, interested in proper use of the Flag, into the America Flag Association. Thirty-four states enacted laws prohibiting desecration. The Supreme Court upheld the constitutionality of the states' flag laws; the opinion was written by Justice Harlan. The SAR continued to promote national legislation for the proper use of the Flag in the United States Congress.

IMMIGRANT EDUCATION FURTHERED

Nine million immigrants entered the United States during this period. The SAR Committee on Information for Aliens was active and prepared a pamphlet, SAR Leaflet #1 — "Information for

A large number of delegates turned out for the 13th Annual Congress held at Washington, DC in 1902.

Immigrants Concerning the United States." The pamphlet presented facts on the United States, the nature of the government, its institutions, privileges, duties and obligations of citizenship. The pamphlet was translated into 15 languages. Over 1,000,000 copies were distributed each year during the decade. Later, Pamphlet #1 was adopted as an official publication of the Department of Commerce and Labor and given to immigrants enroute to America. Credit was given to the SAR for its preparation.

The France Society was originally organized with only American members. French Law required organizations such as the SAR be sanctioned by the French Government. In 1905 the SAR Society in France was authorized by the Ministry of French Foreign Affairs and the Prefecture of Police. The membership immediately increased with French descendants of French officers and soldiers who fought for American Independence. Among the new members were Count Sahune de Lafayette and Count de Rochambeau. Count Sahune de Lafayette was elected Vice President of the Society.

It was ascertained there was no compilation of the records of the French combatants who fought for American Independence. The SAR took the initiative and approached His Excellency M. Delcasse, French Minister of Foreign Affairs, Republic of France, who authorized a search of the French Navy and Army records. Approximately 7,000 officers and soldiers of the land army and 50,000 officers and men of the navy were indexed with Christian and family names, dates of service, places of birth and observations of their participation in the American Revolution. The information was published by the French Government, and subsequently through the efforts of the SAR, the information was reprinted in English by the United States Government. A copy of the text was given to each State Society.

SAR NEWS MEDIUM BEGUN

Information on activities of the National Society and the State Societies was published by THE OFFICIAL BULLETIN. It was first printed on October 15, 1906 as the news medium for the SAR and

In 1901 the Empire State Society dedicated a monument on the site of the Battle of Fort Washington, New York City to mark the 155th anniversary of the Revolutionary War event.

was distributed to all members.

In 1781 Spanish General Don Bernado De Galvez with Spanish regular and Louisiana Militia troops captured Pensacola and British posts up the Mississippi River. In 1903 Compatriot John Dimitry of the Louisiana Society, working through diplomatic channels, obtained the records of the Galvez Army from the Spanish Archives in Madrid. The records gave the personal history of the men of the Galvez expedition. The National Society approved the membership of descendants of officers and soldiers serving under General Galvez.

General Horace Porter, after serving as President General, was appointed Ambassador to France. He organized the SAR Society in France and was keenly interested in patriotic work. He searched for six years and finally in 1905 located the remains of John Paul Jones in the Old St. Louis Cemetery in Paris. The remains were escorted to the United States by a Navy squadron.

During this decade the SAR successfully promoted legislation in the United States Congress authorizing the Quartermaster General of the Army to furnish marble headstones for the graves of Revolutionary War soldiers. Also, the SAR obtained congressional authorization for compilation of the Army and Navy records of the Revolutionary War.

The Revolutionary War patriotic holidays were the basis of State Societies' and Chapters' programs. Normally meetings were scheduled to coincide with the dates of George Washington's Birthday, the Battle of Lexington and Concord, the Fourth of July and the Surrender at Yorktown.

NATIONAL DUES REACH 50¢

In 1905 the National Society annual dues were increased from 25¢ to 50¢.

On November 20, 1909 the Permanent Fund was first established by means of an amendment to the SAR Constitution.

Many REAL SONS were proud to be members and took active part in SAR functions. An example was Compatriot Arra Clark, a REAL SON of the Massachusetts Society, who attended the 18th Annual Congress held in Denver, Colorado, in June 1907.

In 1909 the National Society designed and struck a bronze medal to be awarded by Chapters and State Societies to secondary school students for winning essays on Revolutionary War topics.

The Philadelphia Chapter of the Pennsylvania Society initiated a movement to locate and mark the graves of the Signers of the Declaration of Independence. This promotion resulted in the Pennsylvania Society upgrading the condition of John Morton's grave, a Signer buried in Old Saint Paul Cemetery in Chester. The grave of William Paca, Marylander Signer, was found to be in a neglected condition. The Maryland Society placed a large granite memorial stone over his grave.

The Pennsylvania Society located seven British Revolutionary bronze cannons stored at the Allegheny Arsenal near Pittsburgh. The National Society promoted an Act of the United States Congress for the Pennsylvania Society to place the cannons at the Carnegie Museum in Pittsburgh.

The Pennsylvania Society reinterred the remains of many Revolutionary War soldiers from several isolated locations to a prominent central location in the First Presbyterian Church cemetery in Pittsburgh.

The Empire State Society provided the leadership for New York City to purchase the Morris-Jumel Mansion which served as General Washington's headquarters during the Battle of Harlem Heights. This action saved the house from demolition.

"Nathan Hale on Way to Scaffold" was the title of this handsome statue rendered by Empire State Society Compatriot William Ordway Partridge in 1901.

The Illinois Society Sons of the American Revolution
Chartered 19 March 1890

Salutes with pride
The National Society Sons of the American Revolution
Chartered 17 January 1890

Chapters
American Bicentennial
Elijah Smith
Fort Dearborn
Fox Valley
Gen. Henry Knox
Gen. Jos. Bartholomew
Genl Geo. Rogers Clark
Kishwaukee
John Hancock

1900 ILLINOIS BANNER

Chapters
Lewis and Clark
Little Egypt
Piankeshaw
Prairie's Edge
Shadrach Bond
Spoon River
Springfield
Stephen Decatur

HISTORIC SITES MARKED

This decade was the period when the SAR erected hundreds of tablets and monuments to commemorate the deeds and memory of Revolutionary War events and patriots. Many of these memorials were imposing tributes.

In 1900 in Manhattan, New York City, the Empire State Society placed a marble monument with a bronze tablet surmounted with a Revolutionary War cannon at the site of Fort Washington, where the British captured 3,000 of General Washington's best officers and men along with 150 cannons on November 17, 1776.

On September 3, 1901 the Delaware Society unveiled a handsome Brandywine granite memorial at Cooch's Bridge, where the Stars and Stripes were first unfurled in battle on September 3, 1777. The program included an address by President General Walter S. Logan.

On October 19, 1901 the Maryland Society dedicated the impressive Maryland Revolutionary Monument in the Mount Royal Plaza, the cultural center of Baltimore. The 11-foot bronze statue of the Goddess of Liberty is mounted on a 60-foot high granite shaft, with its broad granite base having a bronze tablet on each of its four sides.

The New Jersey Society erected a monument statue of General Enoch Poor in the churchyard of the Old Dutch Reformed Church in Hackensack and unveiled it in the presence of 400 Compatriots and guests on October 4, 1904.

The Vermont Society dedicated a memorial Tower at Burlington on August 16, 1905 to honor Ethan Allen on a high elevation overlooking Lake Champlain and a part of the original Allen farm. The Honorable Charles W. Fairbanks, Vice President of the United States, addressed the many Compatriots and guests.

The National Congress of 1902 was staged in Washington, DC. A highlight was a program at Mount Vernon honoring George Washington.

Governor Charles Evans Hughes of New York, a member of the Empire State Society, gave the address at the laying of the cornerstone of the Prison Ship Martyr's Monument in Fort Greene Park in Brooklyn on October 26, 1907. The memorial was to honor the 11,500 American prisoners who died aboard British ships.

In 1909 the Massachusetts Society erected a "bay" in the "Cloisters of the Colonies," forming a part of the Washington Memorial Chapel at Valley Forge State Park. The Masachusetts Society was the first State Society to donate a bay to the Chapel.

At the conclusion of this decade (1900-1910) the National Society held a membership of 12,100 active members enrolled in 46 State Societies. Local community Chapters existed in only 17 State Societies; however, 25% of the members of the National Society belonged to Chapters. The Massachusetts Society had the largest number of active members, 1638 enrolled.

THE MARYLAND STATE SOCIETY
OF THE SONS OF THE AMERICAN REVOLUTION
IS PROUD OF ITS 100 YEARS OF
PATRIOTIC SERVICE TO THE NATION,
TO THE STATE OF MARYLAND,
AND TO THE NATIONAL SOCIETY

Governor Edwin Warfield
8th. President General, 1902-1903

Judge Henry Stockbridge
14th. President General, 1908-1909

Mayor James Henry Preston
23rd. President General, 1920-1921

Henry F. Baker
37th. President General, 1935-1936

G. Ridgley Sappington
41st. President General, 1941-1942

Judge Wilson King Barnes
75th. President General, 1977-1978

THE MARYLAND REVOLUTIONARY WAR MONUMENT
MOUNT ROYAL PLAZA, BALTIMORE, MARYLAND
Dedicated to all the
MARYLAND REVOLUTIONARY WAR PATRIOTS

Carl F. Bessent
81st. President General, 1984-1985

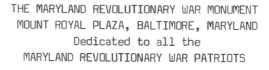

1910–1920: The "Teens" Decade

This decade witnessed continued social changes in America. There were new amendments to the United States Constitution — income tax, popular election of United States Senators and the prohibition of alcohol.

Woodrow Wilson, former President of Princeton University and Governor of New Jersey, was elected President.

The German Empire was determined to expand; when the Crown Prince of Austria was assassinated, this was the excuse for an European explosion. Germany backed Austria; Russia backed Serbia. Soon Germany was at war with Russia's allies — Great Britain, France, Italy.

In 1917 the United States declared war on Germany. There were over 1,000,000 American troops in Europe in 1918, commanded by Compatriot John J. Pershing. Compatriot Bernard Baruch directed America's war industries efforts. Peace came later in the year — the 11th hour of the 11th day of the 11th month.

President Wilson concentrated on the establishment of the League of Nations.

The Sons of the American Revolution continued to concentrate on its patriotic programs.

The SAR purchased one of the three copies of PIERCE'S REGISTER printed in 1786. At the close of the Revolutionary War, Paymaster General John Pierce was instructed to make a final settlement with all officers and soldiers of the Continental Army and to issue certificates for final payments. The original manuscript is preserved by the Treasury Department, and two copies are in the Library of Congress. It is a four-volume set. Each volume is 8 x 13 inches in size, aggregating certificates numbered from 1 to 93,843 issued by the Congress on July 4, 1783. The amount of the certificates totaled $10,650,000.

SAR PROMOTES CRYPT FOR JONES' REMAINS

When Admiral John Paul Jones's body was returned by a naval squadron on July 23, 1905, it was temporarily placed under a stairway in Bancroft Hall at the Naval Academy. The SAR immediately took action and appointed a special committee chaired by Admiral George W. Baird to secure funds to provide a suitable crypt for the Naval hero. The SAR committee's persistent promotion resulted in a congressional appropriation of $75,000 for a fitting sepulcher and the SAR Committee members were honored guests at the ceremonies when the remains were placed in the crypt on Sunday, January 26, 1913.

President General Rogers Thruston and General Lukens Davis, President of the Society of the Descendants of the Signers of the Declaration of Independence, agreed to a joint venture to publish a

Rogers Clark Ballard Thruston was elected President General at the 1913 Annual Congress. Previously President of the Kentucky Society, he always took a great interest in historical, patriotic and philanthropic subjects. The Chapter serving the Louisville area today is named for him.

memorial history on the "Signers." The committee, with appointed members of both societies, worked together and later published a set of eight volumes. During this period 75 descendants of 32 Signers were members of the SAR.

Immigrants, numbering 5,736,000, entered the country between 1910 and 1920. There was a continual demand for SAR Leaflet #1 for these aliens. SAR Leaflet #2 was prepared and distributed: "Naturalization of Aliens in the United States. How to Become a Citizen, What Is Required, Rights and Duties." Both leaflets were used in night schools held for new aliens. Compatriot

President General Louis Annin Ames, a member of the Empire State Society, presided over an observance of Lafayette Day held on September 6, 1918 at Washington, DC.

William P. Dillingham, Chairman of the Immigration Commission, publicly commended the SAR for its efforts in assisting and educating aliens in citizenship.

The SAR Memorial Committee, working with Senator Henry Cabot Lodge, secured the passage of an appropriation of $100,000 for a Thomas Jefferson Statue and Memorial in Washington.

SAR FURTHERS NATIONAL ARCHIVES

A small Congressional appropriation was secured through the efforts of the SAR for the preparation and development of plans for a national archives building for storing and preserving the nation's valuable official manuscripts and records. An Act was approved by the National Congress on March 4, 1913 for a 3,000,000-cubic-feet-of-space structure to cost no more than $1,500,000. The sum of $5,000 was appropriated for preparing plans of the building.

One of the last official acts of Compatriot President William Howard Taft was to approve legislation promoted by the SAR Committee on Military and Naval Records. The Act appropriated $25,000 and authorized the War and Navy Departments to collect, copy and classify the scattered military records of the Revolutionary War.

President Elmer Wentworth prevailed upon the Iowa State Legislature to provide for the general observance of Constitution Day in that state. Thereafter, other states followed this observance. Compatriot David Pierson of the New Jersey Society, Chairman of the Constitution Day Committee, urged each State Society to promote the observance of Constitution Day. A nationwide pattern was established. By 1919 over 5,000 observances were held on Constitution Day through efforts of the SAR.

At the conclusion of this ten-year period, 40 state legislatures, Hawaii, the Phillipines and Puerto Rico had passed laws against the desecration and improper use of the American Flag. This resulted from vigorous SAR promotion of such laws. The SAR successfully promoted legislation requiring the United States Flag to be displayed in all Federal Court Rooms. President General Rogers Thruston, during his term, traveled throughout the country speaking on the origin and evolution of the American Flag. All SAR State Societies and Chapters encouraged the general display of the American Flag on June 14th, Flag Day. The Empire State Society was responsible for the New York Legislature passing a law requiring the American Flag to be displayed at all polling places on election days. The SAR was an active participant in the centennial

Several thousand people turned out for a 1919 Constitution Day celebration sponsored by the New York Chapter.

In June 1914, to commemorate its 25th Anniversary of patriotic service, the SAR conducted a motorcade pilgrimage through five states of General Washington's 1774 journey from Philadelphia to Cambridge, Massachusetts, where he assumed command of the Continental Army. One of the purposes was to foster public interest in the Revolutionary War. Seventy-five members of the SAR and their ladies toured General Washington's route from location to location, arriving on the anniversary dates at each of the night's stopping places. The tour demonstrated General Washington's physical stamina traveling on horseback over poor roads, through fords, averaging 40 miles each day for 11 days. The SAR motorcade was received in the towns and cities with much enthusiasm. The party was met by governors of the states, mayors of cities and towns. Church bells were rung, buildings were decorated. The patriotic adventure received national attention.

CONSTITUTION DAY ESTABLISHED

During the decade, an SAR achievement was establishing the recognition of September 17th as the day commemorating the signing of the United States Constitution. In 1911 Iowa Society

observances of the writing of "The Star-Spangled Banner."

"AMERICAN'S CREED" CREATED

There is a close relationship between the SAR and "The American's Creed." After the declaration of war with Germany, distinguished men of letters sponsored a contest to centralize American patriotism, traditions and aspirations in the form of a creed of citizenship. Over 2,000 creeds were submitted. Compatriot William Tyler Page, Clerk of the House of Representatives, a descendant of Carter Braxton, Signer of the Declaration of Independence, was adjudged the winner. The House of Representatives, through Honorable Champ Clark, Speaker of the House of Representatives, accepted the Creed for the nation.

The SAR Constitution was amended in 1911 to provide for a distinctive President General Badge to be worn during his term of office.

The Delaware Society published the Delaware Revolutionary Muster-rolls which were found in the loft of the old court house in Dover.

Admiral Colby M. Chester, President of the District of Columbia Society, studied the American Navy in the Revolution. There were 64 vessels, carrying 1,242 guns, in the regular Continental Navy. The Colonies' volunteer private armed fleet numbered 1,259 vessels with 18,000 guns. The total number of men who served on the sea was 70,000. There were 797 British vessels captured with cargoes valued at $24,000,000. Seventy percent of the naval engagements were won by the Americans.

In 1915 the Washington Guard was organized as an auxiliary body of the SAR with the purpose to teach patriotism and citizenship to eligible young men. Membership was composed of young men who were sons, grandsons or nephews of SAR and DAR members under the age of 21.

The SAR Annual Congress was held in Portland, Oregon. After the Congress, 40 compatriots and their ladies made a side trip to San Francisco. A banquet was held at the Palace Hotel. A feature of the banquet was a speech by Dr. James Lafayette Cogswell. Dr. Cogswell was the sole survivor of the men who had met at his home on October 22, 1875 and organized the National Society of the Sons of Revolutionary Sires, which in 1889 united with societies of other states and established the SAR.

COMMEMORATIONS CONTINUE

In this decade the SAR continued to commemorate the people, events and anniversaries of the Revolution by commissioning tablets, statues and monuments.

On June 10, 1910 at Compo Beach, Long Island Sound, between Norwalk and Bridgeport, the Connecticut Society unveiled a life-size bronze statue of "The Minute Man" to commemorate the heroism of the patriots who defended the area against the British attack of April 25, 1777.

In 1913 the Connecticut Society placed a bronze tablet marking the site of Colonel Jeremiah Wadsworth's home in Hartford. Colonel Wadsworth was the Commissary General of the Continental Army.

On February 22, 1911 the Maryland Society dedicated a rough-hewn granite block monument at Wye Plantation, Queen Anne County, the Eastern Shore of Maryland. The monument suggests the outline of the desk on which the Declaration of Independence was written. An open scroll bears the inscription, "William Paca, 1740-1799, Signer of the Declaration of Independence."

In 1911 the Massachusetts Society placed a bronze tablet on the Essex Street side of the Hotel Essex, Boston, marking the site of the birthplace of General Henry Knox.

The Massachusetts Society placed a granite monument at Valley Forge State Park to commemorate the service of the Massachusetts troops encamped there in the winter of 1777-78.

On June 19, 1913 the New Jersey Society dedicated a granite monument at Valley Forge to commemorate the service of the New Jersey troops.

A ceremony was held on October 4, 1913 at the Friends burying ground at Stony Brook in the Princeton area by the New Jersey Society. A bronze tablet on a granite block was dedicated to Richard Stockton, Signer of the Declaration of Independence, buried in the cemetery.

In 1912 the Delaware Society erected a granite bay in the Cloisters of the Colonies at the Washington Memorial Chapel, Valley Forge. The marble floor of the bay has an enlarged Colonial Seal of Delaware in the center and the State Seal of Delaware is in the arched ceiling.

In 1915 the Pennsylvania Society unveiled a bronze tablet marking the location of the stockaded Fort Ligonier in Ligonier which withstood attacks by the British and Indians.

In 1915 the Maryland Society placed a memorial stone over the grave of General Mordecai Gist in Saint Michael's Church cemetery, Charleston, South Carolina. The memorial is a flat slab of gray-pink granite, 6 feet long, 3 feet wide, 1 foot thick, upon which is a wreath of oak leaves bearing the insignia of the SAR with the name of General Gist and proper inscription cut into the stone below the wreath.

In 1915 the Vermont Society dedicated a bronze tablet at Burlington, Lake Champlain, at the home of General Ethan Allen and his brother, Colonel Ira Allen. In the same year the Vermont Society unveiled a memorial tablet at the site of Fort Frederick at the village of Winoski, near Burlington.

In 1916 the Rhode Island Society placed a monument to the French troops at the Old North Burial Ground at Prospect Hill, Providence, where many French soldiers are buried.

In 1916 the National Society dedicated a bronze tablet on a ten-foot granite monument at the Revolutionary Barracks, Trenton, New Jersey, to commemorate the capture of Trenton on December 16, 1776.

The SAR continued to attract prominent men. Governor Charles D. Kimball of Rhode Island was elected President of the Rhode Island Society.

Compatriot Curtis Guild, former governor of Massachusetts, was appointed Ambassador to Russia.

Governor Charles S. Whitmen of New York became a member of the Empire State Society.

Compatriot George W. Guthrie of the Pennsylvania Society was the Ambassador to Japan.

WORLD WAR II SUPPORTED

During the World War, Compatriot Elihu Root of the Empire State Society led the American Mission to Russia at Petrograd.

The SAR gave a full measure to the World War effort. The National Society appointed a special War Service Committee.

The Massachusetts Society collected $120,000 to distribute comfort bags to sailors and soldiers passing through Boston.

The members of the Empire State Society subscribed to

One of the ambulances purchased by the Empire State Society.

$15,300,000 worth of Liberty Bonds. In addition the Empire State Society raised funds for three ambulances sent overseas. The Illinois Society and the New Jersey Society each sent one ambulance.

The New Jersey Society sent "Christmas boxes" to each of its 85 Compatriots serving in the armed forces.

Compatriot La Verne Noyes, President of the Illinois Society, gave the University of Chicago $2,500,000 to be used for the education of soldiers and sailors who served in World War I.

At the outbreak of hostilities there were 15,423 active SAR members. One thousand nine hundred and twenty members served in the armed forces. Twenty-two Compatriots were killed in the War.

At the close of this decade there were 16,285 active members. The Permanent Fund totaled $13,609.

South Carolina Society's Thirteen Chapters Salute the Centennial

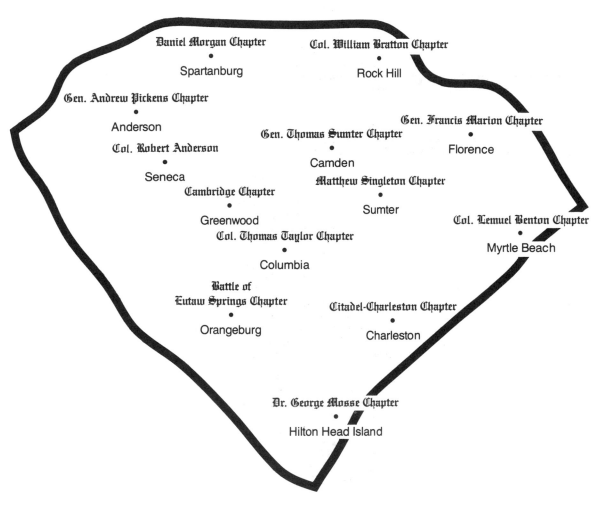

Daniel Morgan Chapter
Spartanburg

Col. William Bratton Chapter
Rock Hill

Gen. Andrew Pickens Chapter
Anderson

Gen. Francis Marion Chapter
Florence

Gen. Thomas Sumter Chapter
Camden

Col. Robert Anderson
Seneca

Matthew Singleton Chapter
Sumter

Cambridge Chapter
Greenwood

Col. Lemuel Benton Chapter
Myrtle Beach

Col. Thomas Taylor Chapter
Columbia

Battle of
Eutaw Springs Chapter
Orangeburg

Citadel-Charleston Chapter
Charleston

Dr. George Mosse Chapter
Hilton Head Island

The South Carolina Society
Of The
Sons of the American Revolution
Organized April 18, 1889

SAR CENTENNIAL HISTORY

PART II: 1920–1940

1920-1930: The Roaring '20s Decade

For the first time in American history, more people were living in towns and cities than in the rural countryside. The United States Congress took action and sharply curbed immigration with a national quota system. The world immediately became smaller when Charles Lindberg (Lucky Lindy) flew solo across the Atlantic to Paris, 3,600 miles in 33½ hours. The Nineteenth Amendment to the Constitution was ratified granting suffrage (right to vote) to women. Prohibition influenced the social life in America. It was a jazz age. Ladies started bobbing their hair, and knee-length skirts became the fashion. Fads became popular, bridge and crossword puzzles. The radio brought Americans closer together. The industrial economy boomed. As the decade ended, there was a downturn, spending declined. The stock market crashed, bringing a depression with business failures and unemployment.

The three Presidents of the United States who served in this decade were all members of the Sons of the American Revolution: Warren G. Harding, Calvin Coolidge and Herbert Hoover.

Compatriot former President William Howard Taft was sworn in as Chief Justice of the Supreme Court.

This was a Golden Age for the Sons of the American Revolution, an expanding and improving society. A National Headquarters was established in Washington. Society membership increased by 27 percent.

CONSTITUTION DAY OBSERVED

The SAR continued to give strong promotion to the observance of Constitution Day, September 17. Thousands of celebrations were held throughout the country to commemorate the signing of the United States Constitution.

The SAR initiated a medals program for grammar and high school students honoring achievement in citizenship and history studies.

In 1921 the SAR Committee on Military and Naval records reported that the Revolutionary War records previously stored in the War and Navy Building had been moved to the Munition Building on B Street and placed under the supervision of the Adjutant General of the Army.

On Flag Day in 1921 the National Society sent a silk American Flag to Sulgrave Manor, the ancestral home of the Washington Family in England. The flag was presented at the Manor Home by Compatriot Charles Dumont of Surrey, Egland.

In 1921 the BULLETIN, which had originated as the SAR publication to all members in 1906, was expanded with a larger format, and additional coverage of State Society and Chapter events, reports of national committees and officers were published. Compatriot Frank B. Steele of the Empire State Society was elected Secretary General and held the office until May 1951. His duties included serving as editor of the BULLETIN.

The Saratoga Battlefield Association, initiated by the Rochester Chapter of the Empire State Society, purchased at a cost of $19,500 the Freeman farm and the Sarle farm comprising 400 acres on which the battle was fought.

REAL SON Dr. Crosby Perry of the Massachusetts Society attended the 33rd SAR Annual Congress in 1922 held in Springfield, Massachusetts.

FRANCE MARKS LAFAYETTE'S GRAVE

Members of the Society in France continued the annual Fourth of July pilgrimage to the grave of General Marquis de Lafayette in Picpus Cemetery in Paris, France.

In the Spring Issue our Society's heritage was traced from its earliest beginnings in the late 1800s through the decade that witnessed World War I. Now, our chronicler — Former President General Carl F. Bessent — describes how the SAR fared during the 20 turbulent years that followed.

On September 17, 1924 the SAR sponsored Constitution Day exercises on the steps of the Sub-Treasury Building in New York City.

General John J. Pershing became a Life Member of the Pennsylvania Society.

The archives of the Bureau of Pensions in Washington were catalogued and preserved the original claims of Revolutionary War pensioners. Over 80,000 separate papers composed the collection.

President Compatriot Harding died suddenly in San Francisco on his return trip from Alaska, and Compatriot Calvin Coolidge was sworn in as President by his father.

Andrew Jackson IV, great-grandson of President Andrew Jackson, joined the Tennessee Society.

Compatriot Frank White, a member of the North Dakota Society, was appointed Treasurer of the United States.

The 1924 SAR Annual Congress was held in Salt Lake City. A train with special cars was made up at Chicago to accommodate the delegates and wives on the momentous trip.

Honorable Charles Evans Hughes, Secretary of State, became a member of the Empire State Society.

Members of the Empire State Society contributed over $10,000 for the restoration of the Cathedral of Saint John the Divine in New York City.

The New Jersey Society offered awards of Fifty Dollar Gold coins to Princeton University and Rutgers University students for the best essays on a Revolutionary War subject.

The National Society Executive Committee in 1924 urged the United States Congress to appropriate funds for repairs to the frigate CONSTITUTION and the resolution was communicated to the President of the United States.

SARS ELECTED PRESIDENT, VP

Two Compatriots, Calvin Coolidge and Charles G. Dawes, were elected President and Vice President, respectively.

Honorable Alanson B. Houghton, President of the Painted Post Chapter of the Empire State Society, was appointed Ambassador to the Court of Saint James.

Compatriot Charles B. Warren of the Michigan Society was appointed Ambassador to Japan.

On the 150th Anniversary of the Battle of Lexington and Concord at the DAR Continental Congress, SAR President General Marvin H. Lewis presented the DAR Flag, designed by former SAR President General Louis Ames, to the DAR.

President General Harvey Foote initiated the custom by Presidents General of making an extensive country-wide tour to visit the State Societies.

The Connecticut Society honored its former President, Honorable Archie Lee Talbot, for the design of the SAR colors — blue, white and buff — at the Stratfield Hotel in New Haven.

REAL SON Nathaniel Jones, age 81, living at the Soldiers Home in Columbia, South Carolina, became a Compatriot, National #41745. His father served as a mounted soldier under General Francis Marion.

Annually on July 4th the France Society commemorates the day and the Marquis de Lafayette by placing a wreath on his tomb in Picpus Cemetery, Paris. This photo shows the 1924 program.

In 1926 the National Society established its first permanent office for the Registrar in the Hill Building at 17th and I Streets in Washington.

On February 18, 1926 the Philadelphia Chapter of the Pennsylvania Society gave a birthday party to REAL SON Compatriot John D. Lewis at his home in Philadelphia. His father, Thomas Lewis, served as a soldier in the Virginia Militia.

A large bronze statue of George Washington was unveiled at Sulgrave Manor in England, a gift of Compatriot Henry Waldo Coe of the Oregon Society.

NEW HEADQUARTERS VOTED

The 37th SAR Annual Congress was held in Philadelphia in 1926 during the Sesquicentennial of the Declaration of Independence. The Congress initiated action to secure a National Headquarters in the nation's capitol and authorized the raising of $250,000. The Bellevue Stratford Hotel served as Congress Headquarters. The church service was held in historic Christ Church with the procession led by the New York Chapter Color Guard. The First Sesson of the Congress was held in Independence Hall. A reception was held later in Independence Hall where President General Remington, Philadelphia Mayor Kendrick and DAR President General Mrs. Brasseau received the delegates and wives. REAL SON Compatriot John D. Lewis placed a special wreath at the Liberty Bell. There was a trip to Valley Forge.

The SAR was active on the Fourth of July. The Empire State Society participated in ceremonies at the historic site of old Fort Washington at Washington Heights in New York City when Honorable Rodman Wanamaker gave the property to the American Scenic and Historic Society. The SAR Colonial Color Guard was featured.

The Western Reserve Chapter of the Ohio Society dedicated and unveiled a bronze tablet on the public square to the memory of Reverend Joseph Badger, a soldier of the Revolution who fought at Bunker Hill.

The Los Angeles Chapter of the California Society promoted a patriotic pageant in the Los Angeles Coliseum on the Fourth with 5,000 participants and over 50,000 spectators. The exciting drama featuring Paul Revere's ride was performed by the famous actor Tom Mix on his wonder horse "Tony".

U.S. SOIL PLACED ON KOSCIUSZKO'S GRAVE

In the Polish city of Cracow on July Fourth, a casket of soil from West Point, Yorktown, Saratoga and Star Fort in South Carolina, was scattered over the grave of Thaddeus Kosciuszko, Engineer Colonel of the Continental Army. The project was sponsored by the New Hampshire Society.

During this period three dormant State Societies were revived: North Carolina, South Carolina and West Virginia.

On September 17, the Sergeant Lawrence Everhart Chapter of the Maryland Society dedicated a five-ton boulder and bronze marker honoring General Lafayette on the east bank of the Monocacy River.

At the Constitution Day dinner at the University Club, the Los Angeles Chapter announced that two REAL SONS had joined the SAR; Leonard Case, 94, National #42781; and Merritt B. Case, 87, National #42782. Their father, Reuben Case, enlisted in the Continental Army at the age of 14, fought at the Battle of Saratoga and saw General Burgoyne surrender. The brothers remembered their father's stories of his role in the struggle for America's independence.

On October 10 the Vermont Society dedicated a bronze tablet at Camp Abnaki, North Hero Island, Vermont on Lake Champlain to commemorate the Battle of Valcour in October 1777.

Thirteen sturdy red oak trees were planted on October 11 in Independence Square as living memorials to the original states. The governor of each of the states was present for the ceremony as well as city officials and leaders of patriotic societies. The program was conducted by the Pennsylvania Society; Compatriot Walter Gabell, served as Chairman of the ceremonies and Marshall of the parade.

In October of 1926 Compatriot Walter Gabell, President of the Pennsylvania Society presented the wreath laid on the statue of George Washington as part of the ceremonies connected with the Planting of Thirteen Trees at the Sesquicentennial Exposition. The trees were placed in Independence Square as living memorials of the staunch unity of the pioneer Commonwealths. Representatives of the Governors of the original 13 states, leaders of national patriotic societies and various government officials participated in the impressive program.

Four Revolutionary War soldiers who were killed in the Battle of Germantown in 1777 were hastily buried following the battle. These graves were uncovered during the bulldozing of a road. The caskets were bourne on flag-draped carriages, passing through the streets of Germantown to the Saint Michael's Lutheran Church graveyard. The soldiers were reinterred in an impressive service conducted by the Pennsylvania Society, which unveiled a bronze tablet at the new burial site.

The New Jersey Society
Sons of the American Revolution

New Jersey SAR - The first SAR - established March 7, 1889, proudly salutes the National on its 100th birthday, April 30, 1989.

Our founder, William Osborne Mc Dowell, National Certificate #1, was not only instrumental in establishing the National Society but was among the founders of the Daughters of the American Revolution as well. Dedicated to world peace, he became chairman of the committee which organized a world wide Liberty Congress, the Human Freedom League, and the League For Peace, a forerunner of the United Nations. For these accomplishments he was nominated for the Nobel Peace Prize. In addition Compatriot Mc Dowell was the catalyst for the campaign to raise money for the construction of the base of the Statue of Liberty

The New Jersey Society, headquartered in the "Cannonball House" around which the battle of Springfield was fought, invites all Compatriots and friends to visit with us, the "crossroads"-"The cockpit of the Revolution" state, to experience the N.J. Revolutionary War battlefields, monuments and historic sites. More than fifty battles and 300 skirmishes were fought on New Jersey soil.

Because of our closeness to these monuments and historic sites the New Jersey Society has vigorously pursued graves registration (6000 registered) and decoration as one of its programs. Additionally, the Society has sponsored or contributed generously to more than sixty monuments and tablets honoring those who sacrificed so much. Our color guard serves at all SAR functions as well as parades and other public events including the 1987 Constitution celebration in Philadelphia.

We welcome those who wish to do genealogical research in our 1000 volume library. Our Executive Secretary is available on Tuesdays and Thursdays during normal working hours.

State luncheon meetings are held in October to honor the DAR, in February to honor the CAR and to celebrate Washington's birthday, and in May for the annual meeting.

TENNESSEE SOCIETY

ORGANIZED DECEMBER 3, 1889

TENNESSEE CHARTER MEMBERS

JACOB ANDREW CARTWRIGHT
JOHN W. EASTMAN
ROGER EASTMAN
LEWIS ROBERT EASTMAN
CHARLES HAZEN EASTMAN
ELIJA EMBREE HOSS
DAVID CAMPBELL KELLY
JOHN PHILLIP WILLIAMS
JOSEPH BUCKNER KILLEBREW
ADRIAN VAN SINIDERN LINDSLEY
GOODLOE LINDSLEY
JOHN TRIMBLE LINDSLEY
WILLIAM EDGAR METZGER
GEORGE C. PAINE
SAML. LEVY ROCHE
FLOURNOY RIVES
JAMES MERRILL SAFFORD
GATES PHILLIPS THURSTON

SIGNERS OF NSSAR INCORPORATION

J.A. CARTWRIGHT

REAL SONS OF THE REVOLUTION

THOMAS V. GREER
GEORGE W. MITCHELL
PETER B. VAUGHN
ALFRED JONES

PRESIDENTS GENERAL

FREDERICK W. MILLSPAUGH 1932-33
HARRY T. BURN 1964

MINUTE MEN

HARRY BURN 1963
EARL L. WHITTINGTON SR. 1966
O.M. WILSON 1970

VICE PRESIDENTS GENERAL

FREDERICK W. MILLSPAUGH 1929-30
LELAND HUME 1930-31
ARTHUR CROWNOVER JR. 1935-36
A. LEA READ 1940-41
FRANK W. ZIEGLER 1942-43
HUGH A. STALLWORTH 1953-54
H. MARTIN NUNNELLEY 1959-61
EARL L. WHITTINGTON 1964-65
O.M. WILSON 1972-74
HORACE A. DONHAM 1980-82
ROBERT A. RAGLAND 1986-87

On October 13 the Connecticut Society dedicated a bronze tablet in the village green in the town of Farmington to the memory of Count de Rochambeau who encamped his troops on the site in June 1781.

BATTLE OF TRENTON COMMEMORATED

On December 29, 1926 the New Jersey Society dedicated a bronze tablet on the main entrance wall of the New Jersey State House to commemorate the 150th anniversary of the Battle of Trenton. The tablet was accepted by Governor Moore. It was unveiled by Compatriot Bayard Stockton, great-great grandson of Richard Stockton, Signer of the Declaration of Independence.

On February 24, 1927 Mrs. A. Howard Clark passed away. From 1892 until her death she reviewed and approved the lineage of all SAR membership applications. She served as first Registrar General of the DAR, and later as Vice-President General and Honorary Vice-President General.

Former Governor of Vermont, Compatriot Percival W. Clement, established a $10,000 trust with the income to support a contest for the best thesis on the principles of the United States Constitution open to juniors and seniors of 18 New England colleges.

Compatriot Cecil B. DeMille produced his famous Biblical movie epic, THE KING OF KINGS.

The 38th SAR Annual Congress held in Richmond in May 1927 authorized the purchase of the Norman William Mansion and its valuable furnishings located at 1227 Sixteenth Street, N.W., Washington, for $145,000. It became SAR National Headquarters.

The National Headquarters purchased in 1927 in Washington, DC boasted a grand reception hall containing elegant furniture.

Compatriot Peter B. Fairchild of the New Jersey Society died on June 19. He was active in the early days of the Society and was the last survivor of the members who were given the same National Number as their State Number.

The Berkshire Chapter of the Massachusetts Society erected a large memorial monument commemorating the militiamen of Berkshire County who helped to turn the tide at the Battle of Bennington. Colonel Jacob Stafford was reinterred under the stone monument. Dedication ceremonies were conducted on the fourth of July.

On August 26, 1927 President General Ernest Rodgers and Compatriot Henry F. Baker of the Maryland Society completed the purchase of the new National Headquarters.

FIRST NAVAL BATTLE SALUTED

On September 10 the Massachusetts Society dedicated a bronze tablet on a rock ledge in Fort Phoenix in Fairhaven Park commemorating the first naval battle of the American Revolution fought on May 14, 1775 between a sloop manned by the men of Fairhaven and two British sloops resulting in the capture of the two British sloops and their crews.

The National Society began operations at the Sixteenth Street Headquarters on October 1, 1927.

Congressman Hamilton Fish of New York joined the Newburgh Chapter of the Empire State Society.

On December 15 President Calvin Coolidge received President General Ernest Rodgers, Secretary General Frank Steele and

Under the auspices of the Connecticut Society's General David Humphreys Branch, ceremonies were held in June, 1928 at East Hartford to dedicate a bronze tablet on a large boulder in memory of Comte de Rochambeau and his soldiers who encamped there on their way to Yorktown. Participating in the program were Branch President Frederic T. Murless, Jr., Society President George S. Godard and Past President General Ernest E. Rogers.

Compatriot William Tyler Page, author of "The American's Creed," in a private audience at The White House.

Governor John S. Fisher of Pennsylvania spoke to the Pennsylvania Society at the Pittsburgh Athletic Club on January 20, 1928. President General Rodgers introduced the Governor, a member of the SAR.

On April 19 the Maryland Society unveiled a tablet honoring Thomas Johnson, first Governor of Maryland, in the State House at Annapolis. The tablet was placed at the entrance to the old Senate Chamber where General George Washington resigned his commission. The tablet was unveiled by Miss Barbara Brooks Dennis, great-great-great granddaughter of Governor Johnson.

United States Senator Arthur H. Vanderburg joined the Michigan Society.

The Western Reserve Chapter of the Ohio Society organized a Colonial Color Guard in the uniform of General Washington's infantry.

PRESIDENT COOLIDGE RECEIVES CONGRESS DELEGATES

The 39th Annual Congress was held in Washington for the members and wives to inspect the new National Headquarters. The church service was held at the Church of the Epiphany, with the New York Chapter again furnishing flags for the event. Delegates and wives were received by President and Mrs. Coolidge at the White House. The DAR National Officers gave a tea in the DAR Memorial Continental Hall for the ladies attending the Congress. A reception was held at the National Headquarters, with the U.S. Marine Band playing throughout the evening. There was a pilgrimage to Arlington National Cemetery where President General Rodgers placed a wreath on the tomb of the Unknown

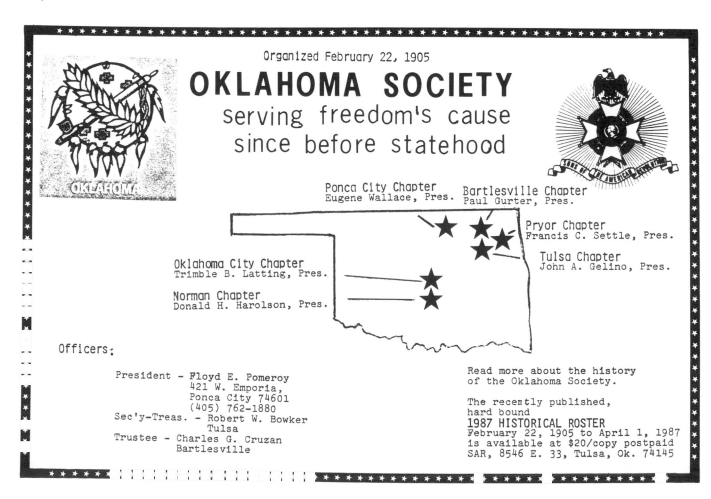

Organized February 22, 1905

OKLAHOMA SOCIETY
serving freedom's cause
since before statehood

Ponca City Chapter
Eugene Wallace, Pres.

Bartlesville Chapter
Paul Gurter, Pres.

Pryor Chapter
Francis C. Settle, Pres.

Oklahoma City Chapter
Trimble B. Latting, Pres.

Tulsa Chapter
John A. Gelino, Pres.

Norman Chapter
Donald H. Harolson, Pres.

Officers:

President - Floyd E. Pomeroy
421 W. Emporia,
Ponca City 74601
(405) 762-1880
Sec'y-Treas. - Robert W. Bowker
Tulsa
Trustee - Charles G. Cruzan
Bartlesville

Read more about the history of the Oklahoma Society.

The recently published, hard bound
1987 HISTORICAL ROSTER
February 22, 1905 to April 1, 1987 is available at $20/copy postpaid SAR, 8546 E. 33, Tulsa, Ok. 74145

Soldier. Compatriot William Tyler Page, Clerk of the House of Representatives, Compatriot Curtis D. Wilbur, Secretary of the Navy, and the Honorable James J. Davis, Secretary of Labor, all addressed the Congress. The North Carolina Society was given its beautiful engrossed Charter and presented a North Carolina silk State Flag. It was the first state flag given to the National Society.

The Minnesota Society strongly promoted the new chapel at Fort Snelling where Compatriot Colonel Walter C. Sweeney was the commanding officer. The pulpit of the chapel was the gift of the Minnesota Society.

On June 14 the New York Chapter observed Flag Day by sponsoring a parade from 59th Street and 7th Avenue to the Central Park Mall. Mounted police and military units participated.

The Pennsylvania Society inaugurated a Flag Day ceremony on Flagstaff Hill, Schenley Park, Pittsburgh with a special sunrise ceremony. There was a 21-gun salute, with the raising of "Old Glory" by the Pennsylvania National Guard field artillery unit. The program included the dropping of flag bombs from National Guard airplanes. Following the ceremonies, breakfast was served at the Carnegie Tech Grill.

The Richard Montgomery Chapter of the Ohio Society unveiled a monument decorated with a long flint-lock rifle and powder horn over the grave of Revolutionary War soldier John Cuppy, buried in Fairfield Cemetery, Green County.

On July 4th at Jensen, Utah, on the banks of the Green River, the Utah Society unveiled a monument to the memory of Father Escalante, the first white man to explore the intermountain country.

On Sunday, September 2, the Pennsylvania Society unveiled a memorial monument to eight Revolutionary War soldiers named McKee in the McKee-Rose Fountain Cemetery, north of Greensburg. The cemetery had been the burial place for the Clan McKee members since 1769. The Clan met at the site in 1775 and decided to fight the British.

By 1929 $110,000 had been pledged to pay the mortgage of the National Headquarters. There was a campaign for 300 pledges of $500 each to clear the debt.

General Charles P. Summerall, Army Chief of Staff, became a member of the SAR.

The Pennsylvania Society presented 150 medals to grammar school students of Pittsburgh. The Ohio Society gave 63 medals to grammar school students in Columbus.

GRAVES OF PATRIOTS MARKED

The Pennsylvania Society continued to mark long-forgotten Revolutionary graves: the grave of Elizabeth Berry, only known woman to have served on enlistment in the Continental Army, buried in Robinson Run cemetery near Sturgeon; the grave of General Francis Nash, killed at the battle of Germantown and buried in the Mennonite cemetery on Surreytown Pike; and the grave of General Peter Muhlenburg, buried in the Trappe Lutheran Church cemetery, north of Collegeville.

On November 1, 1929 President Herbert Hoover visited the SAR National Headquarters where he was inducted into membership as a Life Member of the Pennsylvania Society. His National Number is #47976. He was a descendant of Jacob Wynne, private who served in the New York Militia.

The decade ended with the National Society having a membership of 20,653 active Compatriots. There were 188 Chapters working at the community level.

1930–1940: The Depression Decade

The stock market crash heralded a worldwide business depression. There were 12 million people unemployed in the United States in 1932. Compatriot Franklin D. Roosevelt was elected President and initiated "New Deal" programs which stressed federal support for economic reconstruction. Later, because of the clouds of war, additional funds were appropriated for national defense. Both Germany and Russia invaded and partitioned Poland which triggered the beginning of World War II. Japan continued its undeclared war in China.

The United States population was 122 million people. The "Star-Spangled Banner" was officially adopted as the United States Anthem. Television was being developed and nylon stockings became available for the ladies.

National Society operations were affected by the general economic conditions. Membership and finances suffered. The Society membership in 1930 was 20,398 but declined to 13,167 by 1936. Society operating funds of $15,000 were lost when a bank failed. The Society staff was reduced to four, and salaries were reduced by 10%. The number of annual issues of the Society magazine was reduced to three. A system of issuing Certificates of Indebtedness was established to cover the remaining debt on the National Society Headquarters building. The debt was $40,000 in 1932 and was reduced to $22,000 by 1940.

During the decade the SAR Medals programs were continued. Over 1,000 Good Citizenship Medals were presented in high schools throughout the country each year, while 200 ROTC Medals were awarded annually to ROTC Units in colleges and universities.

A unique feature of the 41st Annual Congress at Asbury Park, New Jersey, in 1930 was the passing of the Graf Zeppelin over the

On February 21, 1932 the France Society staged an impressive ceremony at the statue of George Washington in the Place d'Iena, Paris. The French government permitted the flags of Patriot de Rochambeau to be removed from the Military Museum in order to be at the program. The Society was represented by (from left): Vice-President General Marquis de Rochambeau, Vice President Edward de Neveu, Registrar Comte de Luppe and Secretary C. Benoist d'Azy. They presented a wreath as did other organizations.

TEXAS SOCIETY
SONS OF THE AMERICAN REVOLUTION
Since 8 December 1896

Hon. Ira H. Evans

THEN: Chartered in Galveston, Texas; first President Honorable Ira H. Evans of Austin. Major Evans won the Congressional Medal of Honor for distinguished bravery as a Major in the Vermont Volunteer Infantry at Hatcher's Run, Virginia, April 22, 1865. In 1869 he ran for the Texas Legislature and was subsequently elected as Speaker of the House of Representatives at the age of 25. Fifteen members attended the first annual meeting in Galveston and by March of the next year the Society had twenty members.

PRESIDENTS GENERAL: Texas has been honored with four: Benjamin Powell (1942-43), President TXSSAR 1941; Robert Sonfield (1963-64), President, TXSSAR 1960-61; Walter G. Sterling (1967-68), President TXSSAR 1964-65; most recently Clovis H. Brakebill (1986-87), President TXSSAR 1982-83.

George Washington Birthday Banquet: Paul Carrington Chapter of Houston holds annually and honors outstanding Americans; at 45th Annual Banquet in 1988 Dr. Frank Vandiver, President of Texas A&M University was so honored.

Programs: Graves of Revolutionary War Patriots Marked: in 1976, under the leadership of Colonel R.S.D. Lockwood, five plaques listing the 46 Patriots buried in Texas were cast in bronze and placed in the Texas Capitol in Austin; the Hall of State on the State Fair Grounds, Dallas; at Fort Bliss in El Paso; in the War and Peace House in the Sam Houston Museum, Huntsville; and in the Federal Building in San Antonio.

The Patriot's Fund: in 1977 the Texas Society followed up on an idea provided by Compatriot Howard Jesse and organized a "Patriot's Fund" which would be expended exclusively in stimulating patiotism in the state of Texas. Under the Chairmanship of Brigadier General Graber Kidwell, the fund grew from the initial $4,000 contributed by the Society to $76,000 in 1988 when General Kidwell relinquished the Chair. Only the interest is expended each year for patirotic projects.

The Douglass G. High Oration Contest: Compatriot Robert F. Ritchie of the Dallas Chapter has contributed very generously over the years to the support the awards of this program at the chapter, state, and national level. Several of the Texas winners have gone on to win the national competition, and have included three such winners from the Patrick Henry Chapter in Austin.

The Boy Scout Recognition Program: this program is currently under the leadership of Richard L. Robinett of New Braunfels. An impressive silver eagle trophy is presented each year at the annual State Convention **for** the Texas participant in the national competition. The Liberty 87 Chapter of Brownsville **provided** the Texas winner in 1989.

Billy E. Hightower

National Congresses Held in Texas: Houston and Dallas. The National Congress in 1996 is scheduled to be held in San Antonio, to coincide with the 100th Anniversary of the Texas Society.

NOW: The Galveston Chapter was the first chapter organized in the Texas Society. It hosted the TXSSAR 93rd annual State Convention on 10-11 March 1989. From the original 20 members in 1896 the Texas Society had grown to 2161 members in 35 chapters in late 1988, making up over eight percent of the 24,749 members in the National Society, and making Texas the State Society with the largest number of members. Billy E. Hightower, independent businessman and former teacher in the New Braunfels Public Schools, of New Braunfels serves as the President of the Texas Society.

Congress Headquarters Hotel and dropping a wreath in honor of Baron Von Steuben.

The Maine Society was given a small section in the town of Wells with a trust to care for the small park and fly the United States Flag on patriotic days, including the anniversary of the days the town of Wells was besieged by Indians during the "King William War" in 1692.

NEW YORK GOVERNOR ROOSEVELT SPEAKS

The Empire State Society observed 1931 Flag Day on the village green adjoining Old Saint Paul's Episcopal Church in the quaint Village of Eastchester, Mount Vernon, New York. Compatriot Governor Franklin Roosevelt was the speaker. The program included an elaborate pageant of historical scenes of the early New York colony.

On June 21, 1931 the General David Humphreys Branch of the Connecticut Society decorated the 611 Revolutionary graves in New Haven County and held ceremonies at the grave of General Humphreys in the Grove Street Cemetery in New Haven and at the monument of Nathan Hale on the Yale University campus.

On July 4, 1931 the annual Fourth of July ceremony was held at the grave of General Marquis de Lafayette in Paris, France. Compatriots Marquis de Chamburn and Marquis de Rochambeau spoke to the large group. Compatriot United States Ambassador Walter Edge placed the wreath on the grave.

The Richard Montgomery Chapter of the Ohio Society held ceremonies on Sunday, July 19, marking the graves of eight Revolutionary soldiers buried in Warren County. Descendants of each soldier unveiled each marker and presented sketches of their ancestor.

Flag raising ceremonies were conducted by the Utah Society at sunrise on Ensign Pike on July 24, 1931. This marked the opening of the celebration of the covered wagon days commemorating the placing of the United States Flag on the peak in 1847 by Brigham Young, who claimed the territory for the United States.

In 1931 the Philadelphia Chapter of the Pennsylvania Society held its annual Constitution Day observance on the *U.S.S. Constitution* which was visiting Philadelphia. The Chapter continued its custom of placing a wreath in Constitution Chamber in Independence Hall.

The Massachusetts, Connecticut and Rhode Island Societies held their annual Tri-State meeting on September 24 at Newport, Rhode Island. The luncheon was held at the Hotel Viking with 84 compatriots in attendance.

A ceremony was held on October 4 at Cypress Lawn Cemetery, south of San Francisco, where Colonel Adolphus S. Hubbard, first President of the California Society SAR, and his wife, Sarah Isabelle Hubbard, first Regent of the California Society DAR, are buried. Two similar bronze plaques were placed on a granite gravestone.

SURRENDER AT YORKTOWN CELEBRATED

The National Society was prominent at the Surrender at Yorktown Sesquicentennial Celebration in 1931. The National Society engaged the *S.S. Dorchester,* Flagship of the Merchant and Miners Steamship line fleet. The transportation, accommodations on the steamer and land transportation cost the 225 Compatriots and guests only $55 per person. There was wonderful fellowship from the time the steamship left Baltimore on Friday, October 16, for Yorktown until its return to Baltimore on Tuesday.

The impressive Memorial Arch over the roadway to the Yorktown Battlefield was provided by the National Society for the Sesquicentennial.

The National Society placed a bronze tablet honoring Comte de Grasse for his outstanding contributions in securing American Independence. The tablet was designed by Tiffany and Company and placed on the front wall above the entrance of the colonial Custom House in Yorktown built in 1706. This first Custom House in America was purchased by the DAR Comte de Grasse Chapter in 1924. The tablet was unveiled by Compatriot Archibald Barklie of Philadelphia, a descendant of Admiral Comte de Grasse. Marquis de Chambrun, President of the SAR Society in France, spoke.

This handsome George Washignton Memorial Arch, at the Main Entrance to the Celebration Area of the Yorktown Sesquicentennial, was provided by the National Society.

Later in October a reception was held at the SAR National Headquarters in Washington honoring Marshall Petain of France. Two French Compatriots, Marquis de Rochambeau and Marquis de Chambrun, Marshall Petain and President General Benjamin Johnson received the many guests.

The California Society held its George Washington Bicentennial observance at the Fairmont Hotel in San Francisco on February 10, 1932. The U.S. Army Band for the Presido furnished the music. The occasion was also a birthday celebration for Compatriot Leonard Case, a REAL SON, who attended and celebrated his 100th birthday.

The New York Chapter held its George Washington Birthday observance in the Hotel Lexington on February 19. Compatriot Lowell Thomas, author and radio commentator, related his world experiences. The New York Chapter Color Guard presented its 21 beautiful Revolutionary War Flags.

President General Benjamin Johnson died of a heart attack on February 19. Judge Josiah A. Van Orsdel was elected by the Executive Committee to fill the unexpired term of the last President General.

At the 42nd Annual George Washington Birthday meeting of the Connecticut Society held in Greenwich 180 members of the Society of the Revolution merged into the Connecticut Society SAR.

On May 30 the Pennsylvania Society held a celebration at Fort Palmer in Ligonier Valley at the site of the old fort on the Hoon Farm. Compatriots formed into a parade and marched to Fairfield Presbyterian Church where the graves of 32 Revolutionary soldiers were decorated.

COMPATRIOT DOUGLAS MACARTHUR ADDRESSES SARS

On July 3 and 4, 1932 at the Fort Necessity Memorial Park located 11 miles east of Uniontown, Pennsylvania, on US route 40, the Pennsylvania Society staged an impressive program on land originally owned by George Washington, The Society had initiated and promoted restoration of the stockade and earthworks. Compatriot Major General Douglas MacArthur spoke to the large assemblage.

On September 2 the North Carolina Society dedicated a granite stone and plaque at the grave of Major Francis McCorkle near Denver in Catawba County.

On October 1 the District of Columbia Society planted a black oak tree from Mount Vernon on the National Society Headquarters grounds. The program was held on Navy Day. The U.S. Navy Band played and the Honorable Francis Adams, Secretary of the Navy, spoke.

On October 27th President General Millspaugh visited Canton, Maine, to meet Compatriot Osborn Allen, 96-year-old REAL SON, who was in excellent health. On January 10, 1933 Paramount News interviewed REAL SON Allen; he related Revolutionary stories his father told him including experiences at the Valley Forge encampment. His father also served in the War of 1812. The interview was shown in movie theatres nationwide.

The Society in France gave a French Flag to the Fort Necessity Chapter of the Pennsylvania Society to commemorate the service of the French soldiers who fell on the Great Meadows battlefield in 1754.

By 1933 the Rhode Island Society recorded and marked the graves of 2,000 soldiers of the American Revolution.

Former President General R. C. Ballard Thruston compiled a set of the 32 wills of the Signers of the Declaration of Independence. He presented copies of the wills to the Descendants of the Signers, Historical Society of Pennsylvania, Filson Club in Louisville and the National Society.

NATHAN HALE STATUE DEDICATED

On June 6, 1935 the Connecticut Society commemorated the Tercentenary of the Nutmeg State by dedicating the MacMonnies statue of Nathan Hale in Williams Park in New London. President General Henry Baker was the special guest on the occasion.

Colonel Alva Brasted, Chief of Chaplains of the United States Army, was elected Chaplain General. He was a member of the Minnesota Society.

The Pennsylvania Society held special services in Independence Hall on the 100th anniversary of the cracking of the Liberty Bell on July 8, 1935. On this date in 1835 the bell cracked as it tolled the death knell for the funeral of Chief Justice John Marshall.

The mortgage on the SAR National Headquarters was liquidated on the 26th of August, 1935. Certificates of Indebtedness sold to Compatriots made possible the payment of the mortgage in full.

On May 14, 1936 the 100th birthday of the Honorable Gasius Paddock of the Missouri Society, who served as the first Treasurer General of the National Society, was marked. As a young boy he lived in Springfield, Illinois, and became a personal friend of Abraham Lincoln. He attended all the early meetings of the National Society.

On Memorial Day 1936 the Philadelphia Chapter placed 500 SAR grave flags and American grave flags on the graves of Revolutionary soldiers.

Addressing those attending the ceremony to dedicate the de Grasse tablet at Yorktown on October 17, 1931 was President General Benjamin N. Johnson. Behind him were Marquis de Grasse and Marquis de Chambrun, both members of the France Society.

D.B. Waller   James Menefee   William A. Chenault   Harry V. Davis, Jr.   Col. Benjamin H. Morris

T. Ewing Roberts   L. Duncan Stokes   Gradie R. Rowntree, M.D.   J. Colgan Norman

George Rogers Clark, The George Washington of the West, founded Louisville! Rogers Clark Ballard Thruston was known for many years as "Mr. S.A.R. in Louisville."

When William A. Chenault was elected President, this Chapter evolved into The Louisville-Thruston Chapter. This Chapter has been active for almost half a century, with the following successful leadership:

Fletcher L. Elmore, Jr.   Reed A. Martin, Sr.

Gordon A. Snyder   Reed A. Martin, Jr.

James S. Harriman   Wallace M. Craig, Jr.

Eugene J. Krebs   Everett H. Sanneman, Jr., M.D.

Gen. Frank M. Reinecke   Robert P. Van Ness   Msgr. Charles C. Boldrick   Charles C. Card

Col. Robert C. Jobson   Marshall K. Gilbert, III   William C. Gist, DMD   Dr. Samuel B. Peavey

THE LOUISIANA SOCIETY, S.A.R.

honors

–Louisiana State Museum
New Orleans

DON BERNARDO de GALVEZ
Governor of Louisiana (1777-1785)

"Io Solo"
("I Alone")

Born Malaga, Spain in 1746. Became Governor of Louisiana 1 February 1777 at age of 31.

After Spain declared war on Great Britain in 1779, Galvez undertook operations against British posts in West Florida. With small force and volunteers enlisted along march of 30 days, Galvez captured Fort Bute on Bayou Manchac and, on 21 September 1779, captured Baton Rouge. He took Natchez during same expedition. Captured British garrisons at Mobile in March, 1780 and Pensacola in March, 1781. Capture of British posts enabled Spain to acquire East and West Florida in peace of 1783. Galvez received the thanks of the Congress of the United States in 1785 for having aided the Cause of American Independence.

After death of his father in 1785, Galvez succeeded his father as Viceroy of Mexico. He died at the age of 40 in Mexico.

Many descendants of those who fought under Galvez remain in Louisiana and are members of SAR by virtue of that Service.

LOUISIANA SOCIETY CHAPTERS

ALEXANDRIA Alexandria	GENERAL PHILEMON THOMAS Baton Rouge	GALVEZ Shreveport
CALCASIEU Lake Charles	NORTHEAST LOUISIANA Monroe	GEORGE WASHINGTON New Orleans
	ATTAKAPAS Lafayette	

On December 11, 1936 the Florida Society erected and dedicated a bronze marker on the site of the Revolutionary Battle of Alligator Bridge, the one Revolutionary event on Florida soil. The bridge is east of Callahan, Nassau County.

In 1937 the Ohio Society recruited Compatriot George H. Stevenson, a REAL GRANDSON. His grandfather, John Stevenson, served as a private in the 5th Battalion of the Pennsylvania Militia.

The Texas Society enrolled Congressman Maury Maverick of the San Antonia District. He was a REAL GRANDSON.

On June 14, 1937 President Roosevelt dedicated a Memorial erected to General George Rodgers Clark at Vincennes, Indiana, a Doric Temple in a 20-acre park. The Indiana Society took a leading role at the ceremonies.

On September 2, the President General laid the cornerstone of a monument to commemorate the site where General Washington soothed the dissatisfaction of his officers at the New Windsor, New York Cantonment known as the "Temple".

GEORGIA SIGNERS HONORED

On January 2, 1938 a handsome bronze tablet honoring Georgia Signers of the Declaration of Independence and the Constitution was placed and dedicated in the Capitol Building in Atlanta. This was a joint tribute by both the SAR and the DAR.

The Vermont Society conducted a service on January 10 in Green Mount Cemetery in Burlington on the 200th anniversary of the birth of Ethan Allen, Vermont Revolutionary hero.

The Philadelphia Chapter held a dinner honoring Compatriot Atwater Kent, who promoted and underwrote the expense of renovating the Betsy Ross Home. Compatriot John S. Fisher, Governor of Pennsylvania and President of the Pennsylvania Society, presented the Gold Good Citizenship Medal to Compatriot Kent, who is remembered as an early developer and manufacturer of radios.

On June 25, 1938 the SAR in cooperation with *The New York Journal American* sponsored a program honoring 5,000 young Americans who had attained the age of 21 since the last general election with the administration of an oath of Good Citizenship. Over 25,000 spectators attended. Metropolitan Opera and musical personalities sang patriotic songs. The highlight of the program was the administration of the oath by Federal Judge Vincent L. Leibell to the young people. President General Kendall presided.

In 1938 the San Diego Chapter of the California Society initiated "National Citizenship Day" as part of Constitution Day for all newly naturalized citizens in the foregoing year. The promotion evolved into the "I Am an American" Day programs promoted by the Hearst newspapers.

President General Kendall served for four terms. Nationally, prominent Compatriots served on his Executive Committees, including United States Senator Tom Connally of the Texas Society, United States Senator Arthur Vandenberg of the Michigan Society, former President Herbert Hoover of the Pennsylvania Society, Honorable Wilbur Cross, Governor of Connecticut and Honorable John S. Fisher, Governor of Pennsylvania and President of the Pennsylvania Society.

Colonel James D. Watson, Vice-President General for the South Atlantic District, after a long search located the grave of Colonel William Few, Georgia Signer of the Constitution, in an obscure location near Fishkill on the Hudson River in New York State. Later, the Georgia Society replaced the grave marker. Subsequently he was reinterred in Saint Paul's Church in Augusta, Georgia.

SAR PROMINENT AT WORLD'S FAIR

June 1, 1939 was recognized as SAR Day on the New York World's Fair calendar with the dedication of "Washington Hall" on Franklin Lake on the fair grounds. The colonial-style building was donated by President General Kendall and contained many of his personal George Washington memorabilia and artifacts. Thousands of fair visitors toured the SAR "Washington Hall." The United States Congress by Resolution commended the SAR for providing the patriotic building.

Compatriot Richard C. McMullin, Governor of Delaware, addressed the Delaware Society at the Hotel DuPont in Wilmington on Constitution Day, with 250 compatriots and guests present.

Washington Hall at the World's Fair contained an array of artifacts.

On June 23, 1939 Compatriot John Paul Earnest, a member of the District of Columbia Society, died. He was the last surviving Charter Member of the National Society.

On September 17 the New York Chapter held ceremonies at the grave of Alexander Hamilton in Trinity Churchyard in the Wall Street district. A wreath was placed on the grave by Compatriot Laurens M. Hamilton, President of the New York Chapter, and a great-great grandson of Alexander Hamilton.

On November 21, 1939 the New Jersey Society placed a ten-ton boulder with a bronze tablet at the Cadmus Ford Bridge on New Jersey Highway #9 commemorating the crossing of General Washington's army on November 21, 1776.

The decade ended with television being developed and nylon stockings available for the first time. Neutrality and national defense were the main issues in the country.

1940–1950: War and Peace Decade

The population of the United States was 132 million people. Fifty-six percent of the people lived in towns and cities of over 2,500. Life expectancy was 63 years. The United States was sending surplus war supplies to Great Britain. Japanese naval and air forces made a surprise attack on the United States naval base at Pearl Harbor. The United States declared war on Japan, Germany and Italy. Many American prisoners died in the "Bataan Death March" to a prison camp. The United States naval fleet defeated the Japanese in the Battle of the Coral Sea and the Battle of Midway. There was rationing in the country.

Compatriot Dwight Eisenhower was named Supreme Commander of Allied Expeditionary Forces. The allied forces invaded Europe at Normandy, France on June 6, 1944.

American forces under Compatriot General Douglas MacArthur returned to the Philippines.

Compatriot President Franklin D. Roosevelt died on April 12, 1944 and Compatriot Harry S. Truman became President.

The United States dropped atomic bombs on Hiroshima and Nagasaki. The allies triumphed, and the United Nations was born.

America retooled for peace. The "ranch-type home" became popular. Women were introduced to brief bathing suits called "bikinis."

At the start of the decade there were 13,963 SAR members, with the Empire State Society having 2,050 members.

On January 17, 1940 on the anniversary of the birth of Benjamin Franklin, the Philadelphia-Continental Chapter of the Pennsylvania Society attended memorial services at the Franklin Museum and placed a wreath at Franklin's statue. Later, the Chapter placed a wreath on the grave of the distinguished Patriot in Christ Church burial ground.

FEDERAL HALL DEDICATED

The SAR was a principal participant in the dedication ceremonies of the Federal Hall Memorial Building as a national shrine, with the unveiling of a bronze plaque on the site at Wall and Nassau Streets in New York City. Compatriot Gardner Osborn of the Empire State Society was Director of the building, which is best known as the site where George Washington took his oath as first President of the United States on April 30, 1789.

Three governors became SAR Compatriots: Paul V. McNutt of Indiana, Lauren D. Dickinson of Michigan and John W. Bricker of Ohio.

The Continental Guard of the New York Chapter of the Empire State Society held its Annual Colonial Ball on February 17 at the Hotel Plaza. The Guard was composed of the younger Compatriots, ages 18 to 25, of the Chapter and were uniformed in the regulation Continental uniform of General Washington's staff officers.

President General Kendall created a trust fund in the name of his mother, Florence L. Kendall, for an award to the Compatriot enrolling the largest number of new members in a given year.

The District of Columbia Society celebrated its Golden Anniversary on April 19, 1940. A special exhibit commemorating this event was displayed in the Library of Congress. It featured the DC Society's service and accomplishments.

On April 28 the San Diego Chapter of the California Society again sponsored its annual program honoring men and women who had become citizens during the previous year. National Citizenship Recognition Day was first initiated by the San Diego Chapter.

There was a revival and renewal of the SAR Charter of the Alabama Society at a meeting in Montgomery in May.

Continuing an in-depth review of our Society's activities and accomplishments, Former President Carl F. Bessent leads us from the beginnings of United States involvement in World War II through conclusion of the '50s.

On Monday, May 20, 1940 the 47″ × 34″ bronze Memorial Tablet containing the names of donors to the National Headquarters Fund was unveiled on the north wall of the entrance of the Sixteenth Street National Headquarters and dedicated. Each of the donors had contributed $500 or more to the Fund.

On Sunday, June 16, the Connecticut Society's General David Humphreys Branch of New Haven conducted a memorial service at the Grove Street Cemetery and placed a wreath on General Humphreys' grave. The graves of the 34 members of the Governor's "Foot Guard" and 148 Revolutionary graves were decorated. Wreaths were placed at the statue of Nathan Hale on Yale Campus, at the grave of Colonel John Trumbull in the Rotunda of the Yale Art Gallery and at Memorial Hall where 25 sons of Yale who served in the Revolutionary War are memorialized.

As reported in the January 1940 Issue of the *Quarterly Bulletin* published by the National Society, Beacon, New York was the setting for the dedication of a memorial to Colonel William Few, Georgia Signer of the U.S. Constitution. The Patriot's burial site had been discovered earlier. Participating in the program were William Few Christie (second from left), great-grandson of Col. Few, and President General Messmore Kendall (second from the right). It was stated that the monument was "riven from the ribs of Stone Mountain in Georgia."

The Kentucky Society furnished 103 American Flags for the Selective Service Registration offices in Louisville. The Society participated in the naturalization ceremony held in the United States District Court in Louisville on September 20. Twenty-six newly naturalized citizens were presented with a framed copy of "The American's Creed" printed on parchment in the colors of the SAR.

Compatriot Louis L. Emerson, former Governor of Illinois, passed away on January 13, 1941.

LAST REAL SON DIES

Compatriot William Comfort Wheeler of the Vermont Society, last REAL SON, died on February 1, 1941 at the age of 93. As a youngster he recalled hearing Revolutionary War veterans of his neighborhood retelling tales of battles and experiences of the war. He and his father had voted for every President from George Washington to Franklin Roosevelt.

The Oregon Society celebrated its Golden Jubilee on February 22 with much oratory at a special banquet. Compatriot Thomas G. Greene, only surviving Compatriot of the 15 charter members, was present.

Good Citizenship Medal Certificates were available for the first time at the cost of ten cents each.

On May 18 the Illinois Society sponsored "I Am An American" Day Rally at Soldier Field in Chicago, with 100,000 people gathered to proclaim their American citizenship. William S. Knudsen, U.S. Defense Chief, addressed the multitude.

The grave of Oliver Pollack, unsung hero and an Aide to General Bernardo de Galvez, Spanish Governor of Louisiana and leader of the famous Galvez Expedition in 1779, was marked by the Louisiana Society. The grave is located in the Episcopal Churchyard in Pickneyville, Mississippi.

The New Jersey Society placed a boulder and tablet to the memory of General William Colfax, Revolutionary War hero. The beautiful plaque on the three-ton boulder at the foot of the General's grave is located at Pompton and was dedicated on October 18, 1941. The grave is in a small family cemetery on the Colfax Home, still occupied by the General's descendants.

Illinois Society officers placed a wreath on the statue of George Washington at the entrance to the Art Institute in Chicago on April 30, 1942, commemorating his inauguration as President. Left of the wreath was President Dean Traxler.

Compatriots were reminded by the President General they could support the war effort by serving in the armed forces, enlisting in the Home Guard for home defense, supporting SAR programs to bolster morale and instill loyalty, donating blood, serving as volunteer air wardens and purchasing defense stamps and bonds.

The New York Chapter celebrated George Washington's Birthday with a ceremony on the steps of the Federal Hall Memorial Building. It was broadcast coast to coast. Chapter President Alexander Hamilton, great-great grandson of the first Secretary of Treasury, presided. Compatriot General Louis Stotesbury, U.S. Army, spoke on the Armed forces in the war.

The James Morgan Chapter of the Wisconsin Society held a George Washington Birthday observance at the White House Inn in Milwaukee. The honored guests were Mr. and Mrs. Mayard W. Kuter, parents of Chapter member, Brigadier General Laurence S. Kuter, youngest General in the U.S. Army. His Revolutionary War ancestor was General Kuter, who served under General Anthony Wayne.

On Memorial Day the Illinois Society held a memorial service in Lincoln Park at the grave of David Kennison, participant of the Boston Tea Party, veteran of the Revolutionary War and the War of 1812 and the only Revolutionary War soldier buried in Chicago.

The Louisiana Society engaged a caretaker to improve the condition of the Revolutionary War graves in the old St. Louis Cemetery in New Orleans.

The New Jersey Society unveiled a memorial plaque at the Old Greenwich Church at Stewartsville, in honor of Brigadier General William Maxwell, a distinguished soldier of the Revolution.

The oldest Compatriot and also the oldest retired officer of the U.S. Army died at the age of 103. Compatriot General William H. Bisbee of the Rhode Island Society passed away on June 11, 1942.

By passage of Joint Resolution H.J. 303 approved on June 23, 1942 an official Flag Code was established for the first time. The code stated regulations for the use and display of the Flag of the United States. One item in the code listed days on which the flag should be displayed. Another item gave the Official Pledge with definite instructions as to the proper method of salute.

COMPATRIOTS AID FBI

One of the initial activities of the SAR during the war included a "Corps of Minute Men" whom the Federal Bureau of Investigation could contact to secure information on subversive activities. J. Edgar Hoover, Director of the Bureau, officially commended the SAR for its efforts in preserving internal security.

Compatriots serving in the Armed Forces were exempt from paying the $1 National SAR dues. The SAR carried war damage insurance on National Headquarters.

Senators Albert W. Hawkes of New Jersey, Carter Glass of Virginia, Styles Bridges of New Hampshire, Willis of Indiana, Robert A. Taft of Ohio and Gerald P. Nye of North Dakota were all newly enrolled members of the SAR.

Each SAR Chapter was requested to accept the responsibility of recruiting at least three women for enlistment in the Women's Army Corps. Major General J. A. Ulio, Adjutant General of the U.S. Army, commended the SAR for its efforts in recruiting WACs.

The SAR contributed hundreds of pounds of past issues of THE SAR MAGAZINE to the paper salvage drive.

Two members of the Minnesota Society were on Corregidor when it fell and were prisoners of war: Brigadier General Louis C. Bebe and Lieutenant Wells Hodgson, Jr.

Honorable Frank E. Gannett of New York, publisher, became a member of the Empire State Society.

On February 22, 1943 the Philadelphia Chapter held its George Washington Birthday dinner at the Bellevue-Stratford Hotel. The feature of the evening was presentation of the Gold Good Citizenship Medal to Edward G. Budd, outstanding industrialist in transportation and aviation. Mr. Budd created spot welding, which revolutionized industrial techniques.

The SAR participated in the Thomas Jefferson Memorial dedication at the Tidal Basin in Washington on April 13, 1943 on the 201st anniversary of Jefferson's birth.

Colonel Robert R. McCormick, publisher of *The Chicago Tribune* was accepted as a member of the Illinois Society.

The Massachusetts Society installed "pick-up" stations for servicemen on particularly busy highways to assist servicemen in obtaining automobile transportation.

The Massachusetts Society presented an Altar for use by the chaplains on the aircraft carrier, *U.S.S. Bunker Hill.*

Captain Joseph J. Foss, U.S.M.C., 28-year-old flyer who shot down 26 Japanese airplanes, was honored by the South Dakota Society and inducted into SAR membership at Sioux Falls on May 4, 1943.

In 1943 there were 16,303 SAR members. The largest Society was the Empire State Society with 2,392 Compatriots; 2,321 Compatriots were serving in the Armed Forces.

Brigadier General H. L. Whittaker, Commanding General of Fort Warren, joined the Wyoming Society.

The DC Society mourned the passing of Phineas S. Towne on October 14, 1943. Compatriot Towne was one of the few survivors of the Third Calvary which arrived on the scene of General Custer's last stand on the Little Big Horn soon after the massacre. His life experiences are in his autobiography, *Indian Fights and Fighters.*

In recognition of his outstanding services to our nation, J. Edgar Hoover, Director of the Federal Bureau of Investigation, was presented the Good Citizenship Medal in his Washington, DC office. It was awarded by the Orange Chapter of the New Jersey Society in October, 1942. Doing the honors were Chapter Compatriot Harry L. Bowlby (left) and Frank B. Steele, Secretary-Registrar General of the National Society.

THE DISTRICT OF COLUMBIA SOCIETY, SONS OF THE AMERICAN REVOLUTION SALUTES THE NATIONAL SOCIETY AS WE BOTH ENTER OUR 100TH YEAR OF SERVICE TO THE NATION

ADMIRAL DAVID DIXON PORTER
8 June 1813 - 13 February 1891

In 1890, Admiral David Dixon Porter was installed as first president of the District of Columbia Society, Sons of the American Revolution. Admiral Porter entered the SAR based on the service of his grandfather who was a naval commander in the Revolutionary War. Admiral Porter's father was Commodore David Porter, whose remarkable exploits in the Pacific while commanding the U.S. Frigate Essex, served as a training ground for Admiral Porter's older foster brother, then a Midshipman on the Essex, David Glasgow Farragut. From 1826 to 1829, Commodore Porter commanded the navy of the Republic of Mexico during its war for independence. David Dixon Porter served under his father as a lieutenant of the Mexican Navy, and was once captured and imprisoned by the Spanish. He then entered the U.S. Navy in 1829. In the War with Mexico, he played an important part in the capture of a Mexican fortress. In the Civil War, Commander Porter served under his foster brother, Commodore Farragut, at New Orleans. In 1863, Commodore Porter led the gunboat fleet which ran past the guns of Vicksburg, and later Grand Gulf, for which he received the thanks of Congress for opening the Mississippi. Later, as Rear Admiral, Porter commanded the North Atlantic Blockade Squadron and received his second thanks of Congress for the capture of Fort Fisher, North Carolina. At the end of the war, Porter was elevated to the rank of Vice Admiral, and was Superintendant of the U.S. Naval Academy for four years. In 1870, upon the death of his foster brother, Admiral Farragut, Porter was raised to the highest rank in the U.S. Navy, and served as Admiral for the rest of his life. During his last twenty years, Admiral Porter served as Chief of the Naval Board of Inspections, and also found time to write several volumes of naval history, as well as several novels.

The formal Japanese surrender documents ending World War II were signed aboard the *U.S. Missouri* by Compatriot General Douglas MacArthur. Standing behind him was Compatriot General Jonathan Wainwright. The event took place in early September, 1945 in Tokyo Bay.

The Palm Beach Chapter of the Florida Society raised over $600,000 in the War Bond drive.

Compatriot Henry C. Perkins, Rhode Island Society, was promoted to the rank of Captain in the U.S. Coast Guard. He was the youngest Captain in the Coast Guard.

GENERAL EISENHOWER BECOMES COMPATRIOT

General Dwight D. Eisenhower became a member of the Empire State Society.

Brigadier General William C. Chase, Commanding General of the First Division and a member of the Rhode Island Society, was the first person to enter Manila in the liberation of the Philippines.

Compatriot James Harlan Cleveland of the Ohio Society was presented the Purple Heart Medal. His Revolutionary War ancestor, Sergeant William Brown of the Connecticut Militia, received the Purple Heart Medal from General George Washington on May 3, 1783.

Compatriot George A. Smith of the Utah Society, Vice-President General of the Rocky Mountain District, was elected President of the Church of Jesus Christ of Latter Day Saints on May 21, 1945.

The New Jersey Society promoted Assembly Bill 389, passed by the New Jersey Legislature and signed by Governor Edge, requiring compulsory teaching of two years of American history in New Jersey high schools.

Brigadier General Carl R. Gray, Jr., Minnesota Society, was awarded the Distinguished Service Cross for his outstanding service in Italy and France.

The Jacksonville Chapter of the Florida Society held a regular meeting at the George Washington Hotel. Captain Alanson L.

Bryan, MC, USN, related his experiences as Commanding Officer on the *USS Relief* in the South Pacific.

COMPATRIOTS SERVE IN WORLD WAR II

Two thousand three hundred and twenty-one (2,321) Compatriots served in the Armed Forces in World War II from a membership of 16,303 in 1943. Those who died while on duty were:

Richard E. Armstrong, California Society, killed in France, July 9, 1944.

Lieutenant Ross Beason, Utah Society, killed in Africa, March 1944.

Lieutenant General Simon B. Buckner, Kentucky Society, killed on Okinawa, June 19, 1945.

Ralph E. Conrad, Virginia Society, killed in South Pacific, December 29, 1944.

Edward R. Crone, Empire State Society, died as prisoner of war, April 1, 1945.

Lieutenant Colonel Howard J. Edmand, Massachusetts Society, prisoner of war, lost when a prisoner of war ship was sunk, December 15, 1944.

Charles S. Fazel, Virginia Society, February 2, 1945.

John F. Forhan, Illinois Society, pilot, lost flying B-29 over China, July 29, 1945.

Frederick F. Gundrum, Jr., California Society, killed on Guadacanal, July 25, 1944.

George T. Glover, Ohio Society, March 29, 1945.

George N. Greene, Pennsylvania Society, pilot, lost flying B-17 over Germany, July 7, 1944.

John D. Haudenshield, Pennsylvania Society, killed in Germany, May 8, 1944.

Richard G. Hall, Ohio Society, July 30, 1945.

W. Gardner Hodgeson, Minnesota Society, December 1944.

Major John W. Herbert, Texas Society, killed on bombing mission on New Guinea, November 24, 1942.

Major Edwin R. Harper, Pennsylvania Society, lost on bombing mission, April 4, 1943.

Colonel Henry Lee Kinnison, Missouri Society, killed in Burma, June 3, 1944.

Starbuck Lips, Connecticut Society, killed in France, September 20, 1944.

William D. Liversidge, Massachusetts Society, killed in Germany, April 6, 1945.

Admiral William F. Halsey II of World War II fame became a member of the New Jersey Society in late 1946. His flagship, the *U.S.S. Missouri*, was the site of the signing of surrender documents by Japan in 1945.

Captain Alan Randolph Morehouse, Connecticut Society, killed on D-Day, June 6, 1944.

Charles W. Mylius, youngest member of the Virginia Society, lost flying his B-17 over Germany, November 20, 1944.

William K. Marsh, Empire State Society, killed in France, November 19, 1944.

James W. McKay, Pennsylvania Society, killed in Germany, March 13, 1945.

James R. Myers, North Carolina Society, killed in France, September 8, 1944.

William B. North, New Jersey Society, March 13, 1945.

Captain William Owen II, Iowa Society; taken prisoner with surrender of Corregidor, lost on prisoner of war ship, October 24, 1944.

Griffith R. Paul, South Carolina Society, killed on January 21, 1943.

Brigadier General Theodore Roosevelt, Jr., Empire State Society, died on Normandy, July 12, 1944.

Herbert C. Roberts II, Virginia Society, killed on Okinawa, April 24, 1945.

William M. Royall, South Carolina Society, killed in Germany, November 1944.

Richard S. Stockton, New Jersey Society, April 28, 1944.

Truman A. Shattuck, Michigan Society, killed on Iwo Jima, March 2, 1945.

Seth Sprague, Jr., Massachusetts Society, killed in France, January 13, 1945.

Sanderson Sloane, New Hampshire Society, February 26, 1944.

John R. Upton, Connecticut Society, killed in Belgium, February 25, 1945.

General Douglas MacArthur was enrolled as a member of the Empire State Society.

U.S. FLAGS IN PARIS SURVIVE WAR

After the war ended in Europe a communique was received at the SAR National Headquarters on July 24, 1945 from Vicomte Benoist d'Azy of the Society in France. During the entire occupation, the American Flag flew over Marquis General Lafayette's grave every day and was changed twice to a new flag by the cemetery Warden, Monsieur Bernieres, who must be remembered for his courage. German officers came to the grave, and due to respect for military traditions, never reported the American Flag. On July 4, 1945 the Annual Ceremony at Picpus Cemetery was resumed.

Compatriot Simon Lake of the Connecticut Society died on July 23, 1945 at the age of 78. He was the inventor and builder of the first submarine.

The SAR Annual Congress was not held in 1945 because of the war.

On September 15, over the national radio program "The Mayor of the Town," featuring Lionel Barrymore, the theme was the Constitution of the United States and was arranged through the efforts of Compatriot George A. Bunting of the Maryland Society, founder of the Noxell Corporation.

The Maryland Society sponsored a program on radio station WFBR, Baltimore on Constitution Day. A sketch of the Constitution was presented and was broadcast in every classroom in the state.

General Jonathan Wainwright became a member of the Syracuse Chapter of the Empire State Society.

"I Am An American Day" program was sponsored by the New York Chapter in New York City Central Park, where over 500,000 people gathered on Sunday afternoon, May 19.

Lieutenant Colonel John K. Borneman, who served as General Wainwright's Chaplain and who was also taken prisoner at Corregidor, was released from Santo Tomas prison. Compatriot Borneman attended the 1946 SAR Annual Congress in Trenton, New Jersey, as a delegate. Colonel Borneman was the Charter President of the Niagara Falls Chapter of the Empire State Society.

The Pennsylvania Society enrolled 406 new members during the 1945-46 reporting year. This was the largest number ever recruited in a single year by a State Society.

On July 4 the New Hampshire Society held an inspirational program in the Cathedral of the Pines, a beautiful grove overlooking three lakes and facing majestic Monadnock Mountain. Speakers were Congressman Sherman Adams, President of the New Hampshire Society, and Colonel Albert S. Baker, who led his regiment in the retaking of the Philippines. Later on September 8, the New Hampshire Society dedicated the "Altar of the Nation" which is the central feature and contains stones from every state. The Cathedral was dedicated as a memorial to the late Sanderson Sloane.

The Continental Color Guard of the New York Chapter, which had been suspended during the war as most members were in the service, was revived.

Through the generosity of Compatriot Douglass G. High of Cincinnati, the Ohio Society authorized an award of $100 to the

The Massachusetts Society Color Guard posed before the *U.S.S. Constitution* in the Boston Naval Shipyard in July, 1947 at the celebration of the 200th birthday of John Paul Jones. Note the planes flying overhead.

student best informed on American History. It was named the Douglass G. High Award.

On July 21 the Western Reserve Society of the Ohio Society entered a float in the Founders Day Parade celebrating the Sesquicentennial of Cleveland. The float represented a wagon drawn by oxen and carried members holding Revolutionary War Flags.

The Pittsburgh Chapter of the Pennsylvania Society was a beneficiary under the will of Thomas Mellon II, who died on August 18. Mr. Mellon willed the Forsythe Log House in Pittsburgh to the Chapter and left $10,000 for its maintenance.

Prominent Compatriots enrolled during this period included Admiral William "Bull" Halsey, New Jersey Society; Chief Justice Frederick M. Vinson, West Virginia Society; Governor Clarence Meadows, West Virginia Society; Governor James H. Duff, Pennsylvania Society; and Governor Alfred E. Driscoll, New Jersey Society.

The Philadelphia Chapter held its George Washington Birthday Observance at the Bellevue-Stratford Hotel on February 22, 1947. Compatriot Admiral William Halsey, Third Fleet Commander, was the speaker and was awarded the Gold Good Citizenship Medal.

The California Society conducted a campaign against certain history text books in the California School system which subverted the American institutional system. The campaign was successful and the textbooks were removed.

Famed movie producer, Compatriot Cecil B. DeMille, was appointed Chairman of the SAR Bill of Rights Commemorative Committee.

APPOINTED MAGAZINE EDITOR

Secretary-Registrar General and magazine Editor Frank B. Steele, who became ill in 1949, was relieved of certain duties. Compatriot Gardner Osborn of the Empire State Society was appointed editor of THE SAR MAGAZINE. There was a change in magazine format and size with the July, 1949 issue.

At the 59th SAR Annual Congress in Jacksonville, Florida in 1949 the first historical oration contest for young men was held. The winner was Robert Wood representing the Ohio Society. The contest became known as the Douglass G. High Historical Oration Contest.

A new SAR Insignia Badge was designed and presented to all Former Presidents General.

Compatriot Franklin D. Roosevelt, Jr., was elected to the United States House of Representatives from the New York 20th District.

At the end of this decade the SAR membership was 18,258 Compatriots, with the Pennsylvania Society having the highest number on the roll, 2,246. The Empire State Society was second with 2,229 members.

VIRGINIA
Jennings H. Flathers, Historian

Virginia's top officials, James S. Cremins, Sr., President, (left) and Walter W. Brewster, Vice President, joined the scores of others who come daily to admire what is probably the most priceless marble statue in the United States, the magnificent life size statue of George Washington which Jean Antoine Houdon executed as a tribute to America's foremost Revolutionary War hero. It stands in the Rotunda of the State Capitol, Richmond, and is the one executed from life, June 1784, as a tribute to this great commander. At the request of Governor Benjamin Harrison, Thomas Jefferson who was America's minister in Paris, secured the services of Jean Antoine Houdon, the most noted artist in France. He came to Mount Vernon in the fall of 1785 where he made a plaster bust of Washington's head and took the measurements of his body. The statue is carved from Carrara marble and bears the signature of the master with the date, 1788. Before it was shipped to America in May 1796, it was exhibited in the Louvre in Paris. It was so like the great American hero that Lafayette is known to have said, "That is the man, himself. I can almost realize he is going to move."

The statue depicts Washington as a leader and a gentleman. It has the sword which denotes power but also the cane and the plow which relate to the peaceful life which he admired so much.

Also in the Rotunda is the bust of Lafayette, also of Carrara marble by Houdon. Around the rotunda displayed in nitches are busts of other Virginians — Thomas Jefferson, James Madison, James Monroe, William Henry Harrison, John Tyler, Zachary Taylor, and Woodrow Wilson. To study Virginia History is also to learn more of United States History. The same is true of Time Honored Buildings and Places — Mount Vernon, Monticello, Montpelier, Gunston Hall, Williamsburg, and Yorktown.

Some sixty miles east of Virginia's Capitol, Richmond, is Yorktown where the last major battle of the American Revolution was fought, but still farther east lie the Capes where the French Navy under Comte De Grasse so completely outnumbered the British that they left for the New York area leaving Cornwallis to his own fate. De Grasse also landed 3,000 troops to assist the Americans.

Each year since the surrender of Cornwallis with his British and Hessian Soldiers on October 19, 1781, there has been some kind of patriotic observance marking this historic occasion. For a number of years, the Virginia Society, Sons of the American Revolution, has observed the occasion with Wreath Laying Ceremonies at the grave of Virginia's own Battle of Yorktown hero, General Thomas Nelson, Commander of the Virginia Militia. A number of his descendants annually attend this occasion and lay the wreath on his grave.

When the battle at Yorktown ended, the Virginia Militia was assigned to escort the 7,000 British and Hessian soldiers northward to get them away from the coast and the possibility that the British Navy might rescue them. After taking a few days to organize this large delegation, the entourage began its journey wading the streams and rivers, swollen by the autumn rains. When the Militia and the prisoners reached Alexandria, they were met by the Maryland Militia which took half of the prisoners, ferried them across the Potomac and headed for Frederick and the confinement of the captives.

The Virginia Militia with the remaining prisoners then headed for Winchester where there were barracks left over from the French and Indian War. General Washington knew of these.

It was now late in November when the men reached the Shenandoah River, deep from the autumn rains. Only the officers had horses, but the men had to cross the best they could holding their guns and clothing above their heads with the cold water up to their armpits.

Finally, the tired Militia reached Winchester and were happy to turn their burden over to local Militia and head for home, however humble it might be.

Today, descendants of General Thomas Nelson and the Virginia Militia work together to make the Virginia Society, Sons of the American Revolution, a viable organization.

1950–1960: SAR Growth Decade

The population of the United States was 150 million people with 65% of the population living in cities. In June, 1950 Compatriot President Harry Truman ordered United States military units to Korea as a part of the United Nation forces after North Korea troops invaded South Korea. Compatriot General Douglas MacArthur was removed from his Korean command after making unauthorized policy statements. Compatriot General Dwight D. Eisenhower was elected President. American Indians were finally given full citizenship status. A mammoth 13-year interstate highway construction program was initiated. Black Americans gained a new era of power with constitutional rulings and legislation ending discrimination. Alaska became the 49th state and Hawaii the 50th state. The first atomic powered submarine, *U.S.S. Nautilus*, was launched. Six-million automobiles and one-million trucks were coming off the assembly lines. Television had become the main communication medium in American life. Americans were enjoying "The Honeymooners" and "I Love Lucy."

Secretary-Registrar General Frank B. Steele retired on March 30, 1950 after 30 years in office. The position of Executive Secretary was created and Compatriot Harold L. Putnam, Hearst newspaper executive and former President of the California Society, was employed for the position.

The Annual Colonial Ball of the New York Chapter was held in the Starlight Roof Ballroom of the Waldorf Hotel on February 24th with 600 Compatriots and guests.

The New Hampshire Society held its 61st Annual meeting in Concord. Compatriot Governor Sherman Adams placed a wreath on the General Stark statue at the State House. Compatriot General Ulysses S. Grant III, spoke at the luncheon at the Eagle

Hotel. In addition to the Governor, the President of the New Hampshire Senate, the Speaker of the New Hampshire House and 26 members of the legislature were SARs.

The 60th SAR Annual Congress was held at the Hotel Claridge in Atlantic City, New Jersey, May 14-17. Speakers at the Congress were Compatriot Alfred E. Driscoll, New Jersey Governor, and Compatriot Congressman Hale Boggs of Louisiana. Compatriot Frank Steele was honored on his retirement by being elected Secretary-Registrar General Emeritus. Compatriot George S. Robertson of the Maryland Society was honored for his 22 years of service as Treasurer General.

On July 23, 1950 Compatriot Joseph M. Hill, former President of the Arkansas Society, passed away. He was the last survivor of the Signers of the SAR Charter which was granted by the United States Government.

On June 14 the Pittsburgh Chapter assembled at the historic national shrine, "the Block House," to honor the Flag of the United States. This is the apex of "the Golden Triangle" in Pittsburgh where the Monongahela and Allegheny Rivers unite to form the Ohio River.

Compatriot Captain Irving T. Duke, U.S.N., Commanding Officer of the Battleship *U.S.S. Missouri* and member of the Virginia Society, was participating in naval action off the Korean coast.

The Second National Boy Scouts Jamboree was held at Valley Forge on July 2, 1950, with 47,000 Scouts and Scouters attending. At the opening ceremonies President General Wallace C. Hall presented the SAR Good Citizenship Medal to Dr. Arthur Schuck, Chief Scout Executive.

General Frank Merrill, Commander of Merrill's Marauders in the Far East in World War II, joined the New Hampshire Society.

On January 11, 1951, 15 Compatriots and ladies assembled at the "La Placita" in Albuquerque, New Mexico, for the chartering of the new Albuquerque Chapter.

On February 6 there was a fire on the construction site adjacent to National Headquarters. There was smoke damage to the Headquarters.

The Daniel Boone Chapter of the West Virginia Society contributed a rhododendron to the National Headquarters grounds. It is the state flower of West Virginia.

Dr. Warren G. Harding II, nephew of President Warren Harding, was installed as President of the Benjamin Franklin Chapter of the Ohio Society.

CONGRESS HELD IN SAN FRANCISCO

The 61st SAR Annual Congress was held in San Francisco at the Saint Francis Hotel. The first SAR service Recognition Evening was held at this Congress. The address to the Congress by Fulton Lewis, Jr., noted syndicated columnist, was broadcast nationwide. Mr. Lewis was presented the first Constructive Citizenship Gold Medal. A special committee was appointed to inspect and evaluate Washington area properties suitable for a new Headquarters and to determine the advisibility of selling the Sixteenth Street headquarters.

A bill passed by the United States Congress was signed by the President exempting the National Society from all taxation, real and personal property.

On Easter Sunday, April 13, 1952 Compatriot President Truman attended the tenth annual Thomas Jefferson birthday ceremonies conducted by the District of Columbia Society at the Jefferson Memorial at the Tidal Basin in Washington.

July 4th, 1950 was the date chosen by the New Jersey Society to dedicate a statue of Patriot Thomas Paine in Burnham Park, Morristown. He is noted for authorship of *Common Sense* and *Crisis*.

The Georgia Society
Sons of the American Revolution
Proudly Salutes
The National Society of the Sons of the American Revolution
During Its Centennial Celebration

1989 - 1990

PRESIDENT
Hardwick S. Johnson, Jr.
15 Watson Drive
Newnan, GA 30263
Phone: 404-251-4379

SENIOR VICE PRESIDENT
Robert B. Arnold
64 17th Street
Atlanta, GA 30309
Phone: 404-892-0160

SECRETARY
Earl S. McGilvray, Jr.
216 Sivell Road
LaGrange, GA 30240
Phone: 404-882-8610

TREASURER
Charles Hal Dayhuff, III
P.O. Box 909
Fayetteville, GA 30214

REGISTRAR
G. Edward Buxton, III
3439 K North Druid Hills Road
Decatur, GA 30033
Phone: 404-325-3810

RECORDING SECRETARY
W. Dorsey Stancil

CHANCELLOR
Robert E. O'Neal

CHAPLAIN
George W. Porter

GENEALOGIST
Samuel B. Frank

HISTORIAN
Homer E. Wright

NATIONAL TRUSTEE
Col. Robert B. Vance, Sr.

ALTERNATE N. TRUSTEE
Homer E. Wright

VICE PRESIDENTS
NORTH William E. Adams, Jr.
CENTRAL Robert E. O'Neal
SOUTH Julian D. Kelly, Jr., MD

The Georgia Society:

Remains dedicated to membership growth and patriotic, historical and educational objectives.

Congratulates Georgia's own 1989-1990 NSSAR President General James R. Westlake — a first for Georgia.

Recognizes the last Charter Member of the Georgia Society, Eugene Chapman McLaughlin — National No. 35203, State No. 3.

Recognizes Georgia's only REAL SON of the American Revolution — Compatriot Basil Llewellen Neal, deceased.

1989-1990 GEORGIA SOCIETY

CHAPTERS	PRESIDENTS
Abraham Baldwin	Ernest C. Harris
Athens	William E. Adams, Jr.
Atlanta	Robert M. Pryor, Jr.
Bainbridge	G. Frank Battles, Jr.
Coweta Falls	James L. Holman
Edward Telfair	Julian D. Kelly, Jr.
George Walton	Robert L. Murray
John Dooly	Robert Jeter
John Milledge	Dr. James E. Baugh
Lyman Hall	Dr. James C. Parker
Marshes of Glynn	Rodman E. Scott
McIntosh	Earl S. McGilvray, Jr.
Middle Georgia	Malcom G. McPhaul
Mill Creek	Dr. John R. Lindsey
Rome	John E. Haigwood
William Few	Maj. Charles Bonner
William Miller	Lemuel S. Lee
Marquis de LaFayette	Walter Graves

The Pennsylvania Society was organized in Pittsburgh on November 23, 1893. There were 25 charter members, all of whom were also members of District of Columbia Society.

The names of the charter members who became the Pennsylvania Society's first officers are William A. Herron, President; Howard Morton, Senior Vice President; Thomas S. Brown, Secretary; John C. Porter, Treasurer; and Benjamin Page, Historian. Other members who were elected to the Board of Management included Joseph D. Weeks, Alfred E. Hunt, Hugh Hamilton, Roger Sherman, Albert J. Logan, Oliver O. Page,

mayors are requested to issue proclamations calling for the Pledge of Allegiance to the Flag of the United States to be recited on that day in churches and at all public gatherings.

The state society publishes a quarterly magazine entitled "The Pennsylvania Minuteman". It has maintained a high standard of excellence and is generally recognized as one of the outstanding publications of its kind in the national organization. It has won many NSSAR awards, including the Charlotte Lund Woodward Award in 1986 and 1988.

The state society has many outstanding accomplishments to its credit. The Bake House project

"Book Night" by the Erie chapter. A current book of historical and reference value is presented to each high school library in Erie County. Each school sends a representative student to a dinner to accept the book. The student is required to read the book, give a synopsis to the senior class and then present it to the library.

Other chapters engage in similar activities of a patriotic nature during the year, including annual church services, the marking of graves of Revolutionary soldiers, the awarding of SAR Law Enforcement Commendation Medals, SAR Good Citizenship Medals, and ROTC medals at high schools, colleges, and universities throughout the state. Philadelphia Continental Chapter alone awards 23 SAR ROTC medals annually.

Some years ago a compatriot of the state society developed a "Golden Book" of Revolutionary War graves. It lists over 2,000 names of men buried mostly in Pennsylvania. More than 400 of the graves have been photographed and recorded and the information forwarded to the National Society. Of further interest to researchers throughout the country is the "1955 Year Book of the Pennsylvania Society of the Sons of the American Revolution". It was compiled by Compatriot Floyd G. Hoenstine, the historian of the state society. Its nearly 800 pages are divided into three sections: historical sketches, lineages of past and present members, and an index to surnames. As it stated in the foreword, "The Society is fortunate in having well preserved records of the 5,967 members who have affiliated since the year 1893".

Pennsylvania Society History

Mansfield A. Ross, and Elisha G. Patterson.

Wayne Chapter, located in Erie, was the first chapter to be granted a Pennsylvania charter. Shortly thereafter a chapter was organized in New Castle. Both chapters later became inactive but in later years were reactivated. The third Pennsylvania chapter was Philadelphia, organized in 1901; through merger it later became the Philadelphia Continental, the oldest, largest, and most active chapter in the state society. In 1988, for the sixth consecutive year, it won the NSSAR most active chapter award.

Prior to 1927, new members in the Pittsburgh area were automatically a part of the state society. However, on November 3, 1927, a charter was issued for the Pittsburgh chapter, thus permitting it to function the same as other state society chapters.

From 1893 through 1947, with the exception of 1938, all annual meetings were held in Pittsburgh on or near Washington's birthday. In 1938 the meeting was held in Clearfield. It is interesting to note that at the annual meeting of 1937 the time of meetings was changed from Washington's birthday to October, possibly to avoid the winter weather of Clearfield.

At the Clearfield meeting, it was decided to hold future annual meetings in various cities in different sections of the state. However, the plan was not put into effect until 1948 with the first such meeting being held in the Nittany Lion Inn at State College. Today, the annual meetings are held at the general location of the chapter of which the out-going state president is a member.

Throughout the years many chapters were organized, later became inactive, then reorganized with different names and at different locations. Today, there are 26 chapters, each of them comparatively active when size and geographical location are considered. These chapters are: Blair County, Captain Samuel Brady, Centre County, Conococheague, Continental Congress, Erie, Fort Jackson, Fort Schuylkill, Christopher Gist, Harris Ferry, Governor Joseph Hiester, William Maclay, New Castle, Northeast, Philadelphia Continental, Pittsburgh, General James Potter, General Arthur St. Clair, Shenango, Somerset-Cambria, Susquehanna, Tiadaghton, Valley Forge, George Washington, General Anthony Wayne, and Youghiogheny.

Innovations have become traditional in the Pennsylvania Society. Each year, the outstanding compatriot of the State society is honored with the title, "Mr. SAR". In 1979, Allegiance Sunday was inaugurated and has since been adopted by NSSAR. This is the nearest Sunday to July 4th, at which time the Governor of each state and the city

at Valley Forge Park was begun in 1964. It included a number of hereditary and historical societies which agreed to furnish rooms in the Bake House as a part of the restoration program in the park. The state society raised some $4000 to complete the furnishings in one room, dedicated in July 1967.

A bronze marker was placed in the cemetery at Christ Church in Philadelphia as a memorial to George Ross, a signer of the Declaration of Independence. Three descendents of George Ross were in attendance.

Another bronze marker was erected along the highway near Valley Forge Park to mark the grave of Colonel Timothy Matlack, a fighting Quaker. This took place in June 1969, at the behest of Valley Forge Chapter.

The Pittsburgh Chapter placed a bronze plaque honoring a hero of the Colonial period on each of six Gateway Buildings in that city. These were dedicated between 1951 and 1969. Fort Roberdeau, near Altoona, was restored under the leadership of members of the Blair county Chapter. Plaques have been placed there, also at Forts Ligonier and Necessity, as well as at scores of locations throughout the state.

The Bi-centennial was marked in appropriate fashion by the state society. A hand-forged Commemorative Plate, completely designed and produced in Pennsylvania, depicting Washington at prayer, was issued in 1976.

Individual chapters engage in full programs of patriotic activities. Many are associated with traditional holidays such as Washington's Birthday, Memorial Day, Flag Day, Independence Day and Constitution Day. Washington's Birthday has been a symbolic occasion for Philadelphia Continental Chapter for many years, it being the custom to place a wreath at the statue of George Washington at Independence Hall in Philadelphia, and also at the Tomb of the Unknown Soldier of the Revolution.

Pittsburgh Chapter, in cooperation with the DAR, has for many years fostered a Flag Day program for public and parochial school children. As many as 900 people have attended this affair when 72 SAR Good Citizenship Medals and 144 citations were awarded to students of the eighth grade.

During Constitution Week in September, Philadelphia Continental Chapter annually joins with 25 DAR Chapters in Southeastern Pennsylvania for a luncheon, honoring a distinguished citizen with the SAR Good Citizenship Medal.

Another significant occasion is the traditional

On July 29, 1967, the state society was awarded the Freedoms Foundation George Washington Honor Medal for its outstanding accomplishments in helping to achieve a better understanding of the American way of life.

The Eagle Scout Scholarship program, one of our more recent ventures, is slowly expanding as Boy Scout Troops and the involved chapters realize its importance. With continued effort by all concerned, we should eventually provide a national winner.

But all of the society's patriotic activities have not occurred in recent years. As early as 1902, the society was able to rescue seven Revolutionary cannon from the wreckers when the old Pittsburgh Arsenal was being dismantled. After considerable effort, they were permitted by the Federal Government to turn the cannon over to Carnegie Museum, where they were displayed to the public.

Also in 1902, when Pittsburgh's Presbyterian Church was making material changes in its property, the remains of three known eminent soldiers and citizens – General John Neville, Major Isaac Craig, and Colonel James Johnson – – were about to be abandoned. The society, after obtaining the proper permission, had the remains re-interred at the old church grounds and at the Allegheny cemetery.

Through the gift of SAR member Arthur Atwater Kent, the Betsy Ross Foundation was established to renovate and maintain the Betsy Ross property. The building was saved from destruction in 1937 by this generous act of public concern and its was rededicated as a shrine to American Liberty on Flag Day, June 14, 1937. Since that time it has become one of the historic sites of greatest interest in Philadelphia.

The Pennsylvania Society is honored to have hosted National Congresses on seven occasions: Pittsburgh in 1901; Philadephia in 1905; Philadelphia in 1926; Harrisburg in 1944; Pittsburgh in 1959; Philadelphia in 1976; and Valley Forge in 1987.

Five of our illustrious members have been called to serve as President General of the National Society: James D. Hancock in 1904; Charles B. Shaler in 1948; Kenneth G. Smith, Sr. in 1966-67; Robert D. Savage in 1975-76; and Warren G. Hayes, Jr. in 1983-84.

What is written above is history. Looking ahead to our state society's centennial in 1993, let us vow to make the next century even more exciting than the one which is drawing to a close.

By William G. Dorwart

This was the Connecticut Society's entry in the big Inaugural Parade in Washington, DC on January 20, 1953. Compatriots portrayed famous participants in the Revolutionary War.

The Annual Meeting of the Massachusetts Society was held in Concord in the Masonic Temple. A wreath was placed on the grave of Major John Buttrick, who commanded the Patriots at Concord Bridge. Compatriot Senator Everett Saltonstal addressed the meeting.

Secretary-Registrar General Emeritus Frank Steele died on February 28, 1952.

The 62nd SAR Annual Congress was held in Houston, Texas, May 18-22, 1952. The first Minuteman Awards were presented at this Congress. The first award was made to Judge Ben H. Powell III, of Austin, Texas. Twenty-three Minuteman Awards were presented at this first ceremony. A special award was given to *The Saturday Evening Post* for its patriotic editorial policies.

On June 7, 1952 the New Jersey Society unveiled a bronze plaque at the grave of General Robert Erskine, Surveyor General of the Continental Army, in Ringwood Manor State Park, Passaic County.

The Church of Latter Day Saints was granted permission to microfilm the Leach Manuscripts of the genealogies of the Signers of the Declaration of Independence.

Compatriot former Chief Justice Frederick M. Vinson of the Supreme Court passed away on September 8, 1953.

A hurricane toppled the steeple of the Old North Church in Boston. There was an immediate fund drive to restore the famous church tower. The SAR took an active role in contributing to the restoration of the steeple.

Governor John Lodge of Connecticut and Admiral Jubelin of the French Embassy were honored speakers on June 26, 1954 when the Rochambeau Bridge across the Housatonic River between Newton and Southbury was dedicated under the auspices of the Connecticut Society.

Compatriot Herman Talmadge completed six years as Governor of Georgia. Both his father and grandfather had been members of the SAR. Compatriot Marvin Griffin succeeded him as Governor.

With a record of 105 inches of snow for the winter and ten inches in the preceding 24 hours, 100 Compatriots and wives attended the George Washington Birthday Dinner of the Alaska Society at the Forest Park Country Club in Anchorage.

In 1955 the first SAR Handbook was written and published, with 2,000 copies of the 48-page volume printed. The cost to Compatriots was 50 cents per copy including handling and shipping.

Compatriot Count Philippe de La Fayette, great-great grandson of General Marquis de La Fayette, was honored and awarded the SAR Gold Good Citizenship Medal by the National Society at the Army-Navy Club in Washington.

The Pennsylvania Society published a 1955 Year Book compiled by Historian Floyd Hoenstine. It contained much genealogical information in its 773 pages.

HEADQUARTERS MORTGAGE BURNED

In May, 1955 on Recognition Night at the 65th Annual Congress in Chicago, the mortgage contract on the National Headquarters was burned.

On June 6 the Connecticut Society observed the 200th anniversary of Nathan Hale's birth in the Nathan Hale schoolhouse at East Haddam. *Life Magazine* showed pictures of the meeting in its June 13th issue.

The Indiana Society presented a painting of President Benjamin Harrison to the U.S. Army Finance Center, Fort Harrison, Indianapolis.

The Philadelphia-Continental Chapter of the Pennsylvania Society held its Annual Meeting at the Bellevue-Stratford Hotel in Philadelphia. Compatriot Admiral Richard E. Byrd spoke and was presented the Gold Good Citizenship Medal. Admiral Byrd spoke on the strategic importance of the Arctic.

On August 10 the Oregon Society observed Compatriot President Herbert Hoover's 81st birthday at his boyhood home in Newberg. The Oregon Society restored the home, including furnishings, to its original condition of the 1880s. President Hoover spoke of his early years to the Compatriots and guests.

On November 17, 1955 the Nevada Society was presented its Charter at the Prospector's Club in Reno. As a result the SAR had Societies in all 48 states.

Frank Addison Corbin of the Connecticut Society, National #5421, joined the SAR in 1891 and was still active. He served as Secretary-Treasurer of the Connecticut Society for 50 years.

Seven-hundred Compatriots and guests attended the gala 17th Annual Colonial Ball at the Starlight Roof of the Waldorf-Astoria Hotel in New York on February 17, 1956. The Honor Guard of the Old Seventh Regiment presented the Colors. A stately cotillion by candlelight was danced by junior members of the DAR and members of the SAR Continental Guard.

A special committee was appointed at the February Trustees Meeting to explore the ramifications of selling the Sixteenth Street National Headquarters and purchasing a new facility.

Vice-President General Burt B. Barker and former President Herbert Hoover, an SAR, chatted during the celebration of Hoover's 81st birthday at Newberg, Oregon in 1955. The occasion also marked dedication of the Minthorne House.

SURGEON GENERAL POST CREATED

The position of Surgeon General was added to the General Officers of the Society at the 66th Annual Congress held at the Hotel Sagamore, Lake George, New York, in May 1956.

The General Joseph Hiester Chapter of Reading, Pennsylvania, placed a marker on the grave of Dr. Bodo Otto, Senior Surgeon at Valley Forge.

The National Education Association offered $250,000 for the National Headquarters on Sixteenth Street.

On Flag Day 1956 Compatriot Hubbard Scott of the Ohio Society displayed his historic American flags at the Tomb of the Unknown Soldier as the National Society placed a wreath on the tomb.

The Pittsburgh Chapter conducted Flag Day ceremonies at the Block House at Fort Pittsburgh. A history of various American Flags was given. As each flag was described, a uniformed soldier brought it forward. Mayor David Lawrence of Pittsburgh read his Flag Day Proclamation.

Compatriot A. E. Kellum of Princess Anne County, Virginia, served as County Clerk for over 50 years. His 12 sons became SAR members.

On October 20, 1956 the Ohio Society dedicated a monument in McElroy Cemetery in Nobel County to the memory of John Gray, next to the last surviving soldier of the Revolutionary War. Soldier Gray died on March 29, 1868 at the age of 104.

President General Eugene Carver unveiled a bronze plaque on the wall of the Citadel of Quebec, Canada, marking the burial location of 13 American Revolutionary War soldiers. On New Year's Eve 1775 an American force under General Richard Montgomery stormed Quebec and was met by an overwhelming force. Many Americans including General Montgomery were killed.

On September 6 the District of Columbia Society celebrated the 200th anniversary of the birth of General Marquis de LaFayette at the Patriot's statue in LaFayette Square opposite the White House.

The Connecticut Society SAR and the Connecticut State Society DAR erected 25 historical markers designating the camp sites of Rochambeau's Army as it traveled through Connecticut enroute to Yorktown in 1781.

On October 15, 1957 the District of Columbia Society entertained three distinguished France Society Compatriots at the Statler Hotel in Washington: Count Phillippe de Rahune de

THE EMPIRE STATE SOCIETY
SONS OF THE AMERICAN REVOLUTION

Honors some of its distinguished members

Honorable Chauncey M. Depew	President N.Y. Central Railroad
John D. Rockefeller	Oil Magnate and philanthropist
Nelson A. Rockefeller	Governor State of New York
Thomas E. Dewey	Governor State of New York
Col. John A. Calhoun	Vice-President United States of America
Maj. Gen. Frederick D. Grant	Son of President Ulysses S. Grant
Maj. Gen. Ulysses S. Grant	Grandson of President Ulysses S. Grant
George W. Vanderbilt	Horticulturist and established Biltmore
Robert B. Roosevelt	Uncle of President Theodore Roosevelt
Franklin D. Roosevelt, Jr.	Son of President Franklin D. Roosevelt
Col. James Roosevelt	Son of President Franklin D. Roosevelt
Theodore Roosevelt	President United States of America
Capt. Kermit Roosevelt	Son of President Theodore Roosevelt
Br. Gen. Theodore Roosevelt	Son of President Theodroe Roosevelt
Archibald B. Roosevelt	Son of President Theodore Roosevelt
Dwight D. Eisenhower	President United States of America

The first book of Minutes of the Board of Management contains the original Constitution of the Empire State Society, under which the Society was organized February 11, 1890. It tells of the first annual meeting on February 18, 1892 which was held at the office of ESS President, the Honorable Chauncey Mitchell Depew. He was then President of the New York Central Railroad and a charter member of the Empire State Society holding the society number #2. Now in 1988, ESS numbers are well over 11,000.

MICHIGAN SOCIETY ACTIVE SINCE 1890

On January 18, 1890 the Michigan Society was chartered in Detroit. Since that time five local Chapters have formed to enable local eligible men to help promote the objectives of the Society. The Society has contributed to National Leadership since 1962: 1 President General; 8 Vice-Presidents General; 1 Chancellor General; 2 Genealogists General; 1 Surgeon General; and 9 National Trustees. Our late member Lynn Gordon published the "86th Anniversary Complete Membership Roster, 1890 to 1975" and presented it to the Michigan Society in 1976. A Supplement was published in 1988 and copies are now in the National Library at Louisville. Several members have also made meaningful contributions to the National S.A.R. Museum. Michigan has an active Graves Marking Program. Also there are 15 Perpetual Life Memberships (with five deceased) and six Century Memberships (with funds specified for Law Enforcement, Boy Scouts and Grave Marking). The Annual Meeting in the spring includes a Friday Night Awards Program with speaker. On Saturday a regular meeting of the Board of Managers is followed by the Annual Meeting with election of Officers. A noon luncheon is followed by awards and installation of officers.

CHANCELLOR JOHN LANSING CHAPTER, Ingham County — First called the Ingham County Chapter and chartered on April 15, 1925, it was renamed the Chancellor John Lansing Chapter. The new name was taken from a real Chancellor, John Lansing, who was admitted to law practice in Albany, NY in 1775 and who was prominent in legal and political activities in Albany until his death in 1829. Chapter activities include grave marking for three Patriots, as well as Society Past Presidents. Long-term activities have included working with Boy Scouts in the Lansing area.

DETROIT METROPOLITAN CHAPTER, Detroit Area — This Chapter was chartered March 12, 1913 with its jurisdiction as Wayne County. The name was recently changed to Detroit Metro Chapter. Nine meetings of the Chapter are scheduled annually, with none being held in July, August or January. Programs center around Revolutionary War interests. Ladies are in attendance except for one which is stag. Meetings are held at various places. Special observances include: Washington's Birthday, June Picnic, Allegiance Sunday, July 4, Veteran's Day, Christmas Party and an occasional meeting with Louisa Sinclair Chapter of D.A.R.

KENT CHAPTER, Kent County — This was the first of the Michigan Chapters and was organized in 1897, March 12, as the Western Michigan Chapter, having seven counties in the area. On March 27, 1914 the Chapter was reorganized with territory limited to Kent County. The Chapter has ten meetings a year with programs concerned with the Revolutionary War, Government, Constitution and Military Preparedness. An Annual Awards Banquet includes presenting medals to Boy Scouts, High School Students and Junior ROTC Cadets. A new project is the Flag Award whereby framed Flag Awards are presented annually to individuals and businesses for displaying the U.S. flag on their property regularly. This year special emphasis has been placed on recruiting new members.

NORTHERN MICHIGAN CHAPTER, Northern Michigan, including the Upper Peninsula — This new Chapter was recently organized with former members-at-large and new members residing in the area.

SAUK TRAIL CHAPTER, nine counties in southwestern Michigan — This Chapter was organized in Marshall as Southwestern Michigan Chapter on February 22, 1961 and is now called Sauk Trail Chapter, the name change being recommended to make way for possible other Chapters in this very large area. Nine meetings per year are scheduled including the Annual Meeting. Two meetings are held in cooperation with two D.A.R. Chapters with whom we work closely on membership and other projects. Individual members sponsor and present Bronze Good Citizenship Medals to outstanding high school seniors in 12 different high schools in the area. ROTC Medals are also presented to Cadets in the university units. Ancestor and former members graves markings are researched and accomplished. New member recruiting and meaningful programs have been organized and a 10% increase goal has been set. To accommodate membership participation in meetings, they are scheduled in various places in the service area, because of the distances.

LaFayette, Count Jean de Rochambeau and Marquis George de Grasse. All three were descendants of the great heroes of the American Revolution.

HEADQUARTERS BUILDING SOLD

On February 8, 1958 President General George Tarbox convened a Special SAR Congress in Washington, DC, with 88 delegates present. The Congress discussed and resolved to sell the Sixteenth Street Headquarters property and purchase the General Patrick Hurley home of 8,000 square feet located at 2412 Massachusetts Avenue, Northwest, Washington.

The transaction, the sale of the Sixteenth Street property for $294,000, the purchase of the Massachusetts Avenue property for $165,000 with $52,475 for alterations and improvements, allowed

In May 1957 a bronze plaque was dedicated to mark the burial site of 13 American soldiers of General Montgomery's Army killed in the assault on Quebec in 1775. Offering the marker was President General Eugene P. Carver, Jr. (left). Canadian officials also participated in the program.

$76,000 to be added to the Permanent Fund increasing that fund to a total of $85,000.

An excellent article entitled "The Valiant Men of the Sons of the American Revolution" appeared in the May 1958 issue of the *The American Mercury* magazine.

The first SAR Award to the United States Service Academies was given at graduation ceremonies at the Air Force Academy in 1958.

An SAR Medal of Appreciation was approved to recognize outstanding service rendered to the SAR by members of the Daughters of the American Revolution.

The memory of Thomas Lynch, Signer of the Declaration who was lost at sea in 1779, was honored on the Fourth of July by the Connecticut Society in a ceremony on Coast Guard Cutter CG-83346 with a wreath cast onto the waters of Long Island Sound.

The new SAR National Headquarters was opened for business on September 1, 1958. The first formal reception at the new headquarters was held on October 4, 1958 for General Officers and National Trustees attending the Fall Trustees meeting.

In the previous three years 4,250 graves of Revolutionary War Patriots were recorded, making a total of 9,315 graves on record in 34 states, the District of Columbia, Canada and China.

In observance of the 325th anniversary of the founding of the Town of Windsor, Connecticut, the Colonel Jeremiah Wadsworth Branch of the Connecticut Society erected a bronze plaque on the grave of Sergeant Daniel Bissell, patriotic spy of the Revolution.

On November 11, 1958 the Colonel John Rosenkrans Chapter of the New Jersey Society dedicated a monument to Colonel Rosenkrans, who served as Commander of the Third Regiment, Sussex County Militia. Dr. Edna Rosenkrans, a descendant, unveiled the monument.

The South Carolina Society observed the 178th anniversary of the Battle of Cowpens on January 17th by conducting ceremonies at the battlefield and at the General Daniel Morgan Monument in Spartanburg.

Former President General Messmore Kendall passed away on May 1, 1959. He bequeathed the George Washington signet ring to the National Society with the request that it be used in the installation ceremonies for incoming Presidents General.

At the close of the decade the SAR had a membership of 18,661. The three largest State Societies were Pennsylvania, 1,947 Compatriots; Ohio, 1,663; and Emipre State, 1,540. There were 257 Chapters working at the community level.

The 200th anniversary of the birth of Lafayette was observed by ceremonies at Lafayette Park under the sponsorship of the District of Columbia Society in September, 1957. Wreaths were placed by a number of dignitaries.

The Anthony Wayne Chapter of the Ohio Society erected a memorial flag pole on the new Craig Bridge. The names of all service men and women from Lucas County who served in the various wars were enshrined in a steel safe at the base of the pole.

Bill of Rights Day, December 14, 1959, was observed by the Virginia Society's George Mason Chapter by placing a wreath on the grave of Patriot Mason on the grounds of his home, Gunston Hall. Participating were (from left): S. Cooper Dawson, a Mason descendant, Stephen R. Turner, President; Col. Robert P. Waters, Society President; and Compatriot Frederick J. Griffiths, Director of Gunston Hall. The home is not far from Alexandria.

The Missouri Society of The Sons of The American Revolution
Organized April 23, 1889

Presidents General

Allen Laws Oliver, 1946

M. Graham Clark, 1974

Arthur M. King, 1980

Vice-Presidents General

Gov. David R. Francis, 1889
George H. Shields, 1904
Amedee B. Cole, 1912
Linn Paine, 1919-20
James M. Breckenridge, 1924-25
Cooper S. Yost, 1930-31
Allen L. Oliver, 1940
John W. Giesecke, 1948-49
L. Bentley Cash, 1966
M. Graham Clark, 1971

MOSSAR President, 1989-1990
Rev. & Mrs. Paul T. Butler

Vice-Presidents General

Paul W. Bennett, 1976
Arthur M. King, 1977
James S. Shelby, 1988

Secretaries General

M. Graham Clark, 1972-73
Arthur M. King, 1978

Treasurer General

Gaius Paddock, 1889

Surgeon General

Dr. Charles E. Griggs, 1892

MOSSAR congratulates THE NATIONAL SOCIETY OF THE SONS OF THE AMERICAN REVOLUTION for One Hundred years of patriotic service to America and the ideals of human freedom.

THE SAN FERNANDO VALLEY CHAPTER

Salutes
The National Society
Sons of the American Revolution
on the occasion of its
100th Anniversary

The San Fernando Valley Chapter, S.A.R. was chartered on the 30th of April, 1981 by the California Society, Sons of the American Revolution. Since it was founded, this chapter has created and spearheaded many new and highly successful programs many of which have been adopted throughout the Society as a whole. For a still relatively new chapter it has achieved a level of accomplishment that has rarely, if indeed ever been surpassed. In its ten years of highly kinetic operation the Chapter has dynamically pursued all the programs of the CASSAR and the NSSAR as well as several of its own. It is proud to be a vital part of the National Society of the Sons of the American Revolution and is actively enthusiastic in support of and furtherance for its objectives declared to be historic, educational and patriotic.

The San Fernando Valley Chapter's Color Guard

OUR PAST PRESIDENTS
Donald Norman Moran - 1981 - 83 * LtC James Bellah, II - 1984 * George Sutherland Van Dorn - 1985
Col. George A. Eckert, Jr. - 1986 * Roger E. Robertson - 1986 * DeWille F. Bill Semerau - 1988
Robert C. Emrey - 1989

SAR CENTENNIAL HISTORY

PART IV: 1960–1990

1960–1970: Stormy '60s Decade

The population was 170 million people with the trend to the west. There were 162 million television sets in America; 78 million cars and 16 million trucks were on the road. Communists fought against the South Vietnam Government. The United States assumed a military role with a force of 543,000 servicemen. The Americans suffered heavy losses. Large antiwar demonstrations took place. The East German Government erected a concrete wall separating East and West Berlin. The Soviet Union secretly installed missiles in Fidel Castro's Cuba. The United States showed a strong resolve. The Russians removed the missiles. President John Kennedy was assassinated and Compatriot Lyndon Johnson was sworn in as President. Medicare was established. There were federal actions on behalf of civil rights. Martin Luther King was assassinated and there were racial riots in many cities. Alan Shepard became America's first man in space. John Glenn became the first American to orbit the earth and Neil Armstrong the first man on the moon. Richard Nixon became President on January 20, 1969.

The National Society initiated a national advertising campaign by employing a striking billboard design — "KEEP U.S.A. FIRST" — to encourage a revival of patriotism among the American public; 617 such signs were displayed in this decade. Posters of the design were placed on buses and in store windows.

Compatriot Robert R. Peale, great-great-great grandson of the renowned artist Charles Wilson Peale, presented his painting of General George Washington in uniform to the Colorado Society.

The Michigan Society marked the graves of two Revolutionary soldiers buried in Barry County: John Quick, sergeant in the New Jersey Militia; and Amos Ingram, soldier in the Connecticut Militia.

The SAR Badge of First President General Lucius P. Deming was donated to the National Society by Mrs. Carlton L. Wrench. His National Number was 202.

COLONIAL BALL POPULAR

In every January of this decade the New York Chapter held its Colonial Ball in the Grand Ballroom of the Hotel Plaza. Debutantes who were descendants of Revolutionary Patriots were presented. The Chapter's Continental Guard in Revolutionary uniform and the Honor Guard of the Seventh Regiment presented the Colors. In 1963 Compatriot Count Phillippe de Sahune de La Fayette, great-great grandson of General Marquis de La Fayette, and his wife Countess Catherine were honored guests at the Ball.

Compatriot Colonel H. C. Roberts of the Florida Society donated 12 rhododendron plants to the National Headquarters grounds in memory of his son, Compatriot Herbert C. Roberts of the Virginia Society, who was killed on Okinawa in World War II.

The Washington State Society presented the Gold Good Citizenship Medal to Compatriot Chief Justice Walter B. Beals of the Washington State Supreme Court and Supreme Judge at the Nuremberg trials in Germany after World War II.

The SAR Medal of Appreciation was designed and adopted for presentation to members of the Daughters of the American Revolution who render outstanding services to the SAR.

In 1961 the San Diego Chapter of the California Society collected over 60,000 books for use in the public schools in Mexico.

Compatriot Andrew Eyman, Judge of the Municipal Court of San Francisco, opened each session of his court with the Pledge of Allegiance to the Flag of the United States.

The New York Chapter held its annual Inauguration Day

The final three decades of our Society's first 100 years of varied and unique programs are examined by Former President General Carl F. Bessent in light of what events dominated news around the world.

What may have been the nation's largest George Washington's Birthday Banquet in 1960 was staged by the Texas Society's Paul Carrington Chapter at Houston. More than 800 Compatriots and guests attended.

ceremony at Federal Hall National Memorial, Wall and Nassau Streets, commemorating the inauguration of President Washington as first President. A feature of the ceremony was the Old Guard Fife and Drum Corps at Fort Myer, Virginia, performing the colonial drill as formulated by Baron Von Steuben.

Compatriot Laurens Hamilton donated to the National Society an oil painting by Erik Haupt of Compatriot President Dwight D. Eisenhower.

Charles Rush of Chattanooga, descendant of Dr. Benjamin Rush, Signer of the Declaration, won the Tennessee Society's oratorical contest.

The SAR was successful in having a nuclear submarine named for Connecticut's Patriotic Saint, Nathan Hale.

ACADEMY STUDENTS HONORED

SAR awards were presented to outstanding cadets and midshipmen at the Air Force Academy, Naval Academy and the Coast Guard Academy. In 1962 the first SAR award was made at the Military Academy. This program continued each year through the decade.

Every year the Society in France conducted a memorial ceremony at General Marquis de La Fayette's grave in Picpus Cemetery in Paris. Count Rene de Chambrun, President of the Society, always presided. The United States Ambassador and the Commanding General of United States forces in Europe participated in the programs. The United States Flag has flown continually day and night over the grave since 1834 (when the Patriot died), even in World War II during the German occupation.

The Connecticut Society annually honored the four Signers of the Declaration buried in that state: Roger Sherman, New Haven; William Williams, Lebanon; Oliver Wolcott, Litchfield; and Samuel Huntington, Norwichtown. In 1961 and 1962 a memorial ceremony honoring Thomas Lynch, Junior, Signer of the Declaration, lost at sea in 1779, was conducted by the Connecticut Society on the submarine *U.S.S. Croaker,* with a wreath cast on the waters on Long Island Sound. In the other years the ceremonies were conducted on the Coast Guard Cutter *Awasco.*

Every year the District of Columbia Society conducted Fourth of July ceremonies in the Congressional Cemetery at the grave of Elbridge Gerry, Vice President of the United States and the only Signer of the Declaration buried in the District. A combined Color Guard from the Armed Services and a firing squad always participated in the program.

Thousands of people always attended the New York Chapter's Fourth of July program at the Lower Plaza Level of Rockefeller Center. The First Army Band played patriotic music. The Chapter Colonial Guard and Color Guards from the military were part of the ceremonies.

Compatriot Dr. C. Malcolm was President of the Monmouth Battlefield Association, founded to purchase land to preserve the Monmouth Battlefield. The Association was organized by SAR members from the New Jersey and Pennsylvania Societies.

Compatriot Richard D. Meader of the Rhode Island Society, great-great-great grandson of General Nathanael Greene, cut the ribbon when Rhode Island State Road #117 was renamed General Nathaniel Greene Memorial Highway on May 4, 1961.

SPECIAL JULY 4TH CEREMONIES

The North Carolina Society proposed and initiated the "Ringing of Church Bells" on the Fourth of July in 1961. Many State Societies participated in this program through the years. In 1964 the DC Society arranged for the National Cathedral to ring its bell at noon on July 4th and to provide a program of patriotic music on the great carillon in "The Gloria in Excelsis Tower." There was special emphasis on the program in 1968. The Iowa Society arranged to have every church in Iowa City toll its bells at noon on the Fourth. The Arizona Society obtained an Independence Day Proclamation from Governor Jack Williams. Three major television stations gave extensive coverage of actual church bell ringing. The Society held a special program at the State Capitol Rotunda. Patriotic tunes were presented by the Sun City Bell Ringers. The actual ringing took place from 11 am to 1 pm of the Capitol's Liberty Bell with 50 members, guests, children ringing the bell.

An impressive memorial service, honoring Thomas Lynch, Jr., Signer of the Declaration of Independence who was lost at sea in 1779, was conducted by the Connecticut Society on July 4th, 1961. The solemn program was held aboard the *USS Croaker*, a submarine, from which a wreath was cast upon the waves.

Missouri's original state flag was presented by Compatriot Allen L. Oliver, President of the Missouri Society, on June 14, 1961 to Compatriot Governor John Dalton. The flag was designed in 1911 by Compatriot Oliver's mother.

The New Jersey Society held a program on June 25 commemorating the anniversary of the Battle of Monmouth. The program was held in the battle-scarred Old Tennent Church, Freehold, which served as a field hospital during the battle. The service concluded with the firing of a Revolutionary War cannon.

On November 5, 1961 the Georgia Society presented a Revolutionary War cannon, cast in Philadelphia in 1777, to the Georgia State Archives. The cannon is permanently located on the grounds of the Archives Building in Atlanta.

One-hundred members and guests attended the Alaska Society Annual George Washington Birthday Dinner at the Westward Hotel in Anchorage on February 22, 1962.

The Spring National Trustees meeting was held in Independence Hall, Philadelphia, On May 22.

Compatriot Robert L. Russell took the oath to become a Judge of the Georgia Court of Appeals from his brother-in-law, Compatriot Governor Samuel E. Vandiver. Compatriot Russell's grandfather served as Chief Justice of the Georgia Supreme Court.

The R. C. Ballard Thruston Chapter of the Kentucky Society held a Memorial Day program at the grave of Captain George Gray of the Virginia Militia at Fort George in Louisville. Captain Gray equipped and led a company of 100 horsemen during the Revolution. Presidents James Monroe and Zachary Taylor were his cousins.

On August 19 the Vermont Society commemorated the only Revolutionary battle fought in Vermont at the Hubbardton

Battlefield, Rutland County. The Americans were severely beaten in the battle in 1777.

PATRIOT MEDAL AUTHORIZED

The National Trustees authorized the Patriot Medal for Compatriots who demonstrated outstanding effort for the promotion of State Societies' programs. The rules allowed each State Society a minimum of one medal each year; two medals for Societies of 500 or more members; and Societies over 1,000 members, three medals per year.

Admiral William Furlong, President of the DC Society, prepared a history of the Flag of the United States for the Smithsonian Institution.

President Fred O. Schnure of the New Jersey Society presented SAR scrolls to 27 newly naturalized citizens at the Sussex County Courthouse.

The Palm Beach Chapter of the Florida Society sponsored a colorful and inspiring Massing of the Colors ceremony in Memorial Presbyterian Church, West Palm Beach. Forty-one color guards from military and patriotic societies participated.

The Philadelphia-Continental Chapter held its Annual George Washington Birthday Luncheon at the Bellevue-Stratford Hotel on February 22, 1963; 125 members and guests left the hotel for a wreath laying ceremony at the George Washington statue in front of Independence Hall. The assembly then proceeded to the Liberty Bell where Washington's Farewell Address was read.

Both Senator Barry Goldwater and Governor Paul L. Fannin of Arizona joined the Arizona Society.

The fee for supplemental applications was increased from $3 to $10.

The Maryland Society honored John Hanson on April 6 by dedicating a bronze plaque at Mulberry Grove Plantation, La Plate, Charles County, the birthplace of John Hanson, President of the United States in Congress Assembled 1781-1783.

The Maine Society unveiled a bronze plaque in the First Congregational Church, Deer Isle, in October honoring Peter Powers, a Revolutionary War clergyman.

The DC Society observed Constitution Day, September 17, 1963 by meeting in the National Archives Auditorium and visiting Exhibit Hall where the Constitution and the Declaration of Independence were on display.

The Maryland Society celebrated Constitution Day by rededicating a large bronze plaque which depicted the early Baltimore Inn where the Continental Congress met in Baltimore in mid-December 1776.

Plans were presented at the Winter National Trustees meeting in 1964 for a proposed Memorial Library-Auditorium addition with an estimated cost of $1,500,000. A funding campaign was initiated, but the project never materialized.

At the 75th Annual Meeting of the New Jersey Society held on April 18, 1964 at the Forsgate Country Club, Jamesburg, Lester L. McDowell, grandson of William O. McDowell, exhibited the "Number One" National Membership Certificate issued to his grandfather.

AWARD TO COMPATRIOT LOWELL THOMAS

The New York Chapter presented its Chauncey M. DePew Medal to Compatriot Lowell Thomas, veteran radio and television news commentator and explorer, at the annual Patriots Day smoker held at the Harvard Club on April 17.

A Special SAR Congress met in the John Wesley Powell Auditorium, Cosmos Club, Washington, on October 16, 1964. The Congress amended the SAR Constitution to allow the National Trustees to fix the date and place of Annual Congresses. It also voted to reduce the supplemental fee from $10 to $5.

The posthumous presentation of the first Patriot Medal by the National Society to General Douglas MacArthur was made in an impressive ceremony at the General Douglas MacArthur Memorial, Norfolk, Virginia, on October 19. Executive Secretary Putnam and President General Harry T. Burn presented the medal to Mayor Roy B. Martin who accepted on behalf of the Memorial.

One-hundred fifty organizations participated in the Annual George Washington Birthday Memorial Service and the massing of the Colors held in Grace Cathedral sponsored by the San Francisco Chapter of the California Society on February 22, 1965. The Cathedral was full to its capacity of 2,000.

THE CONNECTICUT SOCIETY of the SONS of the AMERICAN REVOLUTION, INC.

ORGANIZED APRIL 2, 1889
INCORPORATED JANUARY 3, 1890

"A CENTURY OF COMMITMENT TO OUR NATION'S HERITAGE — 1889-1989"

1989   1990

Lucius Parmenias Deming
FIRST PRESIDENT GENERAL
of the NATIONAL SOCIETY of the
SONS of the AMERICAN REVOLUTION

and FIRST PRESIDENT of the
CONNECTICUT SOCIETY of the
SONS of the AMERICAN REVOLUTION

Governor Trumbull War Office
Lebanon, Connecticut

Nathan Hale Schoolhouse
East Haddam, Connecticut

Nathan Hale Schoolhouse
New London, Connecticut

PATRIOTIC, HISTORICAL AND EDUCATIONAL
"ETERNAL VIGILANCE IS THE PRICE OF LIBERTY"

The Annual Colonial Ball of the New Jersey SAR and DAR Societies was held at the Molly Pitcher Hotel, Red Bank, on George Washington's Birthday.

The James Horseshoe Robertson Chapter of the Alabama Society placed a bronze marker on the grave of its namesake in Tuscaloosa on Sunday, April 25th. He served as a soldier in the Revolution. One-hundred members and guests attended the ceremony.

The Colonel John Rosenkrans Chapter of the New Jersey Society presented the Sussex County Library with microfilm copies of the United States Census reports from 1830 to and including 1880.

Three prominent members passed away in the past year: General Douglas MacArthur on April 5, 1964; former President Herbert Hoover on October 20, 1964; and Sir Winston Churchill on January 24, 1965.

The R. C. Ballard Thruston Chapter joined with the Boy Scouts of America in a ceremony to honor the American Flag on its 158th birthday — June 14th, 1962 — at noon before the Jefferson County World War II Memorial in Louisville. Participating in the program were (foreground, from left): Compatriot J. Colgan Norman, guest speaker; Byron C. Grimes, President of the BSA Old Kentucky Home Council; and Chapter President William A. Chenault. An honored guest was Former President General Walter A. Wentworth.

The 75th SAR Annual Congress held in Albuquerque in April 1965 voted to fix the annual dues at $5 per year, with $1 allocated for publishing *THE SAR MAGAZINE.*

The Isaac Shelby Chapter of the Kentucky Society conducted a program in the Frankfort cemetery for Revolutionary War Chaplain John Gano, a Baptist minister who served seven years in the Continental Army. He was the founder of Brown University. In 1788 he resigned from his New York City church to go to the frontier in Kentucky. In 1804 he was buried in the Baptist Churchyard, Elkhorn City. In 1916 he was reinterred in the Frankfort Cemetery by the DAR.

The Massachusetts Society conducted its annual public program at Concord on April 19, 1965 at the Old North Bridge and later placed a wreath on the grave of Colonel James Barrett who commanded the militia forces on April 19, 1775 in the battle which started the American Revolution.

WASHINGTON'S PRAYER DISTRIBUTED

The Montclair Chapter #3 of the New Jersey Society distributed 13,000 copies of George Washington's inaugural prayer to the 44 churches in Montclair. The churches used the prayer in their order of worship.

On Memorial Day the Wisconsin Society marked the graves of Cooper Pixley and Alexander Porter, Revolutionary War soldiers, in Fort Winnebago Cemetery, Portage, Wisconsin.

Economic conditions in the District of Columbia resulted in the appointment of a special National Headquarters Site Search Committee to investigate properties suitable for relocating the National Headquarters. Many sites including Valley Forge, Williamsburg, Brandywine were considered. Later the special committee issued a report, "Keep the National Headquarters in Washington."

The New York Chapter received title to the historic Odell-Rochambeau Home in Hartsdale. Miss Elizabeth Odell, last member of the family, deeded the historic house to the Chapter for a museum. The Odell House was Count de Rochambeau's Headquarters in 1781 where he and General Washington planned the Virginia campaign leading to the surrender at Yorktown. The Chapter immediately started a campaign to raise $160,000 to restore the house.

The Pennsylvania Society presented two antique candlesticks to Independence Hall to be placed on the desk of the Senate President in the Congress Hall.

Foundations Consultants, Inc., was engaged to raise funds for the National Society at a rate of $1,000 per month. A goal of $1,500,000 was established. The effort was unproductive and the contract was terminated after five months.

Compatriot Captain Robert L. Thomas, USN, was on duty in the Aleutian Islands. He was the Organizing President of the Oakland Chapter, California Society.

The grave of a Revolutionary War soldier was uncovered in land clearing on the Whaley Farm, Smithfield in Henry County, Kentucky. It was the grave of Evans Watkins, 1744-1832, a soldier in the Virginia Militia. It was marked by the Kentucky Society on July 18, 1965. He was an ancestor of Col. Benjamin H. Morris, who became President General in 1985.

Compatriot Charles R. Haugh, a REAL GRANDSON, joined the Virginia Society.

The R. C. Ballard Thruston Chapter arranged for Mayor Cowger of Louisville to issue a Proclamation designating November 27th as the day to honor members of the Armed Forces in Vietnam by displaying flags and designating Sunday, November 28, as a day of prayer for Divine protection of our troops and for ultimate victory.

At the Trustees meeting, February 12, 1966, Executive Secretary Harold L. Putnam announced he planned to retire in June, 1966 after 17 years of service.

The New York Chapter established an annual SAR Award at Columbia University to encourage scholarship and research in the field of American History prior to 1789.

JESSE HELMS GIVEN AWARD

The North Carolina Society presented a distinguished service award to Jesse Helms, editorial commentator for station WRAL, for advocating honesty and efficiency in government.

The Maryland Society presented its first Gold Good Citizenship Medal to Lieutenant General Milton Reckord for 65 years of military service. He commanded the famous 29th Division in World War II. The presentation was made at the George Washington Birthday Banquet at the Belvedere Hotel on February 22, 1966. Also honored was Compatriot George S. Robertson, who served as Treasurer General for 28 years and attended every meeting of the State Society in his 53 years as a member.

The Massachusetts Society marked the grave of Henry Jacobs, Jr., 22-year old Minuteman killed at the Battle of Lexington on April 19, 1775 in the woodlands of Peabody. The grave was discovered by a Cub Scout Pack.

Vice Admiral Hyman Rickover, USN, father of the modern nuclear navy, was presented the SAR Gold Good Citizenship Medal by the Empire State Society at its Annual Meeting at the Hotel Thayer, West Point, on April 30.

Twenty-two representatives and 19 senators of the 89th United States Congress were members of the SAR.

The Elizabethtown Chapter of the New Jersey Society held a memorial service at the Rosehill Cemetery on May 22 for British servicemen buried there. It is the only land in the United States owned by the British Government for burial for its servicemen. There are 98 graves with natives of England.

The Connecticut Society held its 75th Annual Meeting on June 11 at Lebanon and rededicated the Governor Jonathan Trumbull War Office. The War Office is owned and maintained by the Connecticut Society. It was the place where 1,100 meetings of the War Council of Safety were held during the Revolutionary War. Connecticut Governor Trumbull presided over the meetings.

The Tompkins County Chapter enrolled the Empire State Society's 10,000th member, Compatriot Samuel C. Rhode. His patriotic ancestor was his great-great-great-great grandmother, Catherine Rentz, of Colleton County, South Carolina. She gave large quantities of beef and forage to the Continental Army.

The Huntington Chapter of the Empire State Society observed Memorial Day by decorating the graves of all the Revolutionary

In 1967 Rhode Island Society President I. Harris Tucker presented a silver punch bowl to Cmdr. Robert Crispin, USN, for the nuclear submarine *Nathanael Greene*. The ceremony took place at the Greene Homestead at Anthony, Rhode Island.

War soldiers in Huntington Cemetery, as it had done since the Chapter was organized in 1911.

COMPATRIOT ROCKEFELLER ADDRESSES ASSEMBLAGE

The Oriskany Battle Chapter of the Empire State Society celebrated the anniversary of the battle on August 6 at the battlefield state park, Rome. It was a very bloody encounter between the Patriot militia and a force of Indians and Tories. Compatriot Governor Nelson Rockefeller addressed the large crowd attending the barbeque event.

On Friday evening, September 30, 1966, in the State Room of the Mayflower Hotel in Washington, the National Society honored retiring Executive Secretary Harold L. Putnam after 17 years of service. He was honored with the title of Honorary President General and received a Past President General's Badge. Compatriot Warren S. Woodward of the Empire State Society, was introduced as the incoming Executive Secretary and Editor of *THE SAR MAGAZINE.*

The Cincinnati Chapter of the Ohio Society continued its program of distributing American Flag bookmarks through libraries, clubs and community organizations. Over 300,000 bookmarks were distributed during 1966.

At the end of 1966, there were 17,335 names in the SAR grave registry.

On Febuary 2, 1967 the SAR Gold Good Citizenship Medal was presented to General Electric Corporation Vice President Willard Sahloff at the SAR National Headquarters. The ceremony was viewed on national television with many ranking government officials, ambassadors and SAR officers present.

In April 1967 the Palo Alto Chapter of the California Society honored Compatriot Alden Ames, Chapter Secretary, with a surprise 82nd birthday party, honoring his 60 years as an SAR member. He served as a Judge in the San Francisco courts for many years.

At the 77th Annual Congress, Columbus, Ohio, Compatriot Harold L. Putnam was presented a specially struck gold Patriot Medal, in recognition of his having conceived the award and being responsible for its design. A proposed amendment that the President General be elected for a two-year term was defeated by the Congress 92 to 49.

In 1967 the price of a 14 karat gold SAR Badge from J. E. Caldwell of Philadelphia was $48.

The Law Enforcement Commendation Medal was adopted to recognize outstanding performance and service.

COMPATRIOTS IN VIETNAM WAR

Many Compatriots answered the call for service in Vietnam. The South Carolina Society eliminated state and national dues of members serving in Vietnam. Four Compatriots gave their lives in the conflict: Victor Ohanesian of the Empire State Society; Howard Carpenter of the Ohio Society, March 6, 1967; Lloyd M. Willson, Texas Society, February 22, 1968; Robert C. Dickinson, Kentucky Society, July, 1968.

Rhode Island Independence Day, May 4, was observed by the Rhode Island Society at the Valley Ledgmont Country Club, West Warwick. The Society presented a silver punch bowl to Commander Robert Crispin, USN, for the nuclear submarine, *U.S.S. Nathanael Greene.*

The New Mexico Society was established on December 11, 1908 while New Mexico was still a Territory. Prior to that the members who started our Society were members of the Colorado Society. The original membership of the New Mexico Society consisted of 28 members, 17 of whom were also members of the Colorado Society.

The growth in the early years was gradual and in 1919 the roster listed 75 members. In 1929 there was a reorganization effort and more emphasis was placed on growth. Since then there has been a constant increase with the Society now having 170 members. Chapters have been organized in Albuquerque, Santa Fe, Roswell, Hobbs and Las Cruces with Albuquerque and Las Cruces the most active at this time.

The Society's exhibit at the New Mexico State Fair

The State Society has had active attendance at the National Congresses and Trustees Meetings. We are also proud of our members who have held National Offices such as our Colonel James R. Calhoun, present Secretary General; Robert G. Norfleet, former Registrar General and Robert G. Luckey, former Treasurer General.

The New Mexico Society actively participates in a number of patriotic and historic programs, namely the R.O.T.C. Awards, Eagle Scout Program, New Mexico State Fair and the Naturalization of new Citizens Ceremonies. We have maintained the booth at the New Mexico State Fair since 1956 for all patriotic and historic items entered by citizens. We also award two SAR prizes in addition to those awarded by State Fair Officials. Another unique program is our participation in all the Naturalization Ceremonies held in New Mexico for the last 20 years. We have awarded approximately 5000 distinctive certificates to newly naturalized citizens welcoming them to our country.

When New Jersey Compatriots gathered for their 1967 Annual Meeting, they related an anecdote to President General Kenneth Smith (second from left). They were (form left): 2nd VP Richard Crane, 3rd VP Vincent van Inwegen and President George Felt.

On June 2, 1967 former President Harry S. Truman was enrolled as a member of the Missouri Society. He was a descendant of Lieutenant James Holmes of the 2nd Virginia State Regiment.

Arkansas Governor Winthrop Rockefeller joined the Arkansas Society.

In June 1968 at the 78th Annual Congress in Williamsburg, Virginia, a revised admission fee of $15 was approved.

Miss Helen C. Hottenbacher was presented the Gold Good Citizenship Medal by the Maryland Society for 46 years of service to the SAR. She served as Assistant to the Credentials Committee of the SAR Annual Congresses from 1928 to 1948. She took and transcribed the minutes of the Annual Congresses from 1932 to 1950 and handled the detailed work of Compatriot George S. Robertson during his 28 years as Treasurer General.

The Empire State Society presented a "Scroll of Appreciation" to *The New York Daily News* at the New York Chapter's annual Patriots Day smoker at the Princeton Club on April 19, 1968. The award was given to the newspaper for the sale of more than 100,000 American Flags and 50,000 flag stickers at cost.

The John Hancock Chapter of Findlay, Ohio, sponsored an unusual Flag Day program. It obtained the support of local businessmen and merchants and gave an American Flag to every individual home in the city, which had a population of 38,000. It was "Flag City U.S.A."

The Colonel F. W. Huntington Chapter of the Texas Society observed Independence Day with a wreath laying ceremony at the Alamo in San Antonio. The bell at the Alamo was rung at noon.

Microfilm copies of SAR membership papers were stored in the vault of the Manufacturers National Bank of Detroit and in the Granite Mountain Records Vault in the Wasatch Mountains in Utah.

The first SAR Law Enforcement Commendation Medal was presented to F.B.I. Director J. Edgar Hoover by President General Walter Sterling at the F.B.I. Headquarters in October 1968.

The Honorable Joseph W. Barr, Secretary of the Treasury, joined the Texas Society. Governor John A. Love of Colorado became a member of the Colorado Society.

Compatriot Admiral Thomas H. Moorer of the Alabama Society was promoted to Chairman of the Joint Chiefs of Staff. Lieutenant General Herman Nickerson, USMC, of the Massachusetts Society, was Commanding General of the III Marine Amphibious Force in Vietnam.

The Miami Chapter's Annual President's Ball was held at the Country Club of Miami on February 1, 1969. Miss Holiday Jones, a 7th generation granddaughter of President John Adams, made her debut at the ball.

The Mississippi Society held its 60th Annual Meeting in Greenwood. The Society was organized on May 10, 1909 with 18 Charter Members. Compatriot Paul L. Lindholm of Lexington, last surviving Charter Member, was given special recognition.

Ninety-nine-year-old Compatriot Dr. Mott Sawyers of the Minnesota Society, former Chaplain General, a regular attendee of SAR Congresses, attended the 79th Annual Congress at Salt Lake City.

The membership at the end of the decade was 19,595. The Permanent Fund assets totaled $93,297.44.

1970–1980: The Traumatic Decade

These were traumatic years. Four students were killed at Kent State University in Ohio by National Guardsmen during a protest against the Asian War. A Postal Reform Act created an independent United States Postal Service; during the decade the postal rate for first class went from 6¢ to 15¢. The Twenty-Sixth Amendment was ratified lowering the voting age to 18 in all elections. The United States incurred a $2-billion trade deficit for the first time and the national debt rose to $450 billion in 1972. Vice President Agnew resigned because of tax fraud; Compatriot Gerald R. Ford became Vice President under the 25th Amendment. Five men broke into the Democratic National Headquarters in the Watergate office complex in Washington. They pleaded guilty and because of the affair, President Richard Nixon became the first President to resign. Compatriot Vice President Gerald Ford became the 38th President. Compatriot

Nelson Rockefeller became Vice President. President Ford granted an "unconditional pardon" to former President Nixon. A total ban on oil exports to the United States was imposed by Arab oil-producing countries after the outbreak of war between Israel and the Arab States. Gasoline shortages caused long lines at gas stations in many states. At the pump, gasoline prices topped $1 per gallon for the first time. The United States celebrated its Bicentennial, marking the 200th anniversary of its Independence, with festivals, parades. The Liberty Bell was moved from Independence Hall to a nearby pavilion. Millions watched as an armada of 225 "Tall Ships" sailed up the Hudson River on July 4th, 1976. Jimmy Carter of Georgia was inaugurated as the 39th President. Walter Mondale became the Vice President. President Carter in his first Executive order granted amnesty to draft evaders.

CALIFORNIA SOCIETY HISTORY

1875 - 1989

OUR BEGINNING

In preparation for the Centennial Exposition and Celebration of the 100th Anniversary of American Independence at Philadelphia, President U. S. Grant signed the first bill for this celebration on 3 March 1871. The Speaker of the House, James G. Blaine, appointed the Committee of Arrangements on 29 December 1872, to have charge of the Celebration of which Aaron A. Sargent of Nevada City, California, was one of the members.

Interest began developing on the Pacific Coast, particularly in San Francisco, when initial plans were laid in the Fall to meet in the offices of Dr. James L. Cogswell on the evening of 22 October 1875 at 230 Kearny Street, San Francisco, California. At this meeting, the primary organization was completed which was called "National Society of Sons of Revolutionary Sires", and Dr. Cogswell briefly stated the objectives for which the meeting was called to establish the Society, and to make preparations for the celebration of the Centennial Anniversary of American Independence. On motion, the following officers were declared elected by acclamation, vis: Dr. James L. Cogswell, National President, Dr. Peter Wilkins Randle, Vice President for California, and Major Edwin A. Sherman, Vice President for the State of Nevada. The other officers served pro tem pending the next meeting.

JULY 4 1876

In the ensuing year more members became affiliated and the Constitution, By-Laws and Articles of Incorporation were unanimously adopted. The Society dates its organization from the 4th of July 1876, with Gen. Albert M. Winn as president, and William B. Eastin as secretary. Its objectives were:

"to unite the descendants of revolutionary patriots; perpetuate the memory of those who took part in the American Revolution, and maintain the independence of the United States of America; to promote social intercourse, mental improvement and mutual benefit of its members; to organise auxiliaries, co-equal branches and representative bodies, at such time and place as the Directors may determine."

Commissions were issued to establish branches in other locations in California, in New York, Illinois, Iowa, Massachusetts, Maine, and Washington, D. C. President Winn held this office through 1880, followed by Caleb T. Fay, Augustus C. Taylor, and Loring Pickering. Col. Adolphus S. Hubbard became president in 1886. The California Society Constitution, along with its circulars and bulletins, were sent year by year to residents in the east. The increased interest in this patriotic organization led to a national Convention, held at Fraunces Tavern in New York City on 30 April 1889. The history of the Sons of the American Revolution as a National Body begins with this convention, and California was an early member. Both Gen. Winn and Col. Hubbard were made Honorary Past Presidents General by later National Congresses.

SOCIETY RECORDS DESTROYED

All records of the California Society were destroyed in the fire that followed the San Francisco earthquake on 18 April 1906. The National Society at its Denver Congress in 1907 approved the cost of replacing the California Society lineage records. These records were completed and received in 1908.

Howard Cortland Rowley was the first member of the California Society to be elected President General. He was elected at the National Congress in Springfield, Illinois in 1929. Compatriot Rowley was a publisher, and it was during his administration that it became necessary to change the name of the SAR Magazine from "The Minute Man" due to copyright restrictions.

HAROLD L. PUTNAM

California Society Past President and Life Member, Harold L. Putnam, was convinced by the NSSAR Executive Committee in the Fall of 1950 to accept the position of Executive Secretary NSSAR following the 28 year tenure of the prior secretary. Compatriot Putnam was one of the longtime leaders of the Anti-Subversive Textbook "Campaign" that the California Society had long conducted. He instituted the "Pledge to the S.A.R." in the California Society in 1938 which was later accepted by the National Society. He originated the Minuteman and Patriot Medals, and was elected Honorary Past President General on his retirement in 1966, the third member in the California Society to be so recognized.

CALIFORNIA SOCIETY TODAY

California Society Past President and Life Member, Calvin E. Chunn, was most active in the state offices he held, and he then proceeded to enter positions on the National Society level. He was elected President General in 1978, and was reelected at the San Diego National Congress in 1979. His activities both on the state and national level were many and varied. One of the major accomplishments was the moving of the National Society headquarters from Alexandria, Virginia, to Louisville, Kentucky.

The California Society now has 23 chapters and over 1,050 members, and has reestablished the SAR Ladies Auxiliary of over 150 members. This activity has been most productive in assisting the state society. Major educational programs include the awarding of Fellowship Grants of $500 to $750 to graduate students in American Colonial History who are worthy and in need, and the "Spirit of America Award" for worthy junior high school students. Our 1989-1990 President, Arthur W. Barrett, the 98th individual to be elected to that position, is continuing to promote the patriotic, historical, and educational objectives of the society.

Carl H. Lamb, Historian

DR. JAMES L.
COGSWELL
1875
Founder

GEN. ALBERT M.
WINN
1876
Honorary Past
President General

ADOLPHUS S.
HUBBARD
1886
Honorary Past
President General

HOWARD C.
ROWLEY
1929
Past President
General

HAROLD L.
PUTNAM
1950
Honorary Past
President General

CALVIN E.
CHUNN
1978
Past President
General

A treaty was signed by the United States and Panama to turn over the Panama Canal to Panama on December 31, 1999.

Fifty United States personnel were held hostage in the U.S. Embassy in Iran.

An economic recession was fueled by double-digit inflation and a 20% interest rate, the highest in history.

At the end of this decade the population was 226,500,000, an increase of 11% in the previous ten years.

In 1970 SAR membership was 19,595 and the Permanent Fund assets were $100,887; fifteen United States Senators and 24 Congressmen were SARS.

Mrs. Carlton L. Wench of the Conahunta Chapter DAR, presented the personal papers of her grandfather, first SAR President General Lucius L. Deming, to the SAR.

The Pittsburgh Chapter of the Pennsylvania Society dedicated the last of six buildings in the Gateway Center project. Each of the buildings has a bronze plaque honoring a Revolutionary War hero.

The new Martha Washington Medal was approved to be presented to any lady who rendered service to the SAR.

Former Chaplain General, Dr. Mott R. Sawyers of the Minnesota Society, attended the 80th Annual Congress in Houston. He celebrated his 100th birthday on July 5, 1970.

Col. Charles M. Duke, USAF, a member of the South Carolina Society, became the first SAR to walk upon the moon. A graduate of the United States Naval Academy, he was an Astronaut on the 1972 mission of Apollo 16.

President General James Gardiner, with President General Seimes of the DAR, participated in Memorial Day services at the grave of General Marquis de Lafayette in Picpus Cemetery, Paris. Comte Rene de Chambrun entertained both Presidents General at Chateau de la Grange, home of Lafayette.

A Bylaw Amendment established the annual per capita dues at $6.

The Raleigh Chapter of the North Carolina Society initiated a program which was later followed by other SAR Chapters and Societies to promote the ringing of church bells at noon on Independence Day.

Compatriot U.S. Congressman Charles E. Bennett of the Jacksonville Chapter, Florida Society completed 20 years in the Congress. During this time, he had not missed any vote in the House of Representatives. In the 20 years he cast 2,467 votes.

SAR TOUR TO EUROPE

The SAR sponsored a month tour of Europe with visits to England, France, Switzerland and Spain. The cost was $815 per person, including transportation, room and meals. Colorful receptions were given by high officials of these countries for the visiting Compatriots and their guests.

Compatriot Howard L. Alcorn became Chief Justice of the Connecticut Supreme Court. The two previous Chief Justices of the Court were members of the SAR: John H. King and Raymond Baldwin.

Chief Warrant Officer Dennis James Brault of the New Hampshire Society was killed in Vietnam in June 1971.

On September 8, 1971 at the Army and Navy Club in Washington President Donald Hays of the DC Society presented SAR Membership Certificate #100,000 to Compatriot C. Tower French.

The New York Chapter unveiled a bronze plaque on the 160 Water Street skyscraper at the site of Revolutionary War spy Hercules Mulligan's home. He passed vital information to General Washington during the British occupation of the city. Compatriot William Mulligan unveiled the plaque honoring his ancestor.

The Lower Cape Fear Chapter of the North Carolina Society unveiled an SAR marker at the grave of Lieutenant William Green in St. James Episcopal Church graveyard, Wilmington.

The Gen. Arthur St. Clair Chapter of the Pennsylvania Society placed a marker at the grave of Corporal Johnann Martin Froelich, who served with the Northampton County Militia. Compatriot W. Branthoover of Fairport, Ohio, a descendant, unveiled the marker.

Governor Robert Scott of North Carolina became a member of the SAR.

Compatriot Colonel Charles M. Duke, an astronaut of the Apollo 16 mission on which he walked on the moon, became a member of the South Carolina Society.

Compatriot Maurice H. Thatcher, former Governor and U.S. Congressman of Kentucky, reached the age of 101.

The SAR "How They Vote" program was initiated and highlighted how U.S. Senators and Congressmen voted on particular issues. Letters were encouraged to legislators asking for explanations of their vote.

Compatriot Roger C. B. Morton, Secretary of the Interior, dedicated historic Federal Hall in New York City. This is the site where President Washington took the oath of office.

President General Ryall Morgan presented the Charter to the newly organized Society in Switzerland at a banquet in Bern on June 9th. Ambassador Shelby C. Davis was the Organizing President. The banquet was sponsored by the Society in France.

STATE PRESIDENTS GROUP FORMED

The Council of State Presidents was organized as a forum for incumbent and former State Society Presidents to exchange ideas for performing their duties and to increase membership.

On Independence Day 1972 the Connecticut Society conducted memorial services honoring the memory of Thomas Lynch, Jr., the youngest Signer of the Declaration, who was lost at sea. The Coast Guard Cutter "Redwood" drifted as a wreath was cast on the waters on Long Island Sound. An Honor Guard of the Governor's Foot Guard fired a volley followed by "Taps."

On January 9, 1973 the Illinois Society hosted a reception honoring 100 new American naturalized citizens in the U.S. District Court in Chicago.

Compatriot Captain Leslie L. Bucklew, a Spanish-American War veteran of the San Diego Chapter, reproduced and distributed thousands of prints of the famous painting, "The Spirit of '76" to school children and organizations.

In 1973 Mrs. Virginia Kagy, Executive Assistant at the SAR National Headquarters, retired after 42 years of dedicated service to the National Society.

The remains of Colonel William Few, Signer of the Constitution for the State of Georgia, were reinterred from a vandalized tomb at Bacon, New York to Augusta, Georgia. Governor Jimmy Carter of Georgia gave credit to the Stony Point Chapter of the Empire State

The Switzerland Society was chartered on June 1, 1973 during a gala ceremony in Bern, Switzerland. Some of the dignitaries present were (from left): Former President General Horace Y. Kitchell, Society President Shelby C. Davis (then U.S. Ambassador to Switzerland), President General Ryall S. Morgan, Secretary General M. Graham Clark and FPG Len Young Smith.

Society for the arrangements that made the reinterment possible. At the personal invitation of the Governor, former Presidents of the Empire State Society Dr. Albert W. Munso, J. Moreau Brown and Harry Schanck were honored guests at the ceremonies in Augusta.

President Gerald Ford joined the SAR with the National Number of 105,000.

Compatriot Ralph A. Beck of the New Jersey Society was elected President of the Prudential Insurance Company of America.

The Annual Banquet of the Stony Point Chapter of the Empire State Society was held at the magnificent Ivy Manor and attended by 200 members and guests. Former Postmaster General Jame A. Farley was the guest of honor and charmed the assemblage with his wit. He recalled that he resigned his cabinet position when President Roosevelt insisted on running for a third term.

Ceremonies were held at Cheshire, Massachusetts, for the transfer of the Stafford Hill Memorial by the Massachusetts Society to the town of Cheshire. The Memorial, a replica of the Old Mill in Newport, Rhode Island, was built in 1927 to mark the grave of Colonel Joab Stafford of the Massachusetts Militia and to honor the Bershire County men he led in the Battle of Bennington.

The Admiral George Browne Chapter of the Empire State Society unveiled a bronze marker at the Saratoga Battlefield with over 300 Compatriots and guests at the ceremonies.

The Indiana Society placed bronze markers on the graves of two Revolutionary War Patriots buried in Adams County: Captain George Emery and Private Thomas Archibold of the Pennsylvania Militia.

The Montclair Chapter of the New Jersey Society cleared, seeded and generally improved the condition of the town's 1690 cemetery as a Bicentennial project.

The Thomas Jefferson Chapter of the Virginia Society celebrated Jefferson's Birthday on April 13, 1975 at the Farmington Country Club in Charlottesville, with 150 attending. Professor Dumas Malone, the University of Virginia Biographer-in-Residence, Pulitzer Prize Winner, spoke on the life of Jefferson.

NOMINATING COMMITTEE AUTHORIZED

A National Nominating Committee was approved by Bylaws additions at the 85th SAR Annual Congress to provide a slate of candidates for the General Offices of the National Society.

The seven sons of Mrs. Paul B. Evans of the New Hampshire State Society DAR became members of the SAR.

The Minute Man Monument in Elizabeth, New Jersey, was damaged in a traffic mishap. The Elizabethtown Chapter SAR raised funds to reset, landscape and provide a traffic barrier for the statue. The location is where the local militia surprised the Hessians.

The Buffalo Chapter of the Empire State Society sponsored a "Bunker Hill Day" program in the Forest Lawn Cemetery with a rededication of the Bunker Hill Battle Monument erected in 1875. The monument was built by Compatriot Elbridge Spaulding, Organizing President of the Buffalo Chapter, to honor the nine Spaulding Family members who fought at Bunker Hill. An SAR grave marker was placed on the gravesite of Captain Levi Spaulding, who fought in the battle.

The Rochester Chapter of the Empire State Society honored the fourth last survivor of the Revolutionary War by placing an SAR marker on the grave of Lemuel Cook who died in 1866 at the age of 107. The marker was unveiled by Compatriot Henry R. Emerson, third generation grandson of the Revolutionary War soldier.

The admission fee for new members was increased to $25.

On George Washington's Birthday 1976 the Elizabethtown Chapter of the New Jersey Society held a ceremony honoring the 100 Revolutionary War soldiers buried in Elizabethtown's First Presbyterian Church graveyard.

Six-hundred Compatriots and guests attended the New York Chapter's 41st Colonial Ball at the Hotel Plaza in New York City. Twenty-five debutantes including Miss Tawney Godin, reigning Miss America, were presented. All the young ladies traced their lineage back to a Revolutionary War Patriot. The Colonial Fife and Drum Corps presented the Colors and executed drill maneuvers.

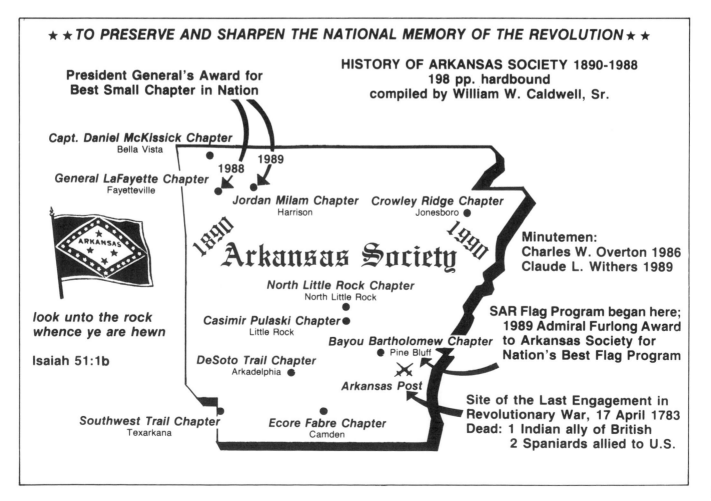

★★ *TO PRESERVE AND SHARPEN THE NATIONAL MEMORY OF THE REVOLUTION* ★★

President General's Award for Best Small Chapter in Nation

HISTORY OF ARKANSAS SOCIETY 1890-1988
198 pp. hardbound
compiled by William W. Caldwell, Sr.

Capt. Daniel McKissick Chapter
Bella Vista

1988   1989

General LaFayette Chapter
Fayetteville

Jordan Milam Chapter
Harrison

Crowley Ridge Chapter
Jonesboro

1890   Arkansas Society   1990

Minutemen:
Charles W. Overton 1986
Claude L. Withers 1989

North Little Rock Chapter
North Little Rock

look unto the rock whence ye are hewn

Casimir Pulaski Chapter
Little Rock

Bayou Bartholomew Chapter
Pine Bluff

SAR Flag Program began here; 1989 Admiral Furlong Award to Arkansas Society for Nation's Best Flag Program

Isaiah 51:1b

DeSoto Trail Chapter
Arkadelphia

Arkansas Post

Site of the Last Engagement in Revolutionary War, 17 April 1783 Dead: 1 Indian ally of British 2 Spaniards allied to U.S.

Southwest Trail Chapter
Texarkana

Ecore Fabre Chapter
Camden

In June of 1975 the Bunker Hill Monument in Buffalo, New York was rededicated in a special SAR ceremony. The structure was erected in 1875 by Elbridge Spaulding, later to become the first President of the Buffalo Chapter; had nine Patriot ancestors who fought at Bunker Hill during the Revolutionary War.

The 86th SAR Annual Congress meeting in Philadelphia authorized the sale of the Massachusetts Avenue National Headquarters. This decision was influenced by the high operating costs in the nation's capitol. A special committee was appointed to investigate properties for the relocation of the National Headquarters.

The Liberty Bell Tour was a Bicentennial project of the National Society. A replica of the Liberty Bell was procured and placed on a special trailer. Former Chaplain General, Reverend Joseph Head of the Minnesota Society, made a tour of 28 states giving the history of the bell, stories on American history and appealing patriotic messages. Compatriot Head appeared in the uniform of a Revolutionary War soldier. Each of the school children was permitted to ring the bell. There was extensive media coverage on the SAR in the local press of the communities visited.

The Binghampton Chapter, Empire State Society, dedicated a memorial plaque to the 400 Revolutionary War soldiers who served from Broome County at the Broome County Community College.

The Huntington Chapter of the Empire State Society placed 80 Huntington Liberty Flags on the graves of the Revolutionary War soldiers buried in the town cemetery. The flag was designed on the Village Green on July 22, 1776 when word of the Declaration reached Huntington. The Flag flew at the Battle of Long Island and was captured by the Hessians.

JULY FOURTH PROGRAMS VARIED

On Independence Day 1976 there were ceremonies conducted by the SAR throughout the country:

• The Maryland Society conducted programs at the graves of Maryland's four Signers: Samuel Chase in Old St. Paul Cemetery in Baltimore; Charles Carroll buried beneath the altar of the chapel of his home, Doughoregan Manor, Howard County; William Paca at the Wye Plantation in Queen Anne's County; and Thomas Stone at Haber de Venture, Charles County.

• The New York Chapter held a Bicentennial program at the Odell House owned by the Chapter. Odell House was the headquarters of Comte Rochambeau where he and General Washington planned the southern campaign of 1781. The French Ambassador presented a life size bust of Rochambeau as a gift from the French people. Compatriot Lowell Thomas was the speaker. The West Point Band furnished the music.

• The North Carolina Society unveiled a gift to the State of North Carolina, a bronze plaque commemorating the four Revolutionary War State Governors. The large memorial plaque is located on a wall of the Rotunda of the North Carolina Capitol.

• The Continental Congress Chapter of the Pennsylvania Society conducted an Independence Day program at the grave of Philip Livingston, Signer, buried in York. Compatriot Philip L. Strong, descendant of the Signer, spoke on his ancestor.

• The Texas Society conducted Bicentennial exercises at the historic Alamo by unveiling a plaque with the names of the 46 Revolutionary War soldiers buried in Texas. The name of each was read and the Alamo Chapel bell struck a single note with the reading of each name.

A "Patriots Plaque" with the names of the 46 Revolutionary War soldiers buried in Texas was placed in the Rotunda of the Texas State Capitol by the Texas Society.

The Empire State Society Bicentennial highlight was "Daniel Bakeman Day" on August 7th at Freedom, New York. Daniel Bakeman, the last surviving soldier of the Revolution, born in 1760, died in 1869 at the age of 109. Services were conducted with U.S. Congressman and Compatriot Jack Kemp as the speaker. Compatriot Alton, third generation grandson of the Revolutionary War soldier, placed an SAR marker on the grave.

The Maryland Society conducted Bicentennial ceremonies at the Revolutionary War Monument in Mount Royal Plaza in Baltimore before a large attendance. Assistant Secretary Vessey spoke on events of the Revolutionary War. The Second Army Band supplied the music.

FUTURE VICE PRESIDENT BECOMES SAR

Congressman J. Danforth Quayle of Indiana, later to become the Vice President of the United States, joined the SAR.

On March 17, 1977 the SAR National Headquarters on Massachusetts Avenue in Washington was sold to the Ivory Coast Government for use as their Embassy. It was purchased for $800,000. Executive Secretary Warren Woodward resigned his position due to the change of operations. Compatriot Lieutenant General Nickerson, USMC (Ret), was appointed Executive Secretary. Temporary National Headquarters of 4,700 square feet was leased in the Huntington Building in Alexandria, Virginia.

On July 4, 1977 the Connecticut Society conducted Independence Day ceremonies in New Haven's Grove Street Cemetery by placing wreaths on the grave of Declaration Signer Roger Sherman and Revolutionary War General David Humphreys. Participating in the ceremonies was the 2nd Company of the Governor's Foot Guard, organized in 1775 and originally commanded by Benedict Arnold.

The Colonel Jeremiah Wadsworth Branch of the Connecticut Society placed a bronze plaque on the grave of Jeremiah Wadsworth located in the Old Burying Ground at the Center Church on Main Street, Hartford, in recognition of his service as Commissary General of the Continental Army.

On September 3 the South Carolina Society sponsored its Annual Colonial Ball at the Carolina Inn in Columbia with 18 debutantes being presented, all descendants of Revolutionary War Patriots. A Guard from the Citadel presented the Colors. Each debutante carried a nosegay in SAR Colors.

On September 3, the Vermont Society placed a Bicentennial monument on a boulder on the Green of North Pawlett School. The plaque commemorated the encampment of 2,500 Continental troops under the command of General Lincoln, where the attack on Fort Ticonderoga was launched ultimately leading to the defeat of General Burgoyne at Saratoga.

Compatriot Harry "Bing" Crosby, noted entertainment personality, died on October 14, 1977. He was a descendant of Private Chillingsworth Foster of the Massachusetts Militia. He was a member of the Washington State Society.

The Maine Society has been faithfully placing SAR grave markers on the graves of Revolutionary War soldiers. By 1978 the Society had placed over 1,500 markers.

On Veterans Day, November 11, 1977, the Massachusetts Society placed American Flags on the graves of four Black Revolutionary War soldiers at the Parting Way Cemetery: Cato Howe, Plato Turner, Prince Goodwin and Quamamy. The Massachusetts Color Guard participated in the ceremony.

The Rochester Chapter of the Empire State Society placed an SAR marker at the grave of Colonel Nathaniel Rochester, founder of the city that bears his name. He had a distinguished career as a Revolutionary War officer.

Two-hundred Compatriots and guests attended the exercises at

THE OHIO SOCIETY

CONGRATULATES
the
NATIONAL SOCIETY
SONS OF THE AMERICAN REVOLUTION
1889 - 1989

On April 10, 1889 a call was issued by the New Jersey Sons of the Revolution for a delegate convention to be held at Frances Tavern in New York City on April 30, 1889 for the formation of a National Society. After a two day session, the National Society, Sons of the American Revolution came into being with eighteen State Societies.

Noting the New Jersey call, the Rev. W. R. Parsons of Worthington, Ohio entered into correspondence with the New Jersey Society. The result a preliminary meeting of interested Ohio citizens was held in the office of Governor Foraker on April 11, 1889. Eleven days later, at a second meeting, Rev. W. R. Parsons was elected the first president of the Ohio Society. Others elected were treasurer, Henry A. Williams and secretary, A. A. Graham. Thus the organization of the Ohio Society on April 22 antedated that of the National Society.

After the convention in New York City, another meeting of the Ohio Society was held on June 4, 1889 at which a constitution was adopted admitting both men and women to membership. All who were present at this meeting were recognized as charter members.

The new National Society looked with disfavor on the Ohio constitution admitting both men and women and ruled that only male descendants of participants in the Revolution would be admitted to membership. As a result, soon after in 1890, there was formed the Daughters of the American Revolution with Mrs. Benjamin Harrison, wife of then President of the United States, as its first President General.

The Ohio Society is proud of the Douglass G. High Historical Oration Contest which originated in Cincinnati Chapter in 1947, then statewide and became National in 1949.

Past Presidents General

James M. Richardson
Loren Edmunds Souers
Charles A. Jones
Charles A. Anderson, MD
Eugene C. McGuire
Nolan W. Carson

Minute Man Awardees

Douglass G. High	Samuel Hubbard Scott
L. F. Ridgeway	Charles A. Anderson
Clarence E. Shriner	Samuel K. Houston
Edward M. Hall	J. Boyd Davis
Loren E. Souers	Eugene G. McGuire
Charles A. Jones	Samuel J. Holt
Warren M. Taylor	Nolan W. Carson

OHIO CHAPTERS

Western Reserve - Cleveland	Constitution - Mansfield
Cincinnati - Cincinnati	Ewings - Athens-Pomeroy
Benjamin Franklin - Columbus	Northeastern - Ashtabula
Nathan Hale - Youngstown	Ethan Allen - Warren
Richard Montgomery - Dayton	Firelands-Bicentennial - Lorain
John Stark - Canton	Samuel Huntington - Fairport Harbor
Lafayette - Akron	Coshocton - Coshocton
George Rogers Clark - Springfield	Rufus Putman - Zanesville
Arthur St. Clair - Chillicothe	

the Brunswick Town State Historical Park sponsored by the North Carolina Society. The program honored the memory of General and later Governor Benjamin Smith by marking his grave with a large bronze plaque.

The George Washington Chapter of the Virginia Society sponsored a 10-foot by 15-foot "KEEP USA FIRST" billboard on U.S. Highway #1 south of Alexandria. The Maryland Society sponsored a similar billboard on the Baltimore-Washington Parkway at the entrance to the City of Baltimore.

Dr. Milton Eisenhower, noted educator and statesman, became a member of the Kansas Society.

Compatriot John Minnick of the Virginia Society promoted the George Mason stamp through the SAR Stamp Committee which was adopted by the U.S. Postal Service.

Compatriot Winston C. Williams of the Wisconsin Society was chosen as Editor of *The SAR Magazine.*

NEW COMMISSION SEEKS HEADQUARTERS

The 88th Annual Congress approved the National Headquarters Acquisition Commission to acquire a property to serve as a National Headquarters.

The Connecticut Society dedicated a plaque on Flag Day, June 14, 1977, marking the site where Greenwich men were mustered into the Continental Army in 1775.

The Arkansas Society SAR and the DAR co-sponsored marking the grave of Revolutionary War soldier Asher Bagley. The grave is located in the Old Union Cemetery in Saline County. Bagley, born in 1751, was a private in the New Jersey Militia, and was given Arkansas land for his military service.

On July 4, 1978 the Indiana Society dedicated grave markers of two Revolutionary War soldiers in the Coltrin Cemetery located northeast of Terre Haute. William Coltrin and his son, John, served in the Connecticut Militia.

On July 4th, the Maryland Society sponsored services at Old St. Paul's Cemetery in Baltimore. A wreath was placed at the grave of Declaration Signer, Samuel Chase, with a musket volley salute. A bronze plaque was dedicated at the tomb of Colonel John Eager Howard, hero of the Battle of Cowpens. A new wrought iron fence was erected at the tomb by the Society. Dr. John Eager Howard placed a wreath on the tomb of his famous ancestor.

The Massachusetts Society marked two Revolutionary War graves on the Fourth of July before a large attendance. In West Abington an SAR marker was placed on the grave of Abington Minuteman Joseph Richards in a hayfield. In the St. Mary's Episcopal Church graveyard the grave of Zibeon Hooker, First Lieutenant of the Massachusetts Militia, was marked.

The Mississippi Society held a grave marking at the grave of Revolutionary War Captain William Causey of the Maryland Militia. The family graveyard is on the family home site in Berwick.

The Empire State Society placed a grave marker on the grave of Private Isaiah Booth of the Connecticut Militia, in Old Welch Churchyard, Nelson, New York.

The New Jersey Society owned a small plot of land in the Monmouth Battlefield Park. It was the spot where General Washington met General Lee in retreat and turned defeat into victory when the British retreated from the battlefield. The Society deeded the land to the State of New Jersey, and it became a part of the Battlefield Park.

Ceremonies were held in Fremont, Ohio, to dedicate a memorial monument at the graves of James and Elizabeth Whitaker. The Whitakers established the first home of white settlers in Ohio in 1782. However, the Indians later gave them this land.

HEADQUARTERS BUILDING PURCHASED

On December 12, 1978, the SAR purchased the Masonic Grand Lodge of Kentucky building in Louisville for $404,000 to serve as its National Headquarters. The structure contains 14,000 square feet of floor space and was completed in 1954.

Colonel Ralph H. Goodell of the Kansas Society was appointed Executive Secretary of the National Society.

The National Headquarters was formally dedicated on Saturday, February 4, 1979 with Mayor Stansbury of Louisville and U.S. Congressman Ramano Mazzoli participating in the program. The SAR employed Ms. Christine Schultz as the SAR Archivist to organize and index the history records of the Society. Compatriots and friends of the Society donated funds to provide the necessary colonial-style tables and chairs for use in the Society Library.

William Joseph Moore, 107-year-old Spanish-American War veteran, joined the Arkansas Society. His ancestor, Thomas Atchley, served in both the New Jersey and the Virginia Militias.

The Oregon Society sponsored an unusual Bicentennial project. Former State President Compatriot Mark Farris prepared and produced "Vignettes of America" program tapes for the blind. The topics included stories ranging from the Liberty Bell and Cornwallis's Surrender to the Declaration of Independence. The cassettes were circulated by the National Federation of the Blind.

The Mississippi Society placed a marker on the grave of Samuel Emory Davis, Revolutionary War officer and father of Jefferson Davis. The grave is located on the grounds of "Beauvoir."

Vice Admiral James B. Stockdale retired after 36 years in the U.S. Navy and became President of the Citadel. He and his cousin, Robert H. Dunlap, were members of the General Henry Knox Chapter of the Illinois Society. Both Compatriots were recipients of the Congressional Medal of Honor.

The 1979 Fall Trustees Meeting was held on October 20th at the Hotel Fort Des Moines, Des Moines, Iowa, with a record attendance.

The Decade closed with an SAR membership of 20,895. The assets of the Permanent Fund were $666,384.

When the National Trustees met in February, 1979, our Society's new Headquarters was dedicated in a colorful ceremony held on the outside. Raising the flag was President General Calvin E. Chunn.

1980–1990: The Final Decade

In the national election of 1980 Ronald Reagan was elected 40th President. The 52 American hostages held in Iran were released. Two hundred and forty-one U.S. Marines were killed when terrorists blew up the Marine Headquarters at the Beirut Airport, Lebanon. Marines and Army Rangers invaded Grenada in the West Indies to evacuate American citizens. Congress passed the Gramm-Rudman Bill to reduce the hugh federal deficit as a means to achieve a balanced federal budget. The space shuttle "Challenger" exploded immediately after liftoff, killing all six astronauts on board. American warplanes struck Libya as a retaliation against Libyan terrorists bombing a West Berlin disco, resulting in the death of American servicemen. William Rehnquist was appointed Chief Justice of the Supreme Court. President Reagan and Soviet leader Gorbachev signed an agreement calling for the dismantling of certain types of missiles. Near the very end of the decade, the vast empire of Communist nations saw intensive revolts against repressive regimes and a turn toward some form of democracy.

There were many anniversary celebrations: Surrender at Yorktown, Signing of the Treaty of Paris, Centennial of the Statue of Liberty, Signing of the Constitution.

A new one-sheet membership application form was adopted, and National Society annual dues were increased from $6 to $8. A looseleaf SAR Handbook with useful procedural information was made available to members.

Compatriot John Minnick, with the support of the George Mason Chapter of the Virginia Society, promoted a postage stamp honoring Revolutionary War Patriot George Mason for his work on the Constitution and the Bill of Rights.

The John Paul Jones Chapter of the Maryland Society promoted a First Day postal cancellation of the John Paul Jones stamp, with proceeds going for the restoration of the John Paul Jones home in Scotland where he was born.

Compatriot John C. Davis was employed as the Executive Secretary of the National Society.

Compatriots Lewis Decker and his son, Randolph Decker, presented a dramatic program on the life and bravery of the average Revolutionary militiaman to the New York Legislature and to many New York schools.

The hostages from Iran were honored by many of the State Societies. The Indiana Society honored Frederick Kupke of Rensselaer and Donald Sharer of Plainfield. The Virginia Society honored Philip Ward.

The National Society designed a special Certificate for presentation to Eagle Scouts together with the Bronze Good Citizenship Medal.

The Fall 1981 National Trustees meeting was held at Williamsburg, Virginia, coinciding with the Bicentennial of the 200th anniversary of the British defeat at Yorktown. There were reenactments of the Yorktown Battle, parades, religious services and wreath laying ceremonies. There were speeches by British

A Brief History of the West Virginia Society of the Sons of the American Revolution

The State of West Virginia was represented at the formation of The National Society of the Sons of the American Revolution in New York City, on April 30, 1889. According to the list of the General Officers published in the National Register of the Society, John J. Jacob was elected Vice-President General representing the state. A subsequent publication of the Society, giving the list of the State Societies, also listed the date of the organization and the officers elected since May 1, 1890. Included therein was the West Virginia Society, organized January 31, 1890 and listed as its officers were: John J. Jacobs, President; George L. Cranmer, Secretary and Registrar; and Robert White, Treasurer. All of these gentlemen were residents of Wheeling, WV. A later list of officers as of July 4, 1891 stated that there were 15 members.

It therefore appears that although citizens participated in the formation of the National Society in 1889 and the State Society in 1891, our State organization was not enduring since there is no evidence that there was any activity in our state for a period of 36 years.

In 1926, through the diligent work and direction of President General Wilbert H. Barrett of

Michigan, a group of men began the task of locating a sufficient number of eligible applicants to organize the West Virginia Society. In early 1927 seven men from West Virginia had qualified and had been admitted to membership. Those seven men were Benjamin Burns, Dabney Caldwell, Jackson Rathbone, Frank Williams, John Giger, William Le Sage and John Ford. The first Chapters organized under the authority granted were George Rogers Clark, Clarksburg, WV and General Andrew Lewis, Huntington, WV. Today we include Daniel Boone, Charleston, WV; James Neal, Parkersburg, WV; General Adam Stephen, Martinsburg, WV; Fort Henry, Wheeling, WV and Greenbrier Valley, Lewisburg, WV.

In the late 1940's the 57th Annual Congress was held at Huntington, WV at which we served as host for the National Society. The Honorable A. Herbert Forman of Virginia was elected President General and at a banquet held in his honor, Colonel Lewis A. Johnson, later Secretary of Defense, served as toastmaster. It is here noted that the largest number of delegates were registered at Huntington than at any other Congress held before 1947.

S.A.R. Society in France

It is in Paris, in the cimetery of Picpus, that the French S.A.R. Society in France has its symbolical origins. There, on July 4th 1834, the American ambassador in France, Livingstone, accompanied by some officials, came to unfurl the American banner over general La Fayette's grave in the presence of the three children of the French hero of the War of Independence. Since then, the colours have been raised on July 4, every year, to commemorate the friendship between the French and the Americans that originated in the French participation in the War of Independence.

That participation had officially begun on February 8th 1778, with treaties of commerce and alliance signed by the Insurgents' envoy, B. Franklin, and King Louis XVI. It was for France a way of admitting the Declaration of Independence de facto and then, its military involvment in the conflict which opposed the British with the Americans, would soon become ineluctable. Even at that time, some young French aristocrats had stood as volunteers to defend the cause against the British. The most prominent among them was the Marquis de La Fayette. Three months after the treaties had been signed, the fleet of Admiral d'Estaing was sailing off to America. In February 1780, an expeditionary force of 6.000 men was sent to America under the Comte de Rochambeau. They were followed by Admiral de Grasse's squadron on March 21th 1781. From 1777 to 1783, several thousand French men shed their blood in the New World, and in addition the French participation cost a lot of money and entailed the budget of Kingdom of France.

As early as its origin, the S.A.R. National Society declared that : "the descendants of the French men who had fought for the Independence of the States could gather and create, in France, sections offically acknowledged by the Society". At first there was only one section gathering the Americans who had settled in France. They organized the ceremony at Picpus, without any French men. After World War I, the section improved notably under the influence of one S.A.R. in France, Edward H. de Neveu, and Ambassador Myrron T. Herrick, a great support of the Franco-American friendship. They both devoted their energy to make the French join them. Thanks to their efforts, some descendnats of the French officers who had fought in America were able to join the Americans and a committee was created. On October 19th 1926, that committee was empowered by the National Society to form an independent State Society in France, and on February 4th 1927, the statutes of the new Society were voted. The French S.A.R. Society was born, and remarkably enough, it was the only non-American Society. It admitted to it, and still does, "the descendants of all those who served the cause of American Independence or proved to be effectively sympathetic towards it".

Since 1926, the French Society has kept growing. Only a few members strong when it constituted, it now numbers about 350 fellows, most of them French, and thus ranks, on account of its growing importance, within the first twenty federal Societies. In France, it has numerous activities, with two climaxes every year : first on July 4th, with the annual celebration on La Fayette's grave at Picpus, then a banquet where numerous French and American officials meet. And the Society also takes part in many festivals. Thus it tries and answers its purpose which is more especially, "to keep up the ties of friendship which united both French and American peoples when the American Nation was born".

Olivier de Luppé

and French dignitaries, including President Reagan and President Francois Mitterand of France. Forty-four members of the France Society attended and carried a French Flag which had been carried by French troops during the siege at Yorktown.

Scores of SARs gathered at Yorktown in October, 1981 to celebrate the 200th anniversary of the end of the Revolutionary War.

The Massachusetts Society marked the grave of Patriot Samuel Sawin in the famous Mount Auburn Cemetery in Cambridge. He participated in the Battle of Lexington and Concord.

Compatriot Harry L. Jeter of the Oklahoma Society sponsored all his male descendants, two sons and six grandsons, for membership in the SAR.

The Virginia Society sponsored a memorial service at the grave of President James Monroe in the Hollywood Cemetery in Richmond, commemorating his 223rd birthday.

SCHOLARSHIPS FOR EAGLE SCOUTS LAUNCHED

The SAR initiated a program to salute Eagle Scouts, with a top Eagle Scout being selected from the State Society. One Eagle Scout was selected from the State Societies winners and awarded a scholarship from the National Society.

The Oregon Society located and placed a grave stone and SAR marker on the grave of "Real Son" Daniel Simmons in Portland's River View Cemetery.

The New Mexico Society sponsored a booth with SAR information and exhibits at the New Mexico State Fair.

Three Compatriots participated in the ground breaking ceremony of the Vietnam Veterans Memorial in Washington: Senator John W. Warner of Virginia, Virginia Governor Charles Robb and Virginia Society President Thomas Burch.

On July 4, 1982 the Huntington Chapter of the Empire State Society placed Betsy Ross Flags on the 100 Revolutionary War Patriots graves in the towns of Huntington, Babylon and Brookhaven.

An organizational meeting of the United Kingdom Society was held in November 1981. On April 8, 1982 President General Richard Thompson presented the Charter to UK Society President Richard Sherman in London. The ceremony was televised by the British Broadcasting System.

Three-hundred Compatriots and guests attended the South Carolina Society's Sixth Colonial Ball at the Carolina Inn in Columbia, with 25 debutantes being presented.

The Mississippi Society placed and dedicated memorial plaques at the Kemper County Court House and the Winston County Courthouse listing the names of the Revolutionary War soldiers buried in each county.

The Virginia Society dedicated a large granite monument at Valley Forge National Park in Pennsylvania to the memory of the Virginia soldiers who served under General Washington in the miserable winter of 1777-1778.

In 1983, despite the worst snowstorm in many years, the New York Chapter held its Annual Colonial Debutante Ball in the Grand Ballroom of the Hotel Pierre. Twelve debutantes were presented to the 250 Compatriots and guests.

The Caloosa Chapter of the Florida Society furnished framed copies of the Declaration of Independence and the Bill of Rights to every high school in Florida's Lee County.

TREATY OF PARIS COMMEMORATED

In September 1983, 170 Compatriots and their guests traveled to Paris to participate in the 200th anniversary of the Signing of the Treaty of Paris. One thousand Americans in recreated Revolutionary War units participated in the ceremonies. There was an SAR ceremony at Picpus Cemetery, where Marquis de Lafayette and his wife are buried.

The SAR members visited the Hotel d'York where the Treaty of Paris was signed. There was a Special SAR Congress and luncheon held at the Hotel Intercontinental. A religious service was held in Notre Dame Cathedral with a mass celebrated by Cardinal Lustger, Catholic Primate of France. A reception followed at the Hotel de Ville, Paris's City Hall, given by Mayor Jacques Chirac.

A dinner was held at the Hotel Trianon Palace and concluded with a historical pageant and a brilliant fountain and fireworks display.

On September 3, the anniversary of the actual signing of the Treaty, there was a gigantic military parade up the famed Champs Elysses to the Arch de Triumphe in Paris. The SAR contingent was the first and largest of the patriotic units, with 96 marchers led by the Massachusetts and Maryland Societies Color Guards. The youngest marcher was six-year-old CAR member, Clarke Bessent. President General Hayes placed a wreath on the tomb of the Unknown Soldier of France.

The Massachusetts Society Continental Color Guard proudly marched at Versailles during the Treaty of Paris commemoration.

The Special Congress concluded with a reception given by U.S. Ambassador Evan Galbraith at the United States Embassy. Many Compatriots toured England following the Paris ceremonies and enjoyed a reception at the London residence of the Minister of the United States, Edward Streator.

From contributions by Compatriots the Eagle Scout Scholarship Foundation reached $50,000.

The Ocala Chapter of the Forida Society placed 100 six-by-eight-foot casket American Flags along the driveways of Woodlawn Cemetery on Memorial Day, Flag Day and the Fourth of July.

Compatriot Leo Leavers of the Buffalo Chapter, Empire State Society, launched a project to restore the graves of a number of Presidents of the United States. The grave of William Howard Taft in Arlington National Cemetery, James Madison at Montpellier Station, Virginia and Grover Cleveland needed restoration.

Annually State Societies conducted Fourth of July ceremonies at the graves of Signers of the Declaration of Independence: The Connecticut Society at the grave of Governor Oliver Wolcott and William Williams; the Delaware Society at the grave of Caesar Rodney; the District of Columbia at the grave of Elbridge Gerry; the Virginia Society at the grave of Benjamin Harrison; and the Maryland Society at the graves of Samuel Chase and William Paca.

The Alabama Society unveiled a new stone at the grave of Revolutionary War soldier, James Butler, at the James-Bailey Cemetery in Shelby County.

The Maryland Society restored its 60-foot-high, 200-ton Revolutionary War Monument in Mount Royal Plaza in Baltimore City and conducted rededication ceremonies.

HEADQUARTERS GAINS FLAG POLES

Two new 30-foot flag poles at the Fourth Street entrance to the National Headquarters were given by former Presidents General Charles Anderson and Eugene McGuire.

On January 14, 1984 on the 200th Anniversary of the Ratification of the Treaty of Paris by the Continental Congress the Maryland Society sponsored ceremonies at Annapolis, Maryland, with French Ambassador Bernard Vernier-Palliez attending.

Former President General Arthur M. King funded a 40-foot by 17-foot addition to the National Headquarters, thereby giving 360 additional square feet for office and library space.

The New Hampshire Society discovered and marked the grave of Reuben Kendall, a Black Revolutionary War soldier, in the Friends' burying-ground in Richmond, New Hampshire.

The SAR joined with other concerned patriotic organizations to successfully lobby the United States Congress to allocate funds to purchase additional land for the Saratoga Battlefield National Park.

On August 19, 1984 the Kentucky Society conducted wreath laying ceremonies at the granite shaft monument of Blue Licks State Park, near Maysville, where 60 Kentuckians died fighting 300 Canadian Rangers in the Battle of Blue Licks.

The Calcasieu Chapter of the Louisiana Society placed 70 casket-size American Flags on the driveways of Orange Grove Cemetery on Memorial Day, Flag Day and Independence Day.

The Missouri Society located the grave of Thomas Terrel, a soldier who served in the South Carolina Militia, in the Macedonia Cemetery, Newton County. A dedication ceremony was held on November 11, 1984 with 300 Compatriots and guests attending.

For the first time since the Post Office Department had issued stamps, it discontinued printing one depicting George Washington. Through the efforts of the SAR a new George Washington stamp was designed and unveiled by President General Carl F. Bessent. Later, President General Benjamin H. Morris was the speaker at the First Day cancellation ceremony for the new stamp.

NEW SAR HISTORY RELEASED

A Second Edition of THE SAR HISTORY was published in 1985.

In 1984 Compatriot George F. Roberts of the Oregon Society sponsored the membership applications of his seven sons which were submitted at one time.

The Hamilton Roddis Foundation of Wisconsin granted funds for colonial doors and doorways off the Long Gallery to the rooms at National Headquarters.

Compatriot General Leonard F. Chapman, Commandant of the United States Marine Corps, spoke on the life of George Washington at the Tennessee Society's George Washington Birthday Dinner.

The New York Chapter of the Empire State Society presented the Chapter's Theodore Roosevelt Award to Defense Secretary Casper Weinberger in May 1985.

The Society purchased an Aubusson rug, originally owned by Robert R. Livingston, Revolutionary War Patriot and United States Minister to France, for the Long Gallery of the National Headquarters.

An expenditure of $90,000 was approved to purchase a computer for the National Society Headquarters to automate a variety of vital information.

A contingent of Compatriots and their ladies toured England and met with the United Kingdom Society at the Savile Club in London in August 1986.

In early 1985 Wisconsin Society President William H. Roddis (right) turned over the key to this colonial door to Museum Board Chairman James A. Williams to symbolize completion of the installation of similar doors and casings throughout the Long Gallery at our National Headquarters. Compatriot Roddis heads the Hamilton Roddis Foundation, which funded the entire project.

The Maryland Society placed a bronze plaque at the Mann Tavern site in Annapolis observing the 200th anniversary of the Annapolis Convention which called for the Constitutional Convention.

The Massachusetts Color Guard participated in special exercises on the *USS Constitution* making its tenth "turnaround" in the Boston Harbor on the Fourth of July 1986.

BETSY ROSS FLAGS PROMOTED

The National Society Flag Committee initiated a program of having the Betsy Ross 13-star Flag flown over each State Capitol and the National Capitol on Flag Day, June 14th and the Fourth of July.

The Arthur & Berdena King Computer Center at National Headquarters was dedicated during the 95th Annual Congress held in Louisville in 1985. The Former President General and Mrs. King, shown cutting a ribbon held by FPG Carl F. Bessent, paid for construction of the Center at the rear of Headquarters.

Compatriots of the Wisconsin Society Proudly Salute Their Patriot Ancestors Who Furthered the Cause of Independence

ABBOTT, Isaac, Jr.
ALLEN, Philip
BAKER, Aaron
BARLOW, Benjamin
BAUMAN, Sebastian
BEAM, Michael, Sr.
BECKLEY, John
BELLAMY, Justus
BENNER, Issac
BOUCHER, Daniel
BOWKER, Daniel
BOYNTON, Capt. John
BRACE, Lt. William
BRISTOW, John
CABLE, Abraham
CALDWELL, Phineas
CAMPBELL, Enos
CHRISTIE, John W.
CLAFLIN, James
CLARK, James
CLARK, John Scott
CLOVER, Philip, Sr.
COBURN, Eliphalet
CONN, John
COPP, Sgt. David
COURTENAY, Hercules
CRAFTS, Edward
CRANDEL, Samuel
CUSHMAN, Daniel
CUMMINGS, Jotham
DEXTER, Samuel
DICKINSON, Daniel
EDDY, James

EVERETT/EVERT, Samuel
FAXON, Thomas
FICKETT, John, Sr.
FISHER, Jonathon
GALL, George
GANNETT, Jacob
GANS, George
GIFFORD, William
GILBERT, Theodore
GOFFE, John
GORTON, Joseph
GRANGER, Elisha
GRANT, James, III
GREGG, Capt. John
GRIDLEY, Thomas
GRIFFIN, Ralph
GOULD, Bazabeel
HALL, James
HAWES, Elijah
HIGBEE, Hendrick
HILL, James
HOYT, Abner
JAMES, Amos
JAQUITH, Ebenezer
JOHNSON, James
JONES, Jasper
JUMP, John
KEEN, Ebenezer
KIMBALL, Caleb
KITTELL, Edmond
KIVETT, Peter
KNOWLTON, Robert
LEDDEL, Dr. William

LEWIS, Maj. Gen. Morgan
LOCK, William
LOOMIS, Benjamin
LUCE, Joseph
MARTIN, Jesse
McARTHUR, Charles
McGRANAHAN, John
MICHIE, Robert
MISKINEN, David
MONTGOMERY, Thomas
MORE, John
MORRILL, Capt. Jabez
NELSON, John
NEWCOMB, Zaccheus
NISBET, James
PALMER, Jedidiah
PARNELEE, Simon
PEALE, Charles W.
POE, Adam
POTTER, William
POWELL, Absolon
PUTNAM, Allen
REED, John
RENCH, John
RITTER, John
ROBERTS, Cornelius
ROBERTSON, Athanasius
ROE, Benjamin
ROGERS, Henry
SEELY, Denton
SESSIONS, Ebenezer
SEVERANCE, Daniel
SHERMAN, Henry

SMALL, Daniel
SMART, Winthrop
SMITH, Reuben
STEARNS, John
STEARNS, Reuben
STEPHENS, John
STEVENS, Oliver
STONE, David
STONG, Jacob
STOVER/STOUFFER, Jacob
STURTEVANT, James
SWIFT, David
TEN BROECK, Leonard
THOMAS, William
TUTTLE, Moses
TWINING, John
ULMER, George
UNDERHILL, Abraham
UPHAM, Jonathon
VAN HOESEN, Gerret
VAN NATTA, John
VOORHIES, Coert
WATERBURY, Daniel, II
WEBSTER, Ephraim
WHEELER, Ephraim
WHITE, Philip
WHITING, Jonathon
WHITLOCK, Robert
WHITNEY, Abraham
WHITTEMORE, Amos
WILSON, David
WOODWORTH, Reuben
YOUNG, Godfrey

We extend warm congratulations to the National Society in its Centennial Year. Since our Society was organized in January, 1890, we have begun our own 100th Anniversary Celebration!

The SAR pressed the Postal Service to reinstitute the program of issuing stamps bearing the likeness of George Washington. A new one was launched in November, 1985. Following the first day of issue ceremonies, President General Benjamin H. Morris (at end of table) autographed souvenir programs. He also addressed those who attended the event in Washington, DC.

The rooms on the east side of the first floor of the National Headquarters were enhanced with period furniture and random length oak flooring.

Every year the New Hampshire Colonial Color Guard placed a wreath and fired a musket salute at the grave of Josiah Barlett, the first delegate at the Continental Congress to vote for Independence. He was a Signer of the Declaration of Independence.

The Western Reserve Society of the Ohio Society provided funds for the restoration of Compatriot Archibald Willard's original "Spirit of '76" painting on exhibit in Cleveland City Hall. Willard was a member of the SAR.

Comedian Bob Hope was presented the first SAR Distinguished Patriot Award by President General Clovis H. Brakebill. The event took place in late 1986 at Mr. Hope's home located in North Hollywood, California. He was recognized for his many years of entertaining members of our Armed Forces.

A secure library vault with compact shelves was a gift of former President General and Mrs. Arthur M. King.

Compatriot Senator Daniel Quayle of the Indiana Society was elected the 44th Vice President of the United States in November 1988 and sworn into office on January 20, 1989.

The George Washington Fund was established to provide financial support to SAR National Committees that do not receive funds from the SAR annual budget.

Believed at the time to be the only man living whose grandfather served in the Revolutionary War, General James Alward Van Fleet, USA (Ret) was awarded his membership certificate in early 1989. A graduate of the United States Military Academy, he had a brilliant career in the Army.

Compatriot Maurice A. Barboza, a member of the District of Columbia Society, established the Black Revolutionary Patriots Foundation. It is to erect a Black Revolutionary War Patriots Monument in Washington.

In January, 1989 President General Charles F. Printz (right) attended a press conference in Washington, DC called to announce a fund raising campaign of the Black Revolutionary War Patriots Foundation. The campaign was initiated to raise the over $4 million that it will take to design and construct a monument on the Mall in Washington to honor the 5,000 black Americans who served in the Patriot cause from 1775 through 1783. Also participating in the conference were (from left); Dr. Marina Whitman, a General Motors Corporation Vice President who presented a check for $25,000 on behalf of the company; Dr. Benjamin Hooks, Executive Director of the National Association for the Advancement of Colored People; and Compatriot Maurice Barboza, a member of the District of Columbia Society who is serving as Foundation Chairman. PG Printz pledged support of the SAR.

The 101st United States National Congress passed and President George Bush signed a Proclamation designating April 30, 1989 as "National Society of the Sons of the American Revolution Centennial Day."

President General Charles F. Printz "kicked off" the Centennial of the SAR with a "Gala" at SAR National Headquarters in Louisville on April 29, 1989. Many Compatriots and their ladies attended in Colonial attire. Mrs. Eldred M. Yochim, President General, of the NSDAR, was an honored guest.

A highlight of the April 29, 1989 Centennial Gala at National Headquarters was the cutting of a commemorative cake by President General Charles F. Printz (left) and Compatriot Thomas B. Williams, a member of the Indiana Society who portrayed George Washington. Our Society was founded on April 30, 1889, the 100th anniversary of Washington's inauguration.

During the SAR Centennial Year President General Charles F. Prinz installed James R. Westlake as the 86th President General at the 99th Annual Congress held in San Francisco, California, on July 2-5, 1989.

The New Decade began with a membership of 25,265 Compatriots and a Permanent Fund of $870,000.

In this next SAR Century, the Sons of the American Revolution must continue to function to meet the objectives that are set forth in the SAR Constitution. For 100 years the National Society has remained steadfast to these ideals and goals. There are no more worthier aims as it moves forward into its Second Century.

Congratulations To The National Society SAR
On The Occasion Of Its 100th Anniversary
From The Florida Society In Its 93rd Year

We Now Have 32 Chapters!

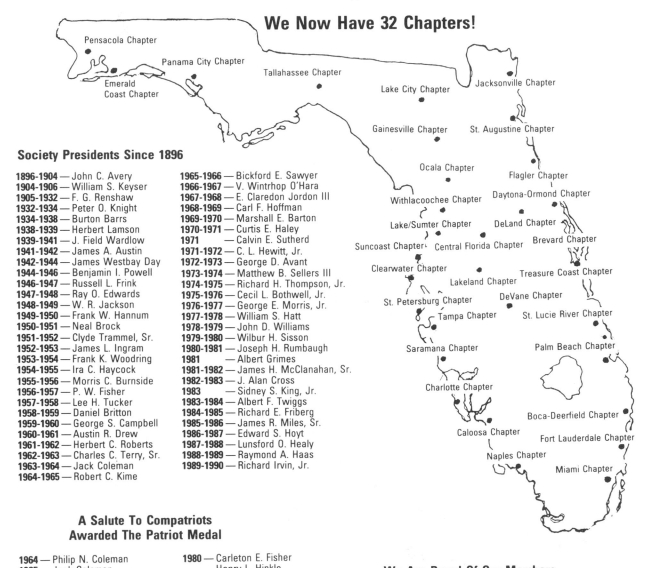

Pensacola Chapter
Panama City Chapter
Emerald Coast Chapter
Tallahassee Chapter
Lake City Chapter
Jacksonville Chapter
Gainesville Chapter
St. Augustine Chapter
Ocala Chapter
Flagler Chapter
Withlacoochee Chapter
Daytona-Ormond Chapter
Lake/Sumter Chapter
DeLand Chapter
Suncoast Chapter
Central Florida Chapter
Brevard Chapter
Clearwater Chapter
Treasure Coast Chapter
Lakeland Chapter
St. Petersburg Chapter
DeVane Chapter
Tampa Chapter
St. Lucie River Chapter
Saramana Chapter
Palm Beach Chapter
Charlotte Chapter
Boca-Deerfield Chapter
Caloosa Chapter
Fort Lauderdale Chapter
Naples Chapter
Miami Chapter

Society Presidents Since 1896

1896-1904 — John C. Avery	1965-1966 — Bickford E. Sawyer
1904-1906 — William S. Keyser	1966-1967 — V. Wintrhop O'Hara
1905-1932 — F. G. Renshaw	1967-1968 — E. Claredon Jordon III
1932-1934 — Peter O. Knight	1968-1969 — Carl F. Hoffman
1934-1938 — Burton Barrs	1969-1970 — Marshall E. Barton
1938-1939 — Herbert Lamson	1970-1971 — Curtis E. Haley
1939-1941 — J. Field Wardlow	1971 — Calvin E. Sutherd
1941-1942 — James A. Austin	1971-1972 — C. L. Hewitt, Jr.
1942-1944 — James Westbay Day	1972-1973 — George D. Avant
1944-1946 — Benjamin I. Powell	1973-1974 — Matthew B. Sellers III
1946-1947 — Russell L. Frink	1974-1975 — Richard H. Thompson, Jr.
1947-1948 — Ray O. Edwards	1975-1976 — Cecil L. Bothwell, Jr.
1948-1949 — W. R. Jackson	1976-1977 — George E. Morris, Jr.
1949-1950 — Frank W. Hannum	1977-1978 — William S. Hatt
1950-1951 — Neal Brock	1978-1979 — John D. Williams
1951-1952 — Clyde Trammel, Sr.	1979-1980 — Wilbur H. Sisson
1952-1953 — James L. Ingram	1980-1981 — Joseph H. Rumbaugh
1953-1954 — Frank K. Woodring	1981 — Albert Grimes
1954-1955 — Ira C. Haycock	1981-1982 — James H. McClanahan, Sr.
1955-1956 — Morris C. Burnside	1982-1983 — J. Alan Cross
1956-1957 — P. W. Fisher	1983 — Sidney S. King, Jr.
1957-1958 — Lee H. Tucker	1983-1984 — Albert F. Twiggs
1958-1959 — Daniel Britton	1984-1985 — Richard E. Friberg
1959-1960 — George S. Campbell	1985-1986 — James R. Miles, Sr.
1960-1961 — Austin R. Drew	1986-1987 — Edward S. Hoyt
1961-1962 — Herbert C. Roberts	1987-1988 — Lunsford O. Healy
1962-1963 — Charles C. Terry, Sr.	1988-1989 — Raymond A. Haas
1963-1964 — Jack Coleman	1989-1990 — Richard Irvin, Jr.
1964-1965 — Robert C. Kime	

A Salute To Compatriots
Awarded The Patriot Medal

1964 — Philip N. Coleman	1980 — Carleton E. Fisher
1965 — Jack Coleman	Henry L. Hinkle
1969 — Francis S. Henderson	Sidney S. King, Jr.
V. Wintrhop O'Hara	1981 — J. Alan Cross
1970 — Eden C. Booth	Wilbur H. Sisson
Carl K. Hoffman	1982 — James F. McClanahan
Bickford E. Sawyer	1983 — Richard E. Friberg
1971 — Curtis E. Haley	James R. Miles, Sr.
1972 — Marshall E. Barton	Joseph S. Rumbaugh
H. D. McKesson	1984 — Carl A. Buechner, Jr.
1973 — C. L. Hewitt, Jr.	S. Floyd Coats
1974 — George D. Avant	1985 — Leo S. LaFontaine
1975 — Austin R. Drew	Albert J. Twiggs, Sr.
Luther F. Gerhart	1986 — Michael R. Gentry
Calvin E. Sutherd	Lunsford O. Healy
James L. Waugh	Edward S. Hoyt
1976 — Matthew B. Sellers III	1987 — Robert C. Foster
Richard H. Thompson, Jr.	John B. Marshall
John D. Williams	1988 — Richard Irvin, Jr.
1977 — Cecil L. Bothwell, Jr.	Floyd D. May
Herbert L. Bowers	Frederick R. Snyder, Jr.
Zack M. Williams	1989 — Russell Ford
1979 — William S. Hatt	Raymond A. Haas
George E. Morris, Jr.	Albert B. Snapp
	Henry E. Winter

We Are Proud Of Our Members
Who Served As National Officers

President General
Ray O. Edwards
Matthew B. Sellers III
Richard H. Thompson, Jr.
Secretary General
Austin R. Drew
Treasurer General
Edward S. Hoyt (current)
Historian General
Herbert C. Roberts
Chancellor General
Carl K. Hoffman
Frederick R. Snyder, Jr. (current)
Chaplain General
Luther F. Gerhart
Leo LaFontaine
Genealogist General
Carleton E. Fisher

Sites of National Headquarters

For many years the subject of a National Headquarters was discussed at Annual Congresses - but no action was taken until 1927. The Congress that year voted to purchase the private residence of Mrs. Norman Williams at 1227 Sixteenth Street, N.W., Washington, DC. This building was sold in 1958 to the National Educational Association, with a move then being made to the Gen. Patrick Hurley home located in Washington at 2412 Massachusetts Avenue, N.W. When the decision was made in the 1970s to leave the Washington area, an extensive search was begun for a new site. This led to the purchase of our present location in Louisville in 1978, at the time Headquarters of the Masonic Grand Lodge of Kentucky.

1227 Sixteenth Street, Washington, D. C.

2412 Massachusetts, Washington, D. C.

1000 South Fourth Street, Louisville, KY

NATIONAL
NEWSLINE

On October 19 re-created British forces prepared to surrender on battlefield.

'Twas a Colorful 200th Anniversary at Yorktown!

The usually sleepy little city of Yorktown, Virginia, came alive with a bang for a while in October to celebrate the 200th Anniversary of the victory of Gen. George Washington, his weary men and allies over Lord Cornwallis and his forces.

Highlighted by four full days crammed with morning to evening events, the celebration was truly a great one. And the SAR was there en masse — from the Trustees that met in Williamsburg and viewed a number of special activities to those Compatriots who were part of 148 re-created military units of the Revolutionary War (they hailed from 23 states and Canada and boasted over 4,000 participants).

The well-planned program featured such diverse things as re-enactments of attacks on battlefield redoubts, visits aboard United States and French naval ships, parades, fireworks displays, band concerts, religious services and wreathlaying ceremonies — over 400 in all. But nothing could top those on Monday, October 19, which commenced with the assembling of every re-created unit on the broad battlefield and ended with a dramatic re-enactment of the surrender itself. In between were a colorful review parade and addresses by United States, British and French dignitaries, including a stirring one by President Ronald Reagan.

On Tuesday, fields of tents and other paraphernalia were removed and Yorktown went back to sleep — not to awaken again for another 50 years to mark the 250th Anniversary.

During battlefield ceremony, a huge United States Flag was unfurled.

This colonial unit passed in review before United States and foreign dignitaries.

A bugler in Banastre Tarleton's British Legion boasted a dramatic uniform.

Speaking from behind a thick wall of glass, President Ronald Reagan discussed the need to restore the balance between the federal, state and local levels as was intended in the Constitution. Also speaking was French President Francois Mitterrand (far left), while observing was Virginia Congressman Paul Trible (far right), an SAR.

A colorful dinner was given by President and Mrs. Reagan for French President and Mrs. Mitterrand. They are shown at the entrance to the Governor's Palace, Williamsburg.

Passing in review was a re-created contingent of French soldiers who served under General Rochambeau. In foreground were photographers representing various news media.

Also passing in review were numerous re-created colonial military units, each clothed in authentic uniforms of the day. They participated in an array of other events during the celebration.

About Yorktown Photos . . .

The cover documents some of the drama that highlighted the Big Celebration. Clockwise from the upper left are: a re-created British unit; colonial fife corps playing at a special ceremony; the SAR Flag on display at a solemn commemoration before the Yorktown Victory Monument, with Virginia Compatriot Thomas Nelson serving as an Honorary Flag Bearer; and Virginia Military Institute cadets passing in review before President Ronald Reagan and other dignitaries.

The photos on these two pages were taken by Stephen Bullock Associates, a professional firm in Williamsburg.

Mrs. Reagan was greeted in the reviewing stand by Senator Harry F. Byrd, Jr., an SAR.

WELCOME HOME, SAR LIBERTY BELL!

The Society's revered Liberty Bell is now permanently enshrined at National Headquarters in Louisville!

This historic event was made official during a solemn dedication ceremony which highlighted the February 20th meeting of National Trustees. Led by President General Richard H. Thompson, Jr., the program featured an address by him, a prayer by Past President General Arthur M. King, brief remarks by Rev. Joseph B. Head and ringing of the bell for all to hear. The full meeting is reported in the Minutes elsewhere in this issue.

At left Benjamin H. Morris, Chairman of the Headquarters Building Committee, thanked Registrar General Howard L. Hamilton for his generous gift to the Society that paid for enshrinement of the bell on a handsome platform.

PG Thompson thanked Compatriot Head for his many years of touring the bell throughout 30 states and bringing its message to 1½ million people, primarily school children. He also announced that the Liberty Bell Foundation has purchased another bell replica which Compatriot Head will take on tour beginning this year. His talk also included quotes from a letter written by Arnold E. Kadue, President of the Foundation: "It is our prayer and hope that many of your fine members will want to lend a hand now and then in scheduling lectures at schools in their locality. Additionally, we trust that many of your members will see the desirability of making some tax-deductible contributions to the Foundation. In the present age of hedonistic comforts, and rock music culture of our youth today, we need to

focus attention on those brave men who are your ancestors and who brought forth upon this land a Constitutional Republic, divinely-inspired."

The SAR bell was cast in Annesty, France by the Packard Foundry and visited

The SAR bell was unveiled by Rev. Joseph B. Head (left) and President General Richard H. Thompson, Jr. Visible from the outside, the bell is located near the Fourth Street entrance to National Headquarters.

the first school in late 1976. The Society paid for the bell and the trailer on which it was hauled by a motor home housing Compatriot Head and his wife, Leona May. A great deal of favorable publicity was generated for the Society.

President General Richard H. Thompson, Jr. (right) reviewed the bell's history and recounted its tours about the country.

Attendees at the Trustees meeting bowed their heads while Past President General Arthur M. King (on platform) gave a prayer.

New Program to Award Eagle Scout Scholarships

The National Society has launched one of its most ambitious programs ever, this time to salute Eagle Scouts all across the country — with the top Scout to be selected each year through a competition among State Societies and awarded a scholarship! SARs are being encouraged to lend backing and financial support.

Approved by the Trustees during their meeting in February, the program has the enthusiastic endorsement of the Boy Scouts of America. To facilitate funding, the NSSAR Eagle Scout Scholarship Foundation has been established. Gifts to the Foundation are tax deductible, with income generated from investments to be used to defray expenses. As of the end of April, over $3,000 had already been donated by various State Societies and Compatriots.

Full details appear in the tear-out brochure on the following two pages (note perforations). SARs are urged to show it to local Scouting leaders. The time is **now** to begin lining up support for this year's competition. Maybe **your** State Society's winner will receive top honors — and be feted at the 93rd Annual Congress in Atlanta, Georgia in 1983!

This important project is the brainchild of the Boy Scout Section of the Public Relations Committee. The Section is chaired by Robert E. Burt, KSSAR. It was successfully tested over the past several months throughout the Kansas Society under the energetic leadership of President Robert O. Dickey. Then it was presented to the Executive Committee by Past President General

Under the test program sponsored by the Kansas Society, Eagle Scout Kris Kobach was awarded a handsome trophy by Past President General King during a special ceremony. The National Society is sending him to the 92nd Annual Congress in Portland, Oregon.

Arthur M. King, who is also a Past President of the Kansas Society. The Committee recommended that it be approved by the Trustees.

To help build the necessary financial base for this program, Chapters, State Societies and others are urged to make contributions.

Prime Examples of How SARs Support Scouting

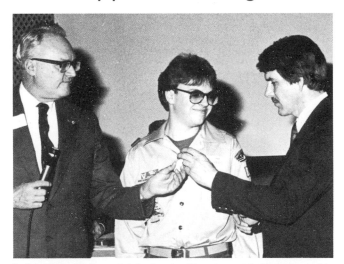

(Left) — Chancellor General John C. Mowbray, a Nevada Supreme Court Justice, has long been active in promoting the Boy Scout movement. This year he was Chairman of Government Day, which saw 80 Scouts from across the state gather in Carson City to learn about how government works. Upon gathering in the Assembly Chamber, they were welcomed by Governor Robert List, who also was the luncheon speaker. Next each paired off with a top official who shared his ideas and conducted a tour through various offices. This photo shows Compatriot Mowbray helping Morty Chinnock into his

judicial robe. The special day is a traditional event in Nevada, as it is throughout the nation. **(Right)** — Every year during the Western Reserve Society (OHSAR) celebration of George Washington's Birthday, the outstanding Eagle Scout from the Cleveland area is presented a Bronze Good Citizenship Medal. The 1982 winner was James L. Gress, who received the award from Compatriot James R. Mecredy (left), while his father proudly observed. Scout Gress raised $500 and constructed a concrete ramp at his church's handicapped entrance.

Treaty Commemorations Draw SARs to France

At the end of August over 100 Compatriots from across the country and some 70 guests winged to Paris, France, to participate in nearly a week of events commemorating the 200th anniversary of the signing of the Treaty of Paris, which concluded the Revolutionary War. Because of the significance of the overall celebration, Trustees voted earlier this year to proclaim it a Bicentennial Congress.

They were joined by several hundred members of various Revolutionary re-enactment units from the United States portraying both American and French forces, collectively referred to as the Expedition Liberte. Many of them had participated in the 1981 Bicentennial program at Yorktown. Also on hand were members of the Daughters of the American Revolution, the Society of the Cincinnati and other hereditary organizations.

The SAR contingent was headed by President General Warren G. Hayes, Jr. Other general officers present were Secretary General Carl F. Bessent, Registrar General G. Arthur Luther, Historian General Harry L. Walen, Genealogist General Augustus di Zerega and Chancellor General Benjamin H. Morris.

Lafayette Honored

On Tuesday, August 30, Picpus Cemetery in Paris was the setting for the first official event: the placing of wreaths by the SAR and DAR on the graves of Lafayette and his wife, Adrienne. This moving cere-

During the ceremony at the Hotel d'York as shown on the left, President General Hayes recounted the efforts of Compatriot John Jay Ide to locate this building where the Treaty of Paris was signed. From the newsmen right were Secretary General Carl F. Bessent; Dr. Joan Challinor, Chairman of the National Committee for the Bicentennial of the Treaty of Paris; Comte Rene de Chambrun, President of the France Society; and Comte Jacques Trudon, Secretary of the France Society. On the right, PG Hayes placed a wreath before a monument in the American Cemetery at Saint Laurent, paying tribute to the U.S. soldiers killed during the 1944 invasion at Normandy.

Colorful re-enactment units participated in numerous events, including a performance on the left at the Hotel de Ville prior to a reception by the Mayor of Paris. On the right, the Massachusetts Society Continental Color Guard marched at Versailles.

mony was preceded with remarks by PG Hayes, DAR PG Mrs. Walter Hughey King and the President of the France Society, Comte Rene de Chambrun (readers are invited to read his interesting talk about Lafayette in an accompanying article). Also participating was the striking Massachusetts Society Continental Color Guard. Later the group visited monuments dedicated to Lafayette, Washington, Rochambeau, de Grasse and Franklin at different locations throughout the city.

President General Warren G. Hayes addressed the large group of SARs and DARs present at ceremonies in Picpus Cemetery. Directly behind him was Mrs. Walter Hughey King, President General of the DAR, while at the far right was Comte Rene de Chambrun, France Society President. Also participating were members of re-enactment units.

Lafayette and his wife were honored by both the SAR and DAR with wreaths at their graves.

Wednesday's activities began promptly at 11 am before the Hotel d'York, 56 rue Jacob, where the Treaty of Paris was signed by representatives of the United States and British governments on September 3, 1783. Visitors were welcomed by Claude Manceron, Chief of Staff to French President Francois Mitterand, while Dr. Joan Challinor recounted the story behind the signing of the Treaties of Paris and Versailles (the latter by representatives of England, France, Spain, Russia and the Holy Empire on the same day in Versailles). She is Chairman of the National Committee for the Bicentennial of the Treaty of Paris, headquartered in Washington, DC. PG Hayes placed a wreath on the hook of a commemorative plaque installed by the SAR on the facade of the Hotel d'York.

Witnessing the program at the Hotel d'York were Robert J. McKenna (left), U.S. Senator from Rhode Island, on behalf of the Governor; Compatriot John W. Warner (second from left), U.S. Senator from Virginia; Claude Manceron (seated), Chief of Staff to France President Mitterand; and Harry L. Walen (right), Historian General.

Comte de Chambrun Recalls Lafayette

As described in the accompanying report of the Treaty of Paris commemoration, Comte Rene de Chambrun, President of the France Society, was the featured speaker during ceremonies at Picpus Cemetery on August 30. Here are selections from his illuminating remarks relative to Lafayette:

"Welcome to this Memorial, lovingly built by Lafayette's wife to perpetuate the memories of her grandfather, her mother, her sister Louise and 1,300 other martyrs beheaded a few hundred feet from here and thrown away into a huge hole a few days before the fall of Robespierre which ended the Terror.

"Freed from her own prison where she was waiting for her turn to die, she crossed Europe with her two daughters and shared Lafayette's miserable life in the donjon of Olmutz. When she returned to France, she found the dreaded hole and with the help of a few families of the martyrs and borrowed money, she bought the ground you will be walking on and built this chapel where; since 1804, night and day, nuns have never ceased to pray.

"She died three years later, on Christmas Eve, from the illnesses she suffered during her five years' imprisonment.

"Twenty-seven years later, Lafayette joined her, on May 23, 1834. He was buried by her side under some soil sent by the State of Virginia and a few weeks later, on July 4, while your national anthem was being played, your representative, Mr. Livingston, placed an American flag on his grave. Since then, the "Stars and Stripes" with a growing number of stars, have always flown at Picpus, even during the years of the German Occupation. No German dared enter this sacred convent.

"Yesterday, I spent a few hours in his home at Lagrange. We treasure there all the documents and souvenirs and my wife does not let anything leave the property. She allowed me for this particular occasion to bring here these two original pages of his words of farewell to the United States. I believe he would approve of my reading

to you from his own pen his first and last words before leaving your country forever.

"Here was his first sentence:

To have been, in the infant and critical days of these States adopted by them as a favorite son, to have participated in the toils and perils of your unspotted struggle for independence, freedom and equal rights, and in the foundation of the American Era of a new social order which has already pervaded this, and must, for the dignity and happiness of mankind, successively pervade every part of the other hemisphere, to have received, at every stage of the Revolution, and during forty years after that period, from the people of the United States and their Representatives, at Home and Abroad, continued marks of their confidence and kindness, has been the pride, the encouragement, the support of a long and eventful life . . .

"And here were the last words:

God bless you, Sir, (Lafayette was addressing President Monroe) *and you all who surround us! God bless the American people, each of their States, and their federal Government! Accept this patriotic farewell of an overflowing heart. Such will be its last throb when it ceases to beat.*

"When walking towards his grave, your thoughts may travel back, as mine sometimes do, to these long and frequent visits he used to make during the twenty-seven last years of his life, sometimes alone, sometimes with one of his daughters, to pay his tribute to the woman he loved. You will then be able to imagine how profound would have been his emotion if on those occasions, he had been able to foresee that on this day, more than a century and a half later, the descendants of his comrades in arms who fought with him for the Independence of your country would begin their sojourn in France by this pilgrimage."

Also in attendance were U.S. Senator John W. Warner, a member of the Virginia Society, who was serving as the personal representative of President Ronald Reagan. The Governor of New Jersey, Compatriot Thomas H. Kean, had planned to be present but had a change in schedule. He named as his representatives for this and other events, New Jersey Society President John E. Flemming, National Trustee Ralph K. Turp and Executive Secretary Howard W. Wiseman.

Business Session Held

Next on the day's agenda was a Congress luncheon at the Hotel Intercontinental. The affair included presentation of the Colors by the Maryland Society Color Guard, toasts to

During the Hotel Intercontinental luncheon, Frazier Draper (left), Cultural Attache with the U.S. Embassy in Paris, was presented a Silver Good Citizenship Medal by Past Vice-President General E. Asa Bates, Jr., who has been Vice Chairman of the SAR Treaty of Paris Bicentennial Committee.

President Mitterand and visiting SARs from the United States, remarks by honored guests and the giving of a Silver Good Citizenship Medal to Frazier Draper, Cultural Attache with the American Embassy, in recognition of his invaluable assistance in making plans for the celebration. Honored guests included Prince Cyrille Makinski, President of France/Etats-Unis; Gen. Richard Hilmer, Defense Attache with the U.S. Embassy, representing our Ambassador to France; French Senator Jacques Habert, who heads a committee responsible for North American affairs; DAR PG King; and Dr. Challinor.

Later the gathering was recessed briefly to permit guests to depart. Then followed a Congress business session, the Minutes of which are capsuled elsewhere in this issue of the magazine. At the end of the afternoon, many Compatriots watched a colorful military parade that featured the Expedition Liberte and French ceremonial units.

Normandy Beaches Visited

Although not an official part of the Congress, a train trip to the Normandy landing beaches was included in the list of activities. This took place on September 1 and was highlighted by a visit to the American Cemetery at Saint Laurent, burial ground

for nearly 10,000 United States soldiers killed during the June, 1944 invasion. It was PG Hayes' honor to place an SAR wreath at a commemorative monument.

Friday began with a religious service in Notre Dame Cathedral in memory of those who died in the Revolutionary War. Sponsored by the SAR and Society of the Cincinnati, the ceremony featured a Mass celebrated by Cardinal Jean-Marie Lustiger, the Roman Catholic primate of France. In his sermon, the Cardinal struck a solemn note, calling the American Declaration of Independence the first true ''declaration of the rights of man'' and urging his audience to ''safeguard man's inalienable rights in today's difficult world.'' The ritual concluded with a Te Deum with 20 singers and music from both the Chapel and Grand Organs.

Next came a reception at the Hotel de Ville (City Hall) offered by Paris Mayor M. Jacques Chirac for SARs, guests, DARs and the Expedition Liberte. In his remarks to attendees, Mayor Chirac recalled how France had helped the colonies in their

PG Hayes brought greetings during the reception hosted by Paris Mayor Chirac.

struggle for independence and emphasized how since then his nation and the United States have been close friends and allies.

Prior to the reception given by the Mayor of Paris, members of the Expedition Liberte performed on the spacious courtyard of the Hotel de Ville (City Hall).

SARs and guests had special seating at the service in Notre Dame Cathedral.

Ceremonies at Versailles

Everyone then traveled via a bus caravan to Versailles for a memorable series of activities marking both the Treaty of Paris and Treaty of Versailles. These included the unveiling of an SAR commemorative tablet, trooping of the Colors by the Expedition Liberte in the Royal Courtyard of the Chateau and tours of the palace. An evening SAR dinner was held at the Hotel Trianon Palace in the same room where President Wilson met with Clemenceau of France, Lloyd George of Great Britain, Orlando of Italy and Hymans of Belgium to present to representatives of the German government the surrender terms that were to end World War I. Special greetings were extended by Versailles Mayor Damien.

The day's events concluded with a spectacular historical pageant recapping the Revolutionary War and climaxed with a brilliant fountain and fireworks display which duplicated the one that marked celeb-

At Versailles, a number of officials addressed attendees, including U.S. Ambassador Evan G. Galbraith.

Units of the Expedition Liberte were kept busy at Versailles, this time in the Royal Courtyard of the Chateau.

rations 200 years ago. The program, in which the re-enactment units participated,

was staged at the magnificent outdoor amphitheatre, Bassin de Neptune.

One of the more significant events of the celebration in France was the unveiling by President General Warren G. Hayes, Jr. of a handsome bronze tablet in what is now the Municipal Library at Versailles (formerly the Foreign Office and Naval Ministry Building). It was made possible through the generosity of Compatriot and Mrs. E. Asa Bates, Jr. and commemorates, in both English and French, the Treaties of Paris and Versailles. All SARs can be justifiably proud of this impressive memorial and are invited to view it when in this famous city.

During his remarks, Versailles Mayor Damien reminded those present that it was at this very site where the brilliant French Foreign Minister, Comte de Vergennes, a chief architect of both treaties, labored so long with representatives of the United States, European allies and George III to produce these historic documents.

A number of dignitaries heard PG Hayes' address when the tablet was unveiled (from left): Mr. Descotils, representing President Mitterand; Versailles Mayor Damien; DAR President General Mrs. Walter Hughey King; Senator Habert, representing the French Senate; Virginia Governor and Mrs. Charles S. Robb (he is an SAR); U.S. Senator John W. Warner (a member of the Virginia Society); Secretary General Carl F. Bessent and his grandson, Clarke.

Observing the tablet were PG Hayes and Versailles Mayor Damien. Note the SAR emblem displayed prominently at the top.

En cet hôtel
fut élaboré le Traité de Versailles
signé au château le 3 septembre 1783
qui mit fin à la guerre d'indépendance américaine
★ ⚜ ★
A tablet under the archway, erected
on behalf of
the Sons of the American Revolution,
commemorates the signing of the
peace treaties of 1783 which consecrated
the independence of the United States

This plaque on the outside of the Municipal Library draws attention to the SAR tablet.

The Bicentennial Congress drew to a close on Saturday, September 3, with a gigantic military parade up the famed Champs Elysses to the Arc de Triomphe in Paris. At the head was the SAR contingent led by SG Bessent and the Massachusetts Society Continental Color Guard. Following were the Expedition Liberte, French units and other patriotic groups. Compatriot Bessent's six-year-old grandson, Clarke, a member of C.A.R., was the youngest marcher participating. Reviewing the parade with other dignitaries was PG Hayes, who later took part in a wreath laying ceremony at the Tomb of the Unknown Soldier.

Festivities concluded with a reception hosted by Ambassador Evan G. Galbraith at the United States Embassy. Everyone from the United States was invited to the affair which featured a bountiful buffet served in a tent erected on the spacious grounds.

In a letter of welcome that accompanied invitations to the week's events, Mr. Galbraith wrote that "the very fact you have come 3,000 miles, at considerable personal expense, to mark the formal entry of our Republic into the family of nations, bespeaks both your sense of history and your gratitude to the French nation, without whose help the victory at Yorktown and the Treaty of Paris, would not have been possible."

In return, the people of France showed their gratitude for what the Americans had done during the week by turning out in large numbers to witness various programs. And the media gave unusually heavy coverage.

The overall program was planned for the SAR by a special committee appointed by then President General Howard L. Hamilton. Serving as Chairman has been Comte de Chambrun, with Col. E. Asa Bates, Jr., as Vice Chairman. They and their committee members are to be highly commended for a job well done. And special compliments must also be extended to the Massachusetts Society Continental Color Guard for their excellent services on numerous occasions during the week.

The reception given by Ambassador Galbraith featured a concert band on the grounds of the U.S. Embassy (left), while on the inside various dignitaries greeted hundreds of visitors. When the photo on the right was taken, the greeters were Virginia Governor and Mrs. Charles S. Robb and President General Warren G. Hayes.

The SAR contingent was proud to lead the parade up the Champs Elysses.

Compatriot's Impressions of Trip Typical

Within a few days after he returned from the Treaty of Paris celebration in France, San Fernando Valley Chapter President Donald N. Moran was guest speaker at a Constitution Day Luncheon sponsored by the Los Angeles and Pasadena Chapters in Pasadena, California. Because his experiences were similar to those of many other SARs who participated in the historic pilgrimage, they are capsuled here:

"We as Americans and members of the Sons of the American Revolution often feel we are the last bastion of Liberty and Freedom, as well as the 'sole' guardians of those all important principles of our founding fathers. NOT SO! The people of France demonstrated time and time again the deepest reverence for those precious ideals.

"On Saturday, September 3rd, the delegates to Operation Liberty were privileged to participate in a full scale parade up the famed Champs-Elysees to the Arc de Triomphe. Led by the numerous re-enactment groups in their Revolutionary War uniforms, along with several colonial-style bands, three Calvary units — again in Revolutionary War uniforms — and elements of elite French military units, we marched to spirited martial tunes and the CHEERS and APPLAUSE of the citizens of Paris. The cheers were punctuated by cries of "VIVA ETATS-UNIS," "VIVA INDEPENDANCE AMERICAINE."

"Unfortunately, space limitations preclude the recounting of every encounter, but the selected few presented here will serve as good examples.

"While viewing the Military Tattoo at the Invalides with Compatriot Jonathan Cook (President, Sacramento Chapter), we were engaged in a delightful, language-impaired, conversation with a Parisian. Loosely translated, his comments were: 'It was very costly to France to help establish the United States, but, twice the debt has been repaid — we are forever in each other's debt.'

"At the wreath laying ceremony at the Tomb of the (French) Unknown Soldier under the Arc de Triomphe, a French Lieutenant remarked: 'The Governments of France and the United States may, at times, be at odds, but the peoples of both countries are as one.'

"Immediately after that encounter, I discovered I was almost out of pipe tobacco. Knowing we were to be transported by chartered bus to the residence of Mr. Evan G. Galbraith, our Ambassador to France, for a reception, I elected to cross the police barricades and find a tobacco shop. Within a block of the Arc de Triomphe I found one. The clerk, a man in his sixties, asked me if I was a participant in the ceremonies at the Arc. I, of course, said yes. He then asked what was happening, and to that I advised we were placing a wreath on the Tomb of the Unknown Soldier. He looked surprised, and stated 'But you are an American!' To which I proudly agreed. He then asked how many of us were there? I responded, 'Over five hundred.' With that comment, he walked out of his store, viewed the proceedings at the Arc, then re-entered. He grabbed me by both arms and 'planted one' on each cheek! He then refused payment for the tobacco, and thanked me again as I left the store.

The majestic Arc de Triomph was the destination of the Saturday parade.

PG Hayes participated in a wreath laying ceremony at the Tomb of the Unknown Soldier.

Compatriot Gerald R. Ford Honored

The Gold Good Citizenship Medal was pinned on President Ford by Michigan Society Compatriot Donald J. Pennell. *(Photo courtesy the Detroit Free Press.)*

On behalf of the National Society in December, the Michigan Society presented the Gold Good Citizenship Medal to Gerald R. Ford, who was President of the United States at the time he became an SAR in 1974.

The award was given to Compatriot Ford during a ceremony at the Detroit Athletic Club by Donald J. Pennell, Chairman of the National Medals and Awards Committee. He is a Past President of the Michigan Society and a Past Vice-President General of the Great Lakes District. In his remarks, Compatriot Pennell stated that the medal is the highest award that can be presented to an SAR and recognizes "unusual and outstanding patriotic achievements of national importance".

President Ford's membership application was signed by Marion H. Crawmer, a Former President General from Michigan, and Dr. M. Graham Clark, Jr., who was then President General. Compatriot Clark presented Mr. Ford his membership certificate at The White House. A descendant of Massachusetts Militiaman Ezra Chase, he was assigned the National Number of 105,000 and the State Number of 2829.

When President Ford was presented his SAR membership certificate by President General M. Graham Clark, Jr., he also received this imported china piece entitled "Signing of Independence". It is now on display in the Ford Museum at Grand Rapids, Michigan. The museum is open daily and attracts visitors from across the country. Eleven Presidents before him were SARs. Compatriot Ford attended the University of Michigan, gained his law degree at Yale Law School and served in the Navy during World War II. He was elected to Congress in 1948 and was named Vice President upon the resignation of Spiro T. Agnew. He became President when Richard M. Nixon resigned. *(Photo provided by Michigan Society Compatriot Dwight L. Coulter.)*

Surrounding Compatriots Ford and Pennell at the awards ceremony were (from left): Detroit Chapter President David Trebing, Nelson C. House, Society Treasurer Larry Blackett, Registrar Harold F. Powell, National Trustee Clyde L. Wolff and President Robert A. Briggs.

The Story Behind the SAR Badge

Our membership badge is steeped in historical significance, as related in this scholarly account by Compatriot Duane L. C. M. Galles

Most Compatriots are familiar with the Membership Badge of the Society of the Sons of the American Revolution. Few perhaps are familiar with the history and significance which underlie it. The badge is not only one of the most beautiful of American hereditary societies, it is also one of the most steeped with history and replete with significance.

The Badge was designed in the very early days of the Society by Major Goldsmith Bernard West, Vice-President of the Alabama Society. The badge consists of a cross of eight points suspended by an eagle. The cross is of white enamel and has four arms and eight points, each point being decorated with a gold bead. Its source is the cross of the ancient chivalric Order of St. Louis, founded by Louis XIV in 1693.

Why the Order of St. Louis

The royal and military Order of St. Louis was part of a package of war veterans' benefits decreed by the Sun King at that time. For disabled or needy war veterans, Louis founded the Hotel des Invalides, the first old soldiers' home of the modern era. Its chapel, the Church of the Invalides designed by Hardouin-Mansart, is today known around the world as a magnificent baroque interpretation of Michelangelo's St. Peter's and as the final resting place of Napoleon. To reward officers for distinguished service and merit Louis established the Order of St. Louis. The Order was named after his namesake and patron, Louis IX, saint, crusader and king of France. It was also richly endowed so that a member received not only a decoration but also a pension. These varied depending on grade and seniority and ranged from 800 to 6,000 livres a year. In addition, a member was exempt from certain taxes.

The cross of the Order of St. Louis is identical to the SAR cross except in three details. The central medallion of the SAR badge bears the image of Washington rather than that of St. Louis; the medallion is surrounded by the SAR's motto "Libertas et Patria" (Liberty and Country) rather than the military order's motto "Bellicae Virtutis Praemium" (the Reward for Virtue in War); and the angles between the arms of the cross lack the French fleurs de lis. Instead, the SAR surrounds the cross with the laurel wreath of republican victory.

French Aid Influential

Several reasons made the St. Louis cross an appropriate pattern for the SAR badge. The Grand Master of the Order of St. Louis, Louis XVI, lent the American rebels material and diplomatic aid which was indispensable for the defeat of the British. Moreover, a great many of the French officers who fought for the Patriot cause were chevaliers of the Order. Beyond that the Order of St. Louis had had a significant presence in North America. During the French Colonial period something like 300 chevaliers of St. Louis saw service in North America. Hence, it was in recognition of the decisive aid of France and the significant presence of the Order in North America that the SAR chose the St. Louis cross as a pattern for its own.

But the adoption of the cross of St. Louis was appropriate for other reasons, too. The Order of St. Louis was the first order of military merit. Earlier orders, like the Order of St. John of Jerusalem and the Order of the Garter were crusading or chivalric orders. They were open to members of the nobility ready to undertake deeds of religion or chivalry. But those deeds were international in scope; all Christendom was to be the beneficiary of the knight's good deeds. By contrast, the Order of St. Louis was established to reward military service to one's own country and it was the first to do so. Since the SAR has as its purpose to remember and recognize the military service of their Revolutionary War ancestors to their country, the adoption of the St. Louis cross seemed most appropos.

Legion of Honour Influence

The laurel wreath is significant, for it is derived from another French order, the Legion of Honour.

Instituted by Napoleon shortly after his advent to power, the Legion of Honour was intended to fill the vacuum left by the disappearance of the old royal orders during the Revolution. Napoleon, like Louis XIV before him, recognized the importance of rewarding faithful public service and recognizing merit. Hence, he instituted the Legion of Honour, which to this day remains one of the most prestigious orders of merit in the world. Napoleon's order, however, differed from the old royal orders. Those either presupposed or conferred nobility. They were inextricably linked to the caste system. But with the Legion of Honour came a new basis for reward — personal merit rather than birth. Thus it will not be surprising that the SAR badge is consciously modeled on that of the Legion of Honour. The laurel wreath is borrowed from the Legion of Honour. Even the size of the badge is designed to be exactly that of the Legion of Honour. But the badge refuses to follow the Legion of Honour in all respects. Unlike the Legion of Honour cross which has five arms, the SAR cross resolutely retains the four arms of the cross of Christ. This is as if to declare that the excesses of deism and atheism of the French Revolution are to be eschewed by an American Patriotic society; America is a nation under God.

Eagle Denotes Patriotism

Distinctly American also is the eagle which suspends the cross. Badges of European orders had used a trophy (a war helmet), a wreath, or a gold loop. These symbolized their chivalric purpose. But the purpose of the SAR was not chivalry, but patriotism. Hence, the SAR appropriately adopted the eagle which the Cincinnati had previously selected for their badge. The SAR was conceived as a society of the Cincinnati, open to all sons of Revolutionary sires without regard to primogeniture. The choice produced a uniquely American badge.

BIBLIOGRAPHY

National Society of the Sons of the American Revolution, *Historical Notes* (New York, 1890) pp. 39-40.

Aegidius Fauteux, *Les Chevaliers de Saint Louis en Canada* (Montreal, 1940).

H. Gourdon de Genouillac, *Nouveau Dictionnaire des ordres de chevalerie* (Paris, 1891).

Hanson, *An Accurate Historical Account of All the Orders of Knighthood at Present Existing in Europe* (London, n.d.).

Paul Hieronymussen, *Orders and Decorations of Europe* (New York, 1967).

Currently Vice-President of the Minnesota Society, Compatriot Galles also serves as President of the Minneapolis Chapter. He holds a Bachelor of Arts Degree from George Washington University, Master of Arts from the University of Minnesota and Doctor of Jurisprudence from the William Mitchell College of Law. He has also studied at the University of Edinburgh and the University of Toronto.

1

"General George Washington's Seal Ring"

President General Howard L. Hamilton describes this most valuable National Society possession.

2

The single most valuable property owned by the National Society of the Sons of the American Revolution is not its Headquarters Building nor even its Permanent Fund. It is a small circular object, about ⅞" in diameter, which rests in darkness, untouched for **364 days of the year**, emerging for only one night when a new President General is installed. It shares its space in a thin safety-deposit box with the deed to the Headquarters Building, an insurance policy, some stock certificates, and an affidavit about its own origins. This precious possession is the Seal Ring owned and worn by General George Washington.

The ring itself is of gold, with a thin band and delicate shank. It is a perfect size 10 on a modern mandrel. There is no maker's mark or any inscription whatsoever on the inside. On each outer surface, the metal of the shank is deeply

incised to give in raised relief a stem, three leaves, and a three-part bud or flower at the top, too worn to identify. The annulus of the crown is oval, surrounding and holding in place the setting of light orange carnelian in which is incised the Washington crest **(Fig. 1)**: a shield with three stars

common variation is, "The end justifies the means."

A seal made by the Washington ring is shown in **Figure 2**. The griffin now faces left and the words of the motto read properly from left to right. The original Washington crest, done in colored glass, could be seen in a window of "what is now the buttery", at Sulgrave Manor, the Washington ancestral home in Northamptonshire, England.[2]

Unusual Box for Ring

Almost as interesting as the ring is its box, which is the original used by General Washington. It is made of varnished wood, possibly birch or fruitwood **(Fig. 3)**, and measures 3⅜" wide, 3-9/16" long, and 1⅛" high. On its cover is a shield, ⅞" long and ¾" wide, inlaid of ivory — much crackled with age **(Fig. 4)**. A small brass knob at the front of the lower half controls the catch.

Inside, the lid is lined with lavendar silk, now brown and hanging in shreds. A pin holds a card loosely in place in the top pad, saying, "General Washington's Seal Ring. Statement and Affidavit under bottom pad." The bottom pad is covered with velvet, once lavendar, but now faded to brown except around a center post where the ring rests snugly.

The affidavit is also in our lockbox and is preserved flat between two layers of plastic, because it is so fragile and cracked from being folded beneath the bottom pad. It gives the history and line of

3

at the top and two transverse bands beneath; surmounted by a crown containing a griffin; underlain by a ribbon bearing the Latin words, **"Exitus acta probat."** These words come from line 85 of the second Heroides of Ovid, and are translated literally as, "The outcome proves the deed," or "The event justifies the deed."[1] A

4

descent of the ring through the Washington family. Being typed, it is easily read **(Fig. 5).**

On the rare occasions that the ring is worn, it attracts the greatest of attention and excitement. People look at it with awe and almost reverence. Their greatest wish is to touch it. The ultimate thrill is to be allowed to slip it over the end of a finger and off again. Occasionally there is a skeptic who questions its authenticity despite the affidavit of William Lanier Washington and the great care given to the ring by the National Society since 1922 when it was presented to us. To these we can only give a very unscientific answer: when you put it on your finger and feel that comfortable fit from decades of wear, and see the inner glow of translucent orange radiance from the authentic Washington Seal, you **know** it is real!

PGs Wear Copies

Presidents General are now permitted to purchase copies of the ring from a franchised jeweler. These are not replicas, for they are different purposely in several respects from the original. Sardonyx, a much darker and more opaque stone, is used for the Seal. There are variations in the gold work and in the carving of the seal. On my copy, the gold work is not as deeply sculptured. The oval Seal is smaller and darker. The griffin has a serpent's tongue and streamlined wings. There is no possibility of confusing the copy with the original.

The value of the Washington ring? Well, that cannot be expressed in terms of

money. Who could place a price on such a rare and historic object? Besides, for security reasons the National Society is not anxious for speculation or publicity on this subject. No amount of money could measure the mystique of this ring nor the aura of grandeur, authority, and dignity it bestows upon the office of President General.

(Photos were taken by Mrs. Howard L. Hamilton)

GENERAL WASHINGTON'S
SEAL RING

The Seal Ring of gold set with carnelian cut with the coat of arms of General Washington, that accompanies this statement, belonged to and was worn by General Washington.

Shortly before his death he gave it to his eldest nephew, Colonel William Augustine Washington, my great great grandfather. It passed from him to his son, Colonel George Corbin Washington, my great grandfather, who gave it to his son, Colonel Lewis William Washington, my grandfather, from whom it was inherited by Major James Barroll Washington, my father.

This ring was inherited by me at the time of my father's death, March, 6th. 1900, and it has never since that time been out of my possession.

William Lanier Washington being duly sworn this sixteenth day of February, 1922, deposes and says that the statement set forth as above is true and correct to the best of his knowledge and belief.

5

FOOTNOTES

1. Communication from Dr. and Mrs. Arthur F. Stocker. Compatriot Stocker is Chairman of the Department of Classics at the University of Virginia and Past-President of the Thomas Jefferson Chapter, VASAR, Charlottesville.

2. Footnote from Vol. 1 of Washington Irving's **Life of Washington.**